The
Ache for
a Child

The Ache for a Child

Debra Bridwell

VICTOR BOOKS

A DIVISION OF SCRIPTURE PRESS PUBLICATIONS INC.
USA CANADA ENGLAND

Copyediting: Afton Rorvik
Cover Design: Joe DeLeon
Cover Photo/Illustration: Image Bank

Library of Congress Cataloging-in-Publication Data

Bridwell, Debra.
    The ache for a child / by Debra Bridwell.
        p.   cm.
    Includes bibliographical references.
    ISBN 1-56476-248-3
    1. Childlessness — United States — Psychological aspects.
    2. Infertility — United States — Psychological aspects. I. Title.
HQ536.B75 1994
306.87 — dc20   03-48902
                                                                                      CIP

Contents

The Ache for a Child is a must-read for couples facing the pain of infertility, miscarriage, or stillbirth. Debra offers a thoughtful, thorough examination of the complex issue of infertility, sharing vulnerably and generously from her own experiences as well as from those of others. With exquisite care and warmth, she walks the reader through the bewildering world facing couples struggling with infertility, offering a welcome beacon of enlightenment, comfort, and reassurance. She gives the reader ample opportunity to personalize the journey by answering questions at the end of each chapter and journaling their own rocky passage toward parenthood.

Debra isn't afraid to address some of the hard ethical questions regarding surrogacy, artificial insemination, embryo reduction, and other complex choices infertile couples may be forced to make. As a mother who has experienced the ache for a child in the loss of my newborn daughter, I identified with what Debra had to share, and I will, without reservation, recommend this book to others who, for whatever reason, ache desperately for a child.

CAROLE GIFT PAGE, Author of 31 books, including *Misty, Our Momentary Child, The Child in Each of Us,* and *House on Honeysuckle Lane.*

Dedication

To Michael, who has consistently loved me
since ninth-grade history class and who
has been my best friend and support
through our journey of infertility and life.

To Justin, our bloom in the desert, and to
Aaron (or Erin), our bud who never had
the chance to bloom.

Acknowledgments

I wish to express my appreciation to the following people.

To those who contributed their time, medical expertise, and experience to this book: David Adamson, M.D., director of the Fertility and Reproductive Health Institute of Northern California, Los Gatos, California; William Brown, M.D., past chairman of OB/GYN at The Good Samaritan Hospital of Santa Clara Valley, California; Marianne Carter, R.N., L.M.F.T., San Jose, California; Patricia Rogers, M.D., Mountain View, California; and Panayiotis M. Zavos, Ed.S., Ph.D., director and chief andrologist of the Andrology Institute of Lexington, Kentucky.

To those who contributed theological and ethical assistance: Dr. Vernon Grounds, chancellor of Denver Seminary; Dr. Alan McNickle, professor of Theology, Moody Bible Institute; Pastor Brian Morgan, PBC Cupertino; Pastor Gary Vanderet, PBC Cupertino; and Pastor Steve Zeisler, PBC Palo Alto.

To Patty Einarson, Cathy Greulich, Don and Helen Gruelle, Barbara Walik, and Eileene Werner for their assistance with the manuscript. To Linda Holland who opened the door to publish this book, Afton Rorvik for editing it, and the others at Victor Books for their help.

And a special thanks to the people in the WE CARE support group, the organization of RESOLVE, and the editors of *Stepping Stones* for being my support; and to the women and men who shared their pain, dreams, and frustrations to help others find healing.

Introduction

My intense desire to be a mother has made infertility very painful for me. During my struggle, I have identified with the deep distress of Rachel in the Old Testament when she cried to her husband, "Give me children or I'll die!" (Gen. 30:1) During the earliest part of my infertility twelve years ago, I felt so isolated and wished I knew just one person who had gone through the same thing.

I wrote *The Ache for a Child* for those of you unable to conceive and for those who are childless because you have lost one or more children during pregnancy. Know that you aren't alone. This book is also written for you who may have other children, but are grieving the loss of a much-wanted, irreplaceable baby before birth.

Because so many of the feelings and even medical treatments overlap, for the sake of simplicity I often use the general term *infertility* within this book to refer both to technical infertility and to the loss of a baby during pregnancy. (I also address the issue of pregnancy loss specifically in chapter 15: Miscarriage and Stillbirth.)

As you read through this book, I encourage you to record your feelings in a journal to help you face and analyze them. If you're honest, what you write may embarrass, depress, or even scare you, but you should write even when you're at your worst. Later when you look back at what you have written, you'll realize how far you've come. To assist you in getting started, I've included questions at the end of each chapter in a section called **Your Personal Journey.** These questions can also be used to stimulate discussion in a support group.

I wish I could share the secret to bypassing the grief process that accompanies infertility. I can't. But, in this book I've shared parts of my journey and the experiences of others who have struggled to have children, in the hope that you will find encouragement while you work through your own struggles and grief. Although at times I've felt uneasy about sharing so openly about the most private areas of my life (my infertility and my spirituality), I've chosen to do so in the hope that my words will help those of you traveling the same path. I also hope that this book will guide you to a place of emotional and spiritual strength where you will grow in the knowledge that God *does* love you, and that He will give you strength and wisdom for today and hope for your future.

Some of you may be reading this book to learn more about infertility and pregnancy loss to support those who are struggling. Your concern will go a long way in comforting them in their struggle and lessening their sense of isolation.

Some names and personal details in this book have been modified to ensure the privacy of individuals. I have also alternated using masculine and feminine articles (he and she) to avoid awkwardness. For help in defining some of the terms used in infertility, see the glossary at the back of this book.

Part I

"We Might Be Infertile."

1

From Naive Excitement to Anxious Uncertainty

We can make our plans, but the final outcome is
in God's hands (Proverbs 16:1).

Lord, when doubts fill my mind, when my heart is
in turmoil, quiet me and give me renewed hope
and cheer (Psalm 94:19).

*wo of our dearest friends, Denise and Eric
turned toward the door as my husband Michael
and I walked in. The country-print wallpaper,
comfortable easy chair by the bed, and lack of visible medical instruments or antiseptic smell in the cozy hospital
room surprised me. Then I focused on Denise who looked
exhausted, but smiled with the glow of someone who had
just succeeded in accomplishing an enormous task. Eric
looked like a man in love as he gently held his brand-new
daughter.*

*Seeing their newborn infant, I really recognized for the
first time what a miracle a baby is. Before that I hadn't
stopped to wonder at the process, but had taken for granted that new babies were born all the time. We had been
involved in the day-to-day progress of Denise's pregnancy
though, and felt privileged, even awed to be included in*

the first hours of this amazing new human being's life. She pulled at our hearts instantly.

This birth also had special significance for us, and we felt an undercurrent of excitement as we held their newborn baby. You see, we had started trying to conceive just two months before and were sure that we would be announcing a new member of our family any day. Little did we know then of the years of heartache we would face in our search for that dream.

Michael and I had thought a great deal about starting our family. We waited two years after we were married and finally felt the time was right. We wanted to share our love and lives with a baby of our own, and thought that raising a child, created from our loving relationship, would be wonderful. We planned to have two biological children, and then adopt one. We couldn't wait any longer to start creating our family and to hold our own baby.

We had plans for Michael to go to seminary and knew it would be difficult financially, but we both still felt the time was right. So in August we packed up and drove a moving van to Colorado—away from family and friends in California. I knew I would miss everyone, but I consoled myself with the idea that a new baby would fill some of that loneliness.

Going about our daily tasks took on a new dimension. It was as if Michael and I shared a joyous secret. To others it looked as if we were going through the normal motions of life, but we knew that, unknown to others, we were also working on creating a new life!

We began to plan: "If we get pregnant this month, then...." So many decisions hinged on getting pregnant—our jobs, the number of classes Michael should take, the size of the apartment we should rent, even the type of insurance we should get. We hoped I would be pregnant by Christmas, then we could fly back home and announce the tremendous news to our families.

Instead, although the visit home eased some of our

homesickness, it was a difficult Christmas. My sister-in-law was now six months pregnant, but I still wasn't. (They had started trying to conceive a few months after we had and were successful on their first attempt.) So much of the talk revolved around the arrival of their baby. Meanwhile, we were feeling a growing concern that something was wrong with our ability to have children. We had so wanted to celebrate and join "the club" of parenthood with them. I wondered briefly why it had been so easy for them and why God had chosen to answer their desire and not ours.

One of the presents Michael bought for me that Christmas was a beautiful navy-blue maternity dress with a white collar. He said he'd passed a maternity shop window and knew I would be needing the dress soon, so he bought it for me. I tried it on for him with a pillow underneath and dreamed of the time when I could really wear it. I hung it carefully in the back of our closet to await the time I would need it.

We emptied the linens out of our wedding hope chest and began to fill it with tiny socks and soft baby clothes. We bought books on what to expect during pregnancy. I changed my eating habits to ensure a healthy baby: no aspirin or other unnecessary medication, more fruits and vegetables, and less junk food. I eliminated caffeine and began to take vitamins. We adjusted our budget. We were preparing our lives to include our baby-to-be.

We knew that we might have a slightly harder time having a baby than some of our friends because I had irregular periods. After stopping birth-control pills, I had gone for as long as six months without a period, but my cycles were usually every five to seven weeks. So after a couple of months with no success, I picked up some basal body temperature charts from my gynecologist to help us determine my fertile time.

We certainly didn't want our lovemaking to become just an attempt to make a baby, so we made a conscious

*effort to always take time to be loving and romantic in our
love-making. The doctor told me that we should have sex
"every day or every other day around ovulation." So, we
began to chart my time of ovulation and to focus on great,
romantic sex every day or at least every other day around
that time.*

*If we were at a friend's house during this "who-knows-
if-I'm-ovulating" time, we would yawn at 8:00 or 8:30
P.M. and say, "Sorry we have to leave so early, but we
need to be going now." We didn't want to tell them we
were trying for a baby—we wanted to wait and tell them
we were expecting. We knew our friends would understand
later when we would be able to tell them our happy news.*

*Living this way was wonderful for a while. People
always joke to infertile couples: "Well at least you have
the fun of practicing!" Well to begin with, it was great fun.
Putting our physical and romantic relationship as top priority over everything else was wonderful. We could be
spontaneous without worrying about using birth control.
We felt close and had the added knowledge that we were
doing something very important—making love to connect
physically, emotionally, spiritually, and create a new life.
When we'd have a wonderfully intimate time of lovemaking, we would share our hope that this would be the moment of conception and that our baby would be born from
this expression of love.*

*The problem was that my temperature was as irregular
as my cycles. It was supposed to hover below 98.0° for the
first two weeks, dip about 4 to 6 tenths of a degree right
before I was to ovulate, then rise about a degree and
remain higher for two weeks until my period came. What
it actually did was go up and down constantly by 4 to 6
tenths of a degree during the weeks before I would ovulate. So, we tried to make love all the time since we never
knew when I might ovulate. (That's a problem with temperature charts, you're only sure you've ovulated when
it's too late to fertilize the egg.)*

For four to eight weeks each cycle, we would wonder whether I was about to ovulate, then I finally would. Then I could spend the next two weeks waiting and hoping that every twinge of nausea might mean I was pregnant. But each time we discovered I wasn't pregnant, the sadness came, and we tried to turn our hope to "maybe next time." As the months went by though, it was harder and harder to carve the hours out of every day. We had other deadlines. I was working full-time. Michael was in seminary full-time and working part-time. For most of the first year he worked in the wee hours of the morning or the graveyard shift before heading off to class. In addition, we helped with the high school youth group at our church.

Stress began to creep in when my temperature dropped (meaning I might be about to ovulate), but we would have other things scheduled. As time went on, it seemed we would almost always have something imperative happening during "the" time. I would have the flu; Michael would be stressed over a midterm or final that required all-night cramming with a study group; or an overnight social was planned with the high-school students. To miss the time of ovulation though, when it might not happen again for a couple of months, would have been so depressing. (Years later we learned that sperm can live up to 72 hours, so with normal sperm, having sex every two to three days around ovulation allows sperm to be constantly available to fertilize any egg that appears.)

As the months dragged by, we started to withdraw from our friends. Who had time for them? Besides, it began to hurt to see them start their families while we were having trouble.

We began to fit sex in between our other priorities and out of necessity allot less time to it. At times our focus turned to "getting the job done." When pressure was on in other areas, sex began to feel like a pressure also. The sadness began to grow with each passing month we failed to conceive. We began to worry we might have a problem having children. Well, I began to worry.

Until now, we'd been united in purpose, united in our idea of timing for children, and united in our plan. Now a distinct difference was beginning to emerge. Michael still thought of having a baby as an important, but secondary event in our lives that would eventually happen while we were pursuing other things. He really didn't see anything to worry about and wanted to give it more time. I wanted to go to the doctor. I knew that people who had trouble conceiving were called infertile. I slowly began to realize that we were in that group. (It took a little longer for Michael.)

The forcefulness of my feelings amazed me. I know infertility was harder on me than some others. I don't know why. Some infertile couples are able to say, "OK, that road is closed, what alternatives do we have?" They just move on. Most though, go through a grieving process. That's what I did during the next few years.

Having a baby had become a driving force in my life. I began to feel desperate, the desire almost overwhelming me. Seeing my blue maternity dress hung in the back of our closet began to hurt too much. I also worried that people might see it and bring up the subject. I folded it gently and placed it in our hope chest with the baby clothes where it would be out of sight.

Daring to Voice the Question

For some couples, the realization of infertility can be signaled by a drastic event, such as a hysterectomy or a semen analysis which shows no sperm. These couples are forced to deal with the issue directly.

But for most couples, like us, the problem of infertility dawns on them slowly because infertility is diagnosed only by something *not* happening over a period of time. In the back of our minds, the question forms: *Why is it taking us so long to conceive?* As the months go by, the realization creeps in that something is wrong.

An estimated one in six couples of child-bearing age in the United States,[1] or approximately four to six million people, deal with the crisis of infertility.[2] Infertility is generally defined as the inability to conceive after a year of uninterrupted intercourse (using no birth control) or the inability to carry a baby to live birth. The statistics describe the number of people, but not the emotions and tears behind the numbers.

Deciding to have a baby — to bring a new life into the world — can be a time of dreaming of the future and the changes a child will bring to your life. Even if the decision is made with some apprehension about what some of those changes might be, there is a sense of excitement, of moving ahead in life. When the wanted baby doesn't come through, your feelings of excitement can quickly change to confusion and sadness.

Your Personal Journey

1. How did you feel when you first decided to try for a baby? (ambivalent? excited? nervous?)
2. When did you begin to realize something was wrong? Was there a time when you finally began to identify yourself as infertile? How did you feel?
3. How did others react to your difficulty conceiving? (your spouse? your family? your friends?)

2

The Desire for a Family

Something to live for came to the place,
Something to die for maybe,
Something to give even sorrow a grace,
And yet it was only a baby.[1]

God made each precious baby
so delicate and small . . .
And of His many blessings,
babies are the greatest gift of all![2]

n our premarital counseling the pastor asked Michael and me the important question: "Have you discussed having children?" He didn't ask the question out of idle curiosity, but because he knew the issue of having children was central to a couple's values, goals, dreams, and view of the world. If Michael had wanted five children, but I didn't want any, we would have been ripe for serious problems. We were so proud when we could answer that we had thoroughly discussed the matter and agreed that we both wanted three children.

Of course we weren't asked to think about, what if you discover you can't have children?

Reasons for Wanting to Have Children
Many positive (and negative) factors influence our desire for children. If we are aware of these influences, we can

better cope with the dilemma infertility brings.

As Michael and I became more certain of our infertility and invested more time, money, and effort into trying to have a baby, we reexamined why we wanted children. We found that our motives were complex. Some were meaningful and realistic. Others were laughable, such as the picture I envisioned of how my life would change if I had a baby.

As I shivered while scraping ice and snow off my car at 6:00 each winter morning in Denver, preparing for a job I hated, I longingly thought of "someday" in the future when I would be able to stay home with my baby. When that finally happened, I would open the curtains in the morning, see it was snowing, and decide to stay in that day. I would cancel whatever plans I had made and spend the day rocking my baby and playing with him or her. Maybe I would invite another nearby mom over for warm cinnamon rolls and let the babies play together. I could *choose* what I wanted to do.

Because there are so many reasons for wanting a baby, it's important to think about the underlying reasons for your desire to have a child. In facing the reasons, you can separate those that are superficial and downright silly from those that have essential worth to you.

This is especially important if you should choose at a later date to follow the path of adoption. You will realize that while adoption fulfills many desires to have children, other desires can only be fulfilled by a biological child. Knowing the reasons behind your desire for a child will help you determine what future action or path to take. The following partial list covers some of the diverse reasons (some admirable and some faulty) people want children.

Growth

- A baby would be the needed catalyst for change and growth in our lives. I want to be motivated to grow as a person, to be worthy of the ultimate trust that my own child would place in me. (Or, I just want to quit my job, but can't do it without more justification.)

● A baby would bring a new dimension into my life and make me (and others) feel that I've become a full-fledged adult. I'm ready to settle down and take my place in society. Starting a family is part of that.

● Like "Always a bridesmaid, never a bride," I'm tired of being "Always a shower attendee, never the mom-to-be."

● I want to fully experience the part of my body that was created for having children. I will feel more fully a man/woman when I've helped conceive/given birth to a child.

Enjoyment
● I want to share and learn from the spontaneity and simplicity of children. They're cute, fun, and inspirational. (For children, kisses seem to heal all hurts. All their emotions are out in the open. They find the joy of life in everything—at least one wonderful thing can be found in any garden or even in the construction of their toes.)

● I'd enjoy the companionship and friendship a child would bring.

● If I didn't have a child, I would feel as if I were missing out on something. There is a certain mystical quality about having a child. It is similar to the mystique about sex. I want to experience it to see if it is really as great as everyone says. Comments like, "I didn't know what the word *joy* meant until I had my child," make me wonder if I've ever really experienced joy.

Altruism

● I want to do something meaningful with my life.

● I want to make the world a better place to live by raising a child with my values. I want to leave something worthwhile in this world when I'm gone (i.e., someone who has love for God and compassion for people).

Passing on wisdom or qualities

● I want to nurture, teach, and raise a child. I enjoy caring for people.

● I had a great childhood so I want to share that example with a child. (Or, I had a horrible childhood so I want to give a child what I didn't have.)

● I think my husband and I have some good physical, intellectual, creative, or emotional traits that we'd like to pass on to a child.

Intimacy, family ties, or security

● I want the permanent relationships that having a family brings.

● I want to have someone to carry on my family name. (In American society this isn't as strong an expectation or pressure, but it's still there. It's especially strong in certain families or cultures.)

● A baby would create a greater bond between my spouse and me. A child would seal our union and be the ultimate symbol of it. (A baby can even be a last-ditch hope to "save" a bad marriage.)

Doing the right thing

● It's the thing to do. I've always assumed I would have kids. My parents, friends, and society expect it.

• God intended us to have children in marriage. Children are a blessing and should be sought.

Unique influences

Of course the reasons for having children are as diverse as the individuals wanting them. Unique experiences in our lives can also contribute to our desire to have children. Rich for instance, longed for a relationship that he missed as a child: "One of the reasons I had always hoped to be a Daddy is because I never knew mine."

In Karen's situation, her abortion before becoming a Christian created the strong desire to have another child within her marriage to help heal the pain and guilt.

> My suffering started with my abortion, so I was obsessed with having a baby. In my mind, that would make things right. I was so relieved and excited when we decided to start trying. I thought that it would take away the pain.

Created to Desire to Create

The intensity of the desire to have children varies among and even within couples, but the desire motivates most couples to try to have children. The reasons listed above account for some of the drive, but still don't seem to account for the depth of loss many people feel from infertility. For these people the desire to procreate is so tied into their self-concept that when their ability to have children is thwarted, they still find it inconceivable to see their lives without children. For them, the word *infertility* is devastating. Why is their desire so deeply rooted? Is the basic desire for children a petty, selfish, or unwholesome thing?

I felt confused about this because of the lack of understanding from others. Like many infertile individuals who chose to share their struggle with others, when I mentioned our problem to people, I sometimes received a blank look that seemed to imply that talking about infertility was indiscreet. (It shouldn't be mentioned in polite society because it was linked to sex or "female problems.") Another response I received was that the problem was incomprehensible: "What's the big deal? Do other things with your life." As a result of these types of reactions, I began to feel that my strong desire for children was inappropriate.

I continued to question why I wanted children so strongly until I studied Genesis with my women's Bible-study group. When I read the verse, "Then God said, 'Let us make a man—someone like ourselves' " (Gen. 1:26), I saw it with a fresh perspective. I saw that God had the desire to create new life; and He wanted to create it in His own image. If He, being perfect and complete had this desire to create, how could it be selfish or wrong? And because He created us in His image, with many of His attributes, it should come as no surprise that we share His desire to create.

If we yearn to take part in the miracle of creating a new life "in our image" with attributes like our own, and want the intimacy of nurturing our child to maturity, that is only natural. This yearning is God-given and a part of how we are created. It's no wonder that we can feel jarred and confused when we are unable to fulfill it.

I felt a piece of the puzzle fall into place once I understood this basic reason for my drive. I still struggled with why I wasn't able to have children and how to respond correctly to that obstacle in my life, but I no longer felt guilty for wanting children.

While there are those couples who choose not to have children, it appears that the vast majority of us feel this desire to create life. If children don't come to us, we can choose to go through extraordinary measures to have a child because we have a "right" to have a child and "deserve" to have one. Or we can work toward the goal of building our family because we believe children are a blessing in God's original purpose for marriage, and after going to God for direction about our particular marriage, we believe He wants us to pursue having a child.

Are our motives always pure? No. Like many couples, the realization of our motivation came by gradual understanding. But we both came to the conclusion that it was a good thing to pursue having children, and just because something didn't come easily, didn't mean it was wrong. As the excitement of "trying" turned into the frustration of no results, we began to search for answers. Along with unceasing prayer, we started medical testing.

Your Personal Journey

1. What are your reasons for wanting children?
2. What or who has influenced you to want them? (Consider marriage, family, society, church, friends, self-image, and view of God.)

Part II
"What Can a Doctor Do?"

3

When Is It Time to See a Doctor?

I thought that something was wrong when I didn't
get pregnant after six months. John thought I
was being obsessive. Finally, after three years,
he agreed to see a doctor. —Karen

*fter six months of charting my resting tempera-
ture, the charts showed clearly that I wasn't ovu-
lating regularly. So, I went back to my gynecologist. The decision to seek medical help was easier for me
than some others because of this distinct physical symptom. The gynecologist prescribed Clomid (a fertility drug
to induce ovulation). Hope sprang anew, but I was more
emotional (a side effect of the drug), so each month that I
learned I wasn't pregnant sent me into deeper confusion,
sadness, and even despair. Still, we hoped a doctor could
find the problem and eventually fix it.*

Do I Have the Right to Tinker
with the Body God Gave Me?

When a baby doesn't come, couples begin to wonder if
there is something medically wrong, but because fertility

involves mysteries and miracles of life such as sex and procreation, some couples feel or are told that they shouldn't seek medical help. Another barrier to deciding to get medical help can be the hope that if you wait until next month, maybe the problem will fix itself.

Is infertility a spiritual problem or a medical problem? Sara had to deal with this question in her family: "My mom would feel I was much more spiritual if I just accepted [my infertility]. My sister believes God promises you children if you just have faith."

Some churches have specific teachings regarding sexual or procreative practices or regarding medical treatment in general. But, generally, most orthodox Christian theologians and churches believe that God gave us medical technology to help us, and we have the option to use it as long as it doesn't contradict our "owners manual," the Bible.

Basically, I believe that infertility is an illness like any other. Someone once told me that he felt it was similar to developing cataracts, a condition in which you gradually lose your eyesight. The medical treatment for the disease is not necessary to continue life, but without the removal of the cataracts, the person will eventually go blind and lose a valued part of his or her life. Infertility is similar in that while it isn't life threatening (although there are studies that indicate a higher incidence of cancer of the ovaries[1] and lining of the uterus in women who have never had children[2], it does involve important organs in a person's body not functioning correctly, which greatly reduces the quality of his or her life.

While infertile couples should be open to God using anything in their lives to draw them closer to Him, that doesn't mean that infertile couples should not use medical treatment to fix their problem. I do believe however, that they need to be careful using treatments that *have the potential to help create life.* The ethical and biblical issues of different medical treatments for infertility are discussed in depth in chapter 5.

A well-meaning church member once told me that if children don't come easily to a couple, they shouldn't go to great lengths to pursue medical treatment, but should just adopt because so many children need a family. She was unaware that there are many more couples in our country waiting to adopt than there are available babies. Although it is good to see trials such as infertility as a time to stop and seek God's guidance, the Bible makes no distinction between infertile or fertile couples in the command to care for orphans (James 1:27). So, every couple, whether or not they can have babies easily, should be open to God's leading about adopting a child. This doesn't mean that it's wrong to attempt to have a biological child.

Investigating on Your Own

If you're hesitant to see a doctor, you can begin some of the investigation on your own. The investigation techniques that can be done at home with temperature charting, mucus testing, and ovulation predictor test kits, focus on finding the wife's most fertile time each month. Knowing for certain that you are having intercourse during your fertile time and presenting your doctor with a BBT chart (see page 134) can also speed up the investigation process once you do visit a doctor.

Basal Body Temperature Chart (BBT)

Charting your basal (resting) temperature doesn't cost anything and because women's temperatures vary slightly according to the fluctuation of reproductive hormones, a chart can show approximately when you ovulate in your menstrual cycle. To do this, take your temperature each morning after you have been asleep at least 4–5 hours, and before you move, eat, or talk. Then mark the temperature on a piece of graph paper which has the temperatures marked down the left hand side and the dates across the top of the page. (These can be obtained from your OB/GYN.) If you ovulate during your cycle, your chart will show two phases. In the phase before you ovulate, your resting temperature is normally near 98 degrees. *After* you ovulate, your resting temperature normally rises about one-half a degree to near 98.5 degrees. Often right before this rise in temperature, there is a dip of several tenths of a degree. Looking at several charts can show a pattern which can help you anticipate the time you will probably ovulate in your next cycle.[3]

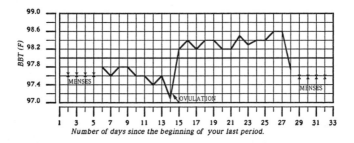

Sample Basal Body Temperature Chart (BBT)

Mucus testing

Cervical mucus also changes according to the fluctuation of reproductive hormones. You can learn to notice this mucus discharge as you wipe yourself after urinating. During non-fertile times, the cervical mucus is opaque, tacky, breaks when stretched or is nonexistent. Just before you ovulate, the properties of the mucus change to provide a better environment for sperm to survive and travel. During this fertile time, the mucus changes to become thinner, clearer, more watery, and looks much like egg white. This fertile type of mucus can last for several days. The most fertile day is the last day of this stretchy, egg-white type mucus.[4]

Ovulation predictor tests

Ovulation predictor test kits are sold over-the-counter in drug stores and cost between $30 and $75 for a five-to-nine-day test kit. They measure the production of the hormone (LH) that triggers ovulation. This surge of LH hormone is evident in a woman's urine 12 to 24 hours before ovulation. So, unlike the BBT chart which shows when you have *already* ovulated, this test helps you to time intercourse for before ovulation occurs.

When It Is Time to See a Doctor

After a year of trying to conceive, the odds of conceiving spontaneously decrease dramatically. If you are in your late 30s or early 40s or have reason to suspect a problem, consulting a doctor makes sense after trying for six months. If the tests show blocked fallopian tubes or a zero sperm count, you may save years of frustration in trying to conceive. (If you have had three or more miscarriages, you may also be helped by seeing a fertility specialist.)

Infertility, in the overwhelming majority of cases, can be traced to a specific medical problem according to fertility specialist Dr. David Adamson: "After a couple has had a thorough history and physical examination, all of the appropriate tests, and a comprehensive evaluation by an infertility specialist, [fewer] than 5 percent of couples could be said to have unexplained infertility."[5]

Going to a doctor can be difficult because with that first appointment, you are admitting there is a problem. Other hurdles you may need to overcome are the invasion of your privacy (physical or emotional), the cost, the time involvement, or the energy needed. These are real parts of the infertility investigation and need to be faced and discussed. You can also make some of the decisions about whether to continue with treatment as you go along.

Many couples can be helped initially by having the wife's *gynecologist* conduct a medical history and physical examination. Because you often already have a relationship with a gynecologist, this can be an easy way to start. However, if your gynecologist doesn't usually treat infertility patients, you might choose to see a *gynecologist with a specialty in infertility,* which means he or she has had extra training in treating infertility. Or if your infertility problem is more difficult, you might need to go to the next level up—a board-certified *reproductive endocrinologist,* a doctor who is trained to treat the more difficult cases of infertility. Some reproductive endocrinologists prefer that you have the preliminary testing done with a gynecologist first. These doctors will either refer your husband to a *urologist* or *andrologist* for testing of the male reproductive system, or they may work directly with a lab for the preliminary male tests.

What to Look for in a Fertility Doctor
If you have a choice of doctors, look for:
- someone with good medical credentials and specific training in infertility testing;
- someone who offers a specific plan for testing and treatment including the total time frame;
- someone who is compassionate about the stress infertility causes;
- someone whose manner or personality makes you feel comfortable enough to ask questions;
- and someone who will take the time to fully answer your questions.

Through interviews or consultations with doctors (on the phone or in person), you should be able to find out many of these things.

If you need help locating a doctor in your area, RESOLVE can help you. (See Appendix A: Resources.)

Questions to ask when deciding on a doctor
Some specific questions to ask a doctor's office staff during a phone interview or the doctor during a consultation appointment include:

- What are the doctor's medical credentials and experience in treating infertility? Who does the actual testing or treatments?
- What percentage of the doctor's patients are infertility patients? (This can be an indicator of the amount of time the doctor is able to spend keeping up with the latest advances in treating infertility. In addition, if the doctor treats pregnant women also, does he schedule infertility patients during specific hours, so they don't have to sit in a waiting room full of pregnant women?)
- What range of services does the doctor's practice provide? Does she suggest an itemized plan with a timetable for tests and treatments?
- What is the doctor's price schedule for the costs of routine tests and treatments? (Also ask for the medical procedure codes to give to your insurance company.)
- How many infertility surgeries (such as laparoscopies or varicocele surgeries) does the doctor perform per year?
- Does he feel comfortable honoring a patient's moral or religious views concerning testing and treatment?
- How available is the doctor for tests or treatments which require critical timing? Does she have backup coverage? (This becomes more important with treatment such as the fertility drug Pergonal which needs to be monitored closely, and intrauterine insemination (IUI), where timing is critical.)

While you are looking for a doctor, it is also a good time to check your health insurance policy, since coverage for infertility treatment varies widely and may even be excluded.

Changing Doctors

At some point you may feel the need to change doctors, but may find it difficult because of the trust you've built or the fear of hurting your current doctor's feelings. But a good doctor will know his limits and refer you to someone with more expertise in your problem area if he has been unable to help you.

You may also feel that you need to change because of specific problems with your doctor. Carole, for instance, decided she wanted to change doctors when she found out that other doctors gave local anesthesia before doing a D & C (dilation and curettage) after a miscarriage. Because her doctor had lacked either the understanding or the training to realize the appropriateness of giving pain medicine before the procedure, she had to deal with unnecessary physical pain in addition to the emotional trauma from her miscarriage.

Vicky found she needed to change doctors because of relational problems.

> Our first doctor was terrible. I can't believe we stayed with him for a year. I think he didn't like or respect women. He talked to me like I was a little girl and to my husband like an adult. When I asked the side effects of a certain drug, he said: "If I tell you, you'll just imagine you have them." He was also rude and rough with the nurses. My second doctor though, was wonderful and understanding.

Don't feel you have to continue seeing a doctor with whom you are unhappy. If you are unable to resolve your concerns after discussing them with your doctor, seeking another opinion might be just what you need. Infertility is stressful enough as it is.

Your Personal Journey

1. Have you prayed about your infertility and asked God to lead you in your decisions?
2. Are you and your husband in agreement on pursuing medical treatments? Do either of you have misgivings?
3. What qualities are important to you in a fertility doctor?

4

The Doctor's Investigation

The medical procedures for infertility are hard
on one's self-esteem. They are a little easier
to bear if your doctor is someone you trust
and respect. — Debbie S.

I wish we had gone to the best doctor we could
find earlier than we did. We basically wasted
the first two years. — Michael

*A*fter six months of charting, then six months
of the fertility drug Clomid with continued charting, I still wasn't pregnant. The gynecologist
asked Michael to see a urologist, and ordered a sperm
analysis (which turned out fine). He then prescribed
stronger doses of Clomid to make me ovulate more regularly.

About six months later we moved back to California. I
started over with a new gynecologist. He told us to continue the now irritating task of temperature-taking; and he
began infertility testing for me, which included blood
work, a hysterosalpingogram, and a diagnostic laparoscopy. During these tests, he prescribed six more months of
Clomid. By this time I was having extreme emotional ups-
and-downs and fatigue as side effects from the Clomid.
With the laparoscopy, the doctor found I had a small

amount of endometriosis, but said he would need to do major abdominal surgery to remove it. So instead, he suggested we just try Clomid again. Emotionally, I couldn't handle more Clomid because the side effects seemed to get worse the longer I took it. About that time, we heard of a reproductive endocrinologist who was skilled at doing the same surgery using a laser. Since laser surgery wouldn't require a full abdominal operation (and our insurance would cover seeing this new doctor), we decided to switch doctors.

When we first visited the reproductive endocrinologist, we felt that we'd finally found someone who understood our struggle and had the expertise to investigate the problem. This doctor was familiar with the latest technology and found that there were tests we had missed. During the consultation he listened, looked at our records, then outlined 12 steps (of tests and treatments) we could take. He then told us that we should know within a year and a half what our chances were of having a biological child. That sounded great. We were tired of the merry-go-round.

The additional tests showed I had a high prolactin level, and Michael had a mycoplasma organism; both my hormone level and Michael's microorganism were corrected with medicine. The doctor was able to do the laser surgery to remove my endometriosis and also open up my right fallopian tube (which had been blocked since birth and hadn't shown up on the hysterosalpingogram). After a break, I ended up taking a few more cycles of Clomid, and eventually also tried eight cycles of other fertility drugs, including Pergonal and Lupron, accompanied by progesterone shots. The whole ordeal frustrated us, wore us out, and took as much time as a part-time job. But, we were compelled to find out if there was a medical answer for our problem.

So many things have to go right for a baby to be created, that it is truly a miracle the process ever works. In the man, the sperm must be produced in sufficient quantities, in the correct shape, and be able to move in a fairly straight fashion. Then the sperm must be transported from the testicles to the penis and ejaculated into the vagina.

In the woman, a mature egg needs to develop and be released from the ovary, then the fimbriae on the end of the fallopian tube need to catch the egg and transport it down the tube. When the sperm is introduced, it needs to be able to cross the cervical mucus, swim up to meet the egg, and penetrate it. Finally, the fertilized egg needs to implant in the wall of the uterus and continue to grow there until the baby is able to live on its own. Any problems with egg or sperm production, egg or sperm transport, egg and sperm joining, or the fertilized egg implanting can contribute to infertility.

The tests for infertility focus on determining where the breakdown occurs in the reproductive process. (Appendix B: Further Reading lists recommended books which cover the fascinating intricacies of the reproductive process.)

The purpose of these medical chapters is to introduce you to the medical side of the fertility process, but they are not meant to be used as a basis for treatment. Consult with a medical professional for any decisions regarding infertility treatment.

History Evaluation

To obtain clues about the reasons for your infertility, the doctor will question both spouses about prior exposure to toxins, previous illnesses, injuries, accidents, operations, and diseases (including those sexually transmitted), the use of prescription medications or illegal drugs, alcohol or tobacco use, caffeine consumption, and the health of extended family members. He or she will also want to know your age, and if you've had significant weight changes, previous abnormal pap smears, and any pregnancies, including miscarriages and tubal pregnancies.

After your consultation, history evaluation, and general physical, the doctor should give you a list of the tests or treatments he or she recommends for you and an estimate of how long it will take to complete them.

Tests for the Wife

Fertility problems are divided fairly evenly between the man's reproductive system and the woman's reproductive system. In many cases, it is a combination of both. So testing of the husband and wife should begin at the same time. Presently, there are a wider variety of tests and treatments available to women.

The pain associated with these tests depends on your sensitivity and on the doctor's expertise. For some patients, the pain on a test is minimal, while for others it can be significant. (Isn't that a nice, calm way to say it?) If you are anxious about pain for any test or know you have a low pain threshold, feel free to ask your doctor for medication prior to any procedure.

Blood of both the husband and wife can be tested for many of the diseases or infections that the doctor asked about in your history evaluation. Blood tests can also evaluate hormone levels and identify certain antibodies which can attack sperm.

Ultrasound
This can be used to check the physical characteristics of the woman's ovaries and uterus.

Post Coital Test (PCT) or Hüner Test
Prior to the PCT, the couple has intercourse, then the wife visits the doctor within a specified number of hours. Cervical mucus is taken from her vagina and analyzed under a microscope to evaluate the existence and behavior of any live sperm in the cervical mucus.

Hysterosalpingogram (HSG)
In this procedure, radio-opaque dye is injected through the cervix into the uterus. Then, if the fallopian tubes are

open, it will spill out the ends of the tubes. X-rays are taken during this procedure to check for open fallopian tubes or abnormalities in the uterus that might interfere with the implantation of a fertilized egg.

Endometrial biopsy
A small piece of uterine lining is removed in the doctor's office and then evaluated under a microscope. This tests the uterine lining to see if it is developing adequately to allow a fertilized egg to implant.

Laparoscopy
This outpatient surgery is done under general anesthetic. The doctor makes one or two small incisions in the woman's abdomen, inserts a small scope, and fills the abdomen with gas to better separate and view the reproductive organs. A surgeon skilled with a laser can also do minor surgical repairs such as remove endometriosis or scar tissue. (It can take between two days and a week to normally recover from this test; some women experience pain in their shoulders from the dissemination of the gas that is introduced into their abdomen.)

A *hysteroscopy* is sometimes also done at this time to look at the inside of the uterus with another scope through the cervix.

Tests for the Husband

Semen analysis
This evaluation of the husband's sperm is usually one of the first tests a doctor orders in the infertility workup. This test requires obtaining a sample of the husband's sperm that has (usually) been masturbated into a specimen cup. The husband should have more than one sperm analysis because sperm counts normally fluctuate between specimens. If collection by masturbation poses a problem or sperm parameters test low, there is also the option of

using a *sterile* condom during intercourse to obtain the specimen. (See the section "Special Seminal Collection Condoms" in chapter 7 for more about this option.)

The semen analysis will show three main things.

Count: The number of sperm per cubic centimeter of semen. Below 20 million is often considered too low for normal fertilization to take place.

Morphology: The shape of the sperm, which is a good indication of its ability to fertilize an egg. At least 60 percent of the sperm should be normal, with an oval head and long tail.

Motility: The ability of the sperm to swim, preferably in a straight line. At least 60 percent should be able to do this.[1]

Hamster-egg penetration assay

In this test, the husband's sperm are placed in a dish with the egg from a female hamster to see if his sperm have the capability to penetrate the egg's surface. (Michael and I had some ethical questions on this one at first because of our concern about life beginning at conception, even though we were assured that the egg could not divide to grow and become a "manster." We realized though, that at no point was it ever a human life, so it never held that status.) Recently, the reliability of the results of this test have come under question. With in vitro fertilization (IVF), doctors have found that even with zero penetration on the hamster egg test, the husband's sperm can sometimes still fertilize his wife's eggs. In addition, a man who has a positive hamster egg test can still fail to fertilize his wife's eggs during an IVF attempt.

Other male tests

If the sperm analysis shows problems with low count (number), motility (ability to swim), or morphology (shape), a urologist and andrologist should investigate further to determine the reason. Additional tests can be done by the doctors to check for problems such as sperm antibodies, high scrotal temperature, or obstructions.

Treatments for the Wife

There are a wide range of treatments for infertility. I will simply highlight the most common areas of treatment.

Fertility drugs

Fertility drugs are often prescribed to induce, time, or regulate ovulation. They will not help a woman with blocked fallopian tubes or uterine abnormalities and can have strong physical and emotional side effects. (Researchers continue to study fertility drugs, and some have raised questions about safety, but so far there has been no conclusive evidence that fertility drugs increase the risk of problems with the mother[2] or child.[3] Long-term effects on the mother or child haven't been studied yet because these drugs are still fairly new. I would recommend that you read the latest studies done on a particular drug before taking it. Ask your doctor for the latest articles or look up the fertility drug's name at a medical library to check the results of the most recent studies. Appendix B also lists some infertility books that focus more on the medical process. Also, if you are planning to take a fertility drug that has the potential of multiple births as a side effect, think through the issues in the *Pregnancy Reduction* or *Embryo Reduction* section in chapter 7.

Clomiphene citrate (Clomid or Serophene) is a synthetic hormone derivative of the drug diethylstilbestrol (DES) that is often taken orally to induce and regulate ovulation. Some of the more common side effects of Clomid include: mild to severe mood swings; fatigue; reduced cervical mucus quality;[4] thinning of the endometrial lining[5]; hot flashes; and about a 10 percent chance of multiple births, mostly twins.

Pergonal (FSH & LH) is an injectable medication as is *Metrodin (FSH alone)*. (FSH is the abbreviation for Follicle Stimulating Hormone and LH stands for Luteinizing Hormone). These drugs also stimulate ovulation. Using these drugs requires a number of daily injections (often administered by the husband and/or wife) and close monitoring of the ovarian follicles which requires several office visits. The cost is usually well over $1,000 per cycle. Some of the more common side effects of Pergonal and Metrodin include: mood swings; breast tenderness; the possibility of over-stimulating the ovaries, causing abdominal pain, bloating, and in rare cases requiring hospitalization; and an elevated multiple birth rate (approximately 20 percent or higher multiple births, most of these twins).[6]

Natural progesterone is often prescribed as a vaginal suppository or as an injectable drug to supplement a woman's own progesterone hormone production. (Progesterone aids in preparing the uterine lining so a fertilized egg can properly implant.)[7] This drug is taken *during* pregnancy. So, although no studies to date have shown that *natural* progesterone (which is different from *synthetic* progesterone) has caused problems with babies who were introduced to it in utero, discuss the need for it carefully with your doctor. Some of the more common side effects of progesterone include: breast tenderness, nausea, fatigue, and vaginal dryness or irritation.

Bromocriptine (Parlodel) is taken orally to reduce a high prolactin hormone level. (Prolactin is the hormone that causes milk production in nursing mothers.) Similar to the reduced fertility in nursing mothers, women with a high prolactin level show reduced fertility. Some of the more common side effects of Parlodel include: nausea, feeling lightheaded, headaches, and nasal congestion.

Leuprolide (Lupron) is an injectable drug, and *Nafarelin (Synarel)* is a nasal spray. They are both used to suppress the production of estrogen. These types of drugs can be used to reduce endometriosis (often in combination with laser surgery) or assist in treatment with Pergonal and Metrodin. *Danazol (Danocrine)* is often prescribed to reduce endometriosis and is a male hormone which has been altered to remove most of the male side effects.[8] Some of the more common side effects of these drugs include: symptoms associated with menopause, oily skin, acne, and an increased appetite.

Surgery
Besides an operative laparoscopy (mentioned earlier in this chapter) the following surgeries may be suggested.

A *laparotomy* is major abdominal surgery in which problems with the ovaries, fallopian tubes, or uterus can be surgically corrected under fiberoptic aided vision.

Tubal surgery involves removing scar tissue or correcting congenital deformities in the fallopian tubes. Because the fallopian tubes are so delicate, the pregnancy rate following tubal surgery is lower than that following surgery on others parts of the woman's reproductive system. It also increases the risk of ectopic (tubal) pregnancies.

A blockage in the fallopian tube can sometimes be opened using a *balloon tuboplasty*. This is an outpatient procedure in which a deflated balloon is inserted into the tube to the place where the blockage occurs. Then it is inflated, resulting in reopening of the tube.

Treatments for the Husband

Sperm washing or processing
Sperm washing or processing can concentrate the healthiest sperm together and reduce detrimental substances in semen, such as sperm antibodies which can inhibit sperm from fertilizing an egg. The washed or processed sperm are used with intrauterine insemination (IUI) or other assisted reproduction techniques (ART).

Fertility drugs
Fertility drugs, such as **Clomiphene citrate (Clomid or Serophene)** are sometimes prescribed for men to increase

sperm production, but studies regarding their effectiveness have been divided.

Surgery

If a varicose vein is found in the scrotum, it is possible it could raise the scrotal temperature sufficiently to cause problems with sperm production. In a ***varicocele operation*** which usually takes about 20 minutes, a small incision is made in the scrotum and the varicose vein is tied off.

This procedure is also being done now without surgery by embolization, in which a soft catheter is fed into one of the gonadial veins where small coils or balloons can be placed to block off the blood flow of the varicose vein.[9]

Further Treatments for Both Husband and Wife

Alternative Treatments

Some couples also choose to explore alternative methods for treating infertility, such as Chinese herbal medicine, acupuncture, homeopathic medicine, chiropractic medicine, relaxation therapy, mega-vitamins, aromatherapy, and so on. If you consider using any of these unregulated alternatives to western medicine, first research their effectiveness. Second, a few of these alternatives may carry religious teaching that is contrary to Christianity. So, just as knowing our moral limits is important when pursuing traditional western medicine, comparing the ideology of nontraditional treatment to biblical truth is also important.

Decision Making within Testing and Treatment

Once you decide to investigate a medical answer, you may either feel a surge of hope or a stab of anxiety brought on by stepping into a strange, uncomfortable new world. Most couples are diagnosed and treated without the need for the "heavy guns" of assisted reproduction. Even so, going to your doctor having done research to know your moral limits, praying about each decision, and feeling assured that you are following God's intention for your lives is vital.

Infertility testing and treatment is difficult because you have to be informed, confident in your knowledge, and assertive about your choices during a time when you are very vulnerable. Information can help you make knowledgeable decisions. If you've asked your doctor about a treatment and don't feel you've received a complete answer, ask again *before* having the treatment done. Or, go to another doctor for a second opinion.

An example of this need for specific information is the time I was told that our insurance wouldn't cover intrauterine insemination (IUI), so I asked the nurse again how much this procedure would help our specific situation. I remembered the doctor referring to it previously as "helping a small percentage of couples." The nurse came back the second time and said it would help our particular problem, maybe 1–2 percent. I was amazed. I had translated "small percentage" as meaning about 35 percent. Knowing this new and much more specific information, made it easier for us to decide about the treatment that month.

I believe that the majority of medical personnel assisting infertile patients are in the field because they genuinely want to help couples have a baby. But, doctors are only people. They may naturally lean toward suggesting their specialty because they know they do it well. If the doctor is a top-notch surgeon, he may recommend surgery more often than another doctor. So we need to be careful consumers and join in the decision-making process.

Infertility is still a new field. New information and studies are being conducted and published around the world. So, in addition to talking with your doctor, check libraries, bookstores, contact RESOLVE, and if you're lucky enough to live near a medical university, use a medical library. Most of them will allow access to the public. If you don't have access to a medical library or don't have time to do the research yourself, the research librarians can often search the literature for you (for a fee) and send the information to you.

What are the financial risks?
In deciding about medical choices, ask yourselves: Will medical insurance cover part or all of the test or treatment? Is this where God would have us spend our financial resources at this time? Since the costs for treatments can range from fifty dollars to several thousand, this can be a major consideration.

What are the physical risks?
The further we get into fertility treatment, the more our bodies are taxed. Take time before and during treatment to ask: Am I worn out physically? Am I taking care of my body? Will these procedures harm my health? There isn't much known about the effects of some of the treatments because the field is so new, such as the effects on monitoring follicle growth by ultrasound or long-term effects of fertility drug use on the adult (or the baby for that matter).

What are the emotional risks?
The hope-and-despair cycle of infertility can make someone who lives on an even keel feel unbalanced very quickly. Introducing the side effects of fertility drugs can add to the imbalance. Before and during treatment, ask yourselves: have we been putting enough emotional energy into caring for our marriage? Are we strong enough to handle the grief if this procedure doesn't work? Do we have emotional support through the process?

Questions to ask the doctor about a particular test or treatment
It is also helpful to make a list of questions to ask the doctor before each visit, test, or treatment. This will en-

sure that your questions will not be forgotten in the stress of the moment. Some questions you might consider are:

- What will this test tell us? Will the results lead to a particular treatment? (The doctor may just be looking for an answer to your infertility or conducting a medical study, but there might be no change in proposed treatment in spite of the results.)

- How many patients are you currently treating with this method who have my particular infertility problem? And has this treatment been shown to improve pregnancy rates for couples in our situation? (It is better not to be one of the first patients or one of a very few.)

- Are there any side effects from this test or treatment? What could go wrong? (One doctor I went to opened up a box of medication, threw away the papers inside, then handed me the pills. When I asked what he'd thrown away, he replied, "Oh, those are just alarmist warnings. You don't need them." I realized at this point that I wasn't being treated like a participant in my treatment and decided not to go back to that doctor.)

- Where can I get literature that more fully explains these proposed tests and treatments?

Your Personal Journey

1. How far do you and your spouse want to pursue medical treatment before pursuing other options?
2. Are you making any sacrifices to become pregnant about which you don't have peace?

5

Examining Assisted Reproduction Techniques

He healeth those that are broken in heart: and giveth medicine to heal their sickness.[1]

As soon as questions of will or decision or reason or choice of action arise, human science is at a loss.[2]

I waited early in the morning in a cold little hallway outside the teaching hospital's lab. Two other women had come before me, and I wondered if they were there for the same reason. Soon a technician showed up to open the door. The woman before me reached under her coat and brought out a little specimen cup. Ah, so she was here to have her husband's sperm washed also. When they called me, I took out my little jar that I'd been keeping warm and watched them write my husband's name on it. While I waited the two hours for the wash to be done, I read in the hospital's library, then went back to pick up my husband's newly washed sperm. (I smiled at the thought of the little guys singing in the shower as they all scrubbed up.)

Holding the vial of sperm, I sped down the road to my doctor's office (getting lost on the way) and arrived upstairs breathless and stressed. The nurse did the insemination, which was simple and painless, and after 20 minutes I went home. I kept feeling strange that Michael wasn't with me. I felt disconnected from him. I decided that if we did this again, I would ask him to come too.

I was astonished when my period didn't come. I felt pregnant, but didn't want to run the risk of another negative pregnancy test, so I waited—at least a full day. I couldn't believe it when the nurse said the test was positive. I was thrilled, but later a thought suddenly popped into my mind. I hope they didn't mix up the sperm samples at the lab. I hope this child is Michael's.

I had never even considered this possibility before. I probably wouldn't have thought of it then, if there hadn't been two other women waiting with semen specimens at the lab. I think I was blocking myself from believing this sperm might actually become a baby. The first reason was because it was difficult to believe that it actually might work after the trouble we'd had conceiving. Secondly, I was protecting myself. I went through the medical motions trying not to think of the outcome, hoping that if it failed, my emotions wouldn't plummet so low.

Then, when the procedure actually worked, I realized I had never thought it through. Because of the hospital's reputation, I had assumed that everything would be fine, but I now realized that my parenting responsibility had started with watching over our eggs and sperm because of their potential. I wish I had asked more questions before the procedure. I wish I had met the lab personnel who would do the procedure. I wish I had asked to watch.

(A few months later I miscarried.)

Assisted reproductive techniques are ethically complex. It isn't wise to treat them just as medical procedures, such as setting a broken arm, because they involve the most intimate part of a marriage relationship and the beginning of a human life. But to condemn them simply because they are complex doesn't do justice to those suffering from infertility's damaging effects.

Before going further, I would like to say that there should be increased effort in the medical community toward finding solutions which actually fix reproductive problems (such as tubal repair, hormone balancing, and methods to raise sperm motility), rather than the new assisted reproduction techniques which bypass the problems, treat the symptom, but place the control in others' hands. I haven't yet found an infertile couple who prefer to go through an "unnatural" process if they don't have to.

Once assured that God would have us pursue medical treatment to have a child, we may be faced with the option of using assisted reproduction techniques and the ethical dilemmas they raise.

I've included some of the evaluations that Michael and I did on each option to help your thinking process. This isn't meant to imply that everyone should come to the same conclusion, but hopefully our thoughts will spark discussion between you and your spouse.

Artificial Insemination
with Husband's Sperm (AIH)

In AIH, the husband's sperm is washed (separated from the seminal fluid), concentrated, and placed within the wife's vagina, cervix, or uterus.

Critics of this procedure believe that it is morally wrong to separate the act of making love from procreation. Although the most conservative Christians reject AIH as not being "natural," generally this procedure does not generate much discussion in most evangelical circles because it involves the husband's sperm and the wife's egg(s) and conception happens inside the wife's body.

Personally, Michael and I had little ethical problem with this procedure. We tried AIH once. If we ever used this technique again, I would be more vigilant with Michael's sperm, and we would both plan to be present for the insemination procedure.

Thinking it through

1. Because the sperm is processed in a lab, there is a remote possibility of a mix-up of sperm or problems from the manipulation of sperm. Do you feel comfortable with the professionalism of the lab?

2. Can you accept the clinical nature of this procedure? (This procedure can involve masturbation and takes the creation of life from the bedroom to the lab and the doctor's office. This may be unacceptable to some couples.)

Gamete Intrafallopian Transfer (GIFT) with Husband's Sperm and Wife's Eggs

In this procedure the wife is usually given fertility drugs, then her mature eggs are taken from her ovaries and placed in a sterile syringe. The husband's sperm are added to the syringe and the contents of the syringe are immediately transferred to the wife's fallopian tube(s) during a laparoscopy in hopes that fertilization will occur within her fallopian tube(s). The main ethical advantage of GIFT over in vitro fertilization (IVF) is that since the sperm and egg are replaced before fertilization occurs, the embryo is never under an outsider's control or vulnerable to exploitive manipulation.

In a variation of this procedure called *Zygote Intrafallopian Transfer (ZIFT)*, the sperm are allowed to fertilize the egg(s), then (usually 24 hours after retrieval) the fertilized eggs (zygotes) are transferred to the wife's fallopian tube(s).

Either of these procedures typically cost between $9,000 and $12,000.

Thinking it through

1. The previous questions raised with AIH, also apply to GIFT and ZIFT because the sperm must be washed for this procedure.

2. How many mature eggs would you choose to have placed back into the fallopian tube(s) with the sperm?

(GIFT is almost always done during a cycle when the wife has taken fertility drugs because the success rates using a single egg are discouragingly low.)

3. The cycle of drugs and the retrieval procedure can be emotionally and physically difficult. Are you and your spouse able to handle this? Because the GIFT procedure also normally requires a laparoscopy for the wife, is she physically able and emotionally ready to handle an operation?

In Vitro Fertilization and Embryo Transfer (IVF/ET) with Husband's Sperm and Wife's Eggs

With IVF the wife is usually given fertility drugs, then the mature eggs are taken from her ovaries and placed with the husband's sperm in a sterile solution in a petri dish. After approximately 48–72 hours the eggs are checked to see if they have fertilized and the fertilized eggs can be transferred into the wife's uterus. This procedure typically costs between $8,000 and $11,000.

The opinions about IVF within Christian communities are varied. Echoing one common belief among evangelical Christians, Steve Zeisler, a pastor at Peninsula Bible Church in Palo Alto, California, said, "I don't think in vitro fertilization is wrong in and of itself. . . . That conception should take place in a dish and then the [fertilized] egg is placed back in the woman, does not seem to be beyond what is [biblically] proper."

Yet in the Roman Catholic Church, this procedure is considered wrong because it doesn't allow natural conception in the wife's body. Lori even found that the stigma against the procedure extended to her child. "When I went to have my baby baptized [in the Roman Catholic church]," said Lori with her eyes wide, "I was told that she was less 'ensouled' than a natural-born child because she was conceived by IVF."

Rather than having problems with the idea of fertilizing a human egg in a dish, many Christians are more concerned with whether the resulting embryo is being treated with respect. What about the number of embryos that don't develop or aren't allowed to develop after fertilization has occurred? Dr. Alan McNickle, a Professor of Theology at Moody Bible Institute voiced his concern: "In the matter of [IVF], one problem is that the technology appears to be indiscriminate in what happens to the harvested eggs that are fertilized, but then are essentially lost. This seemingly casual attitude toward the value of human life is disturbing."

Is it possible to use IVF, while still respecting the immense value of human life? Could couples who believe that life begins at conception use IVF without compromising their ethics? The deciding factor depends on the decisions couples make within IVF treatment. In the book *From Infertility to In Vitro Fertilization,* the authors list some of the questions a couple face within the IVF process.

> [These decisions] include: (1) how many eggs they wish to have fertilized; (2) what they want to do with any excess eggs; (3) how many embryos they want to have transferred into the uterus; (4) how they wish to dispose of any excess embryos; and (5) how they would deal with a large multiple pregnancy (quadruplets or larger), should that occur. . . . You must be prepared to deal with the consequences of a multiple pregnancy or else transfer no more embryos than you have are willing to have develop into babies.

The authors also say that if you want to be sure of only one baby, you have to transfer only one embryo, "but you then only have an 8 percent chance of getting pregnant."[3]

The reason for using more eggs in IVF is that usually not all of the eggs retrieved will fertilize, not all of the fertilized eggs will divide correctly, and not all the embryos transferred will implant. The concept is to fertilize more eggs than needed in order to give a better chance at pregnancy. But, as with all odds, there are times when nothing works and times when everything works. (The problem of

too many embryos is discussed in the "Pregnancy Reduction or Embryo Reduction" section later in chapter 7.)

IVF adds a few more options because the embryos are
outside of the woman's body for a short period of time.

• *Option 1: Freezing extra embryos (cryopreser-*
vation) for transfer to the woman's uterus later.

The problem with freezing embryos is that up to 50
percent of them may be destroyed in the freezing process.[4]
(With newer freezing techniques, some labs are reporting
increased survival rates of thawed embryos to 72 percent.[5]

Some doctors see the fertilized eggs that don't survive
the freezing process as the ones that probably wouldn't
have survived the natural fertilization/implantation process. They feel that if there are more embryos than the
couple wants to transfer, freezing the embryos follows the
principle of giving them every possible chance of survival.

Another viewpoint, held by Dr. Vernon Grounds, chancellor at Denver Seminary, considers it immoral to participate in any process that allows human life to perish. Dr.
Grounds views freezing embryos as "initiating a process
which is inevitably bound to kill some of them. You deliberately fertilize some eggs, then deliberately allow some of
those eggs to die. Isn't that in fact killing off potential
human life as in an abortion?"

The reason that the embryos don't survive remains a
gray area. It is believed that a large percentage of eggs that
fertilize within a woman's body also don't survive and are
sloughed off with her monthly period.

Another consideration in freezing embryos is the legal
problems that have occurred when couples divorce or die,
leaving frozen embryos in limbo. "Custody" battles and
even the right to destroy frozen embryos are currently
being fought in our courts.

• *Option 2: Donating the extra embryos to another*
infertile couple.

The dilemmas with giving away extra embryos to another infertile couple are similar to that of a woman giving up

her baby for adoption: ensuring that the child will be raised in a godly home, always wondering if the child is OK, and the trauma of mourning the loss of your child. An additional concern would be the possibility that you might remain childless, yet would always wonder if you have a genetic child living somewhere.

As Christians, we are responsible for the children that are created from our sperm or eggs. Just as with a Christian placing a child for adoption, it would be a tragedy to participate in the creation of a life, then not take steps to ensure that the child will be introduced to a relationship with God. We are not only responsible for our children's earthly development but also for their spiritual development.

• *Option 3: Transferring all of the embryos into the wife's uterus, no matter how many.*

The problems with this are discussed in the "Pregnancy Reduction or Embryo Reduction" section later in chapter 7.

• *Option 4: Letting the "extra" embryos die.*

While we believe from the Bible that God is involved with children in the womb, the Bible doesn't pinpoint whether the exact moment of "ensoulment" is conception or sometime during the early weeks or pregnancy, such as implantation. Since we don't know, the repercussions of letting embryos die are enormous. At best, choosing to purposefully let embryos die does not respect the immense value of human life.

Michael and I believe IVF could be an ethical choice for us depending on the way we proceeded with it. One way we feel that the IVF process would be within our Christian ethics is to ask a trusted doctor to guarantee that he or she would try to fertilize only the number of embryos we would be willing to carry to term then transfer all of the embryos. We would check out the clinic's success rate to make sure our embryos had the best chance of survival, but of equal importance in our decision to use a particular

clinic would be how they treat the embryos in the lab.
Other options are available with IVF, such as micro manipulation in which a small hole is made in the outer layer
of an egg to allow a single sperm to penetrate it, micro
injection in which a sperm is inserted directly into an egg,
or assisted hatching where a small hole is made in the
outer layer of the embryo to aid in its attachment to the
uterine wall. These procedures are so new that we don't
yet know if the children they produce will have problems.

Thinking it through

1. The previous questions raised with AIH also apply to
IVF because the sperm must be washed for this procedure.
2. How many eggs would you try to retrieve, fertilize, and
transfer? (IVF is almost always done during a cycle when
the wife has taken fertility drugs because the success rate
using a single egg is discouragingly low.)
3. If you are thinking of freezing embryos, have you investigated how the freezing/thawing process will affect the
embryos? What would happen to the frozen embryos if
something were to happen to you before they could be
thawed and transferred? What if you hit a "home run" on
the first attempt and became pregnant with triplets, but
had frozen ten "extra" embryos. If you would be happy
with two children, will you go through the effort and expense to go back and follow through with transferring the
remaining frozen embryos?
4. If you choose to implant three or more embryos, think
through the issues in the "Pregnancy Reduction or Embryo
Reduction" section in chapter 7.
5. The cycle of drugs and the retrieval procedure can be
emotionally and physically difficult. Is the wife able to
handle this? (Normally the eggs can be retrieved trans-
vaginally, but occasionally, the IVF procedure might require a laparoscopy for the wife. Is she physically and
emotionally able to handle surgery?)

6. Based on the success rates and the experimentation still being done, IVF is still in its early stages. Are you informed enough about the safety of the procedure to feel comfortable creating a child this way?

Using Donated Sperm or Eggs

When a husband's sperm or wife's eggs are not healthy enough for conception, donor sperm or eggs can be introduced to obtain a pregnancy.

In the Donor Insemination (DI) procedure, the donor's sperm (usually from an anonymous donor) is washed, concentrated, and placed within the wife's vagina, cervix, or uterus using a sterile syringe. This procedure is relatively inexpensive.

In IVF with donor egg(s) (from either an anonymous or known donor), the donor egg(s) are fertilized with the husband's sperm using the same process as "normal" IVF. The cycles of the donor and recipient are synchronized; the donor is given fertility drugs while the wife is given hormones to prepare her uterus. Then the embryos are transferred to the wife's uterus. The cost is about twice as much as regular IVF, but offers a higher *overall* success rate.

In IVF with donor egg(s) *and* donor sperm (sometimes referred to as embryo adoption), the procedure is the same, except that the couple doesn't contribute genetically to the child at all.

Is using a donor equal to infidelity?

While the procedure of using donors within DI and IVF differ, the unique ethical issue they raise is the introduction of a third party within the marriage. Many Roman Catholics and conservative Protestants view DI as a violation of the "one flesh" that God originally intended in marriage, and believe it is similar to infidelity. To many in the Christian faith though, there is no direct correlation between infidelity and using donor eggs or sperm because sex is not involved. As Dr. Grounds stated in a telephone conversation:

> Some would say that if two are joined together, it is God's intention *they* produce children, that if they cannot produce children, then the use of donated sperm or eggs is, in effect, a violation of their relationship as a married couple. But, I don't see how you could oppose it as in any way violating the nuptial bond, because there is no physical contact whatever—nothing of a sexual or amorous nature.

There are Christian couples who have thoughtfully investigated using donor eggs or sperm. They have earnestly prayed about it, sought guidance from pastors or those well-versed in Scripture, then decided to proceed. Donna and her husband Joe decided on donor insemination after discovering Joe's zero sperm count. They now have two boys conceived through donor insemination.

> We went to a lawyer and started the adoption paperwork, but didn't feel any peace about it. It was expensive and uncertain. We prayed about donor insemination, talked to a pastor, and felt that God had put us in an age where it was one of our options.
>
> We chose not to make it public, just to tell a couple of family members because we thought that would be better for our children's relationship with their father. The sperm bank sent us a list of donor characteristics. For both children, the process was similar. We chose as many of Joe's characteristics as possible, like hair color, height, and blood type (so if our children ever needed a transfusion, they wouldn't learn about their genetic paternity during a crisis). I had to sign forms saying that although the sperm bank screened for AIDS, if I contracted it, they weren't responsible. Joe also had to sign a form saying that he could never claim the child wasn't his.
>
> We had the sperm delivered from the sperm bank to my gynecologist's office. Joe was present during the inseminations in the doctor's office. With our first baby, we didn't

conceive until after the third set of inseminations. That night of the last insemination, we went out and had an incredibly romantic evening. The pregnancy may have come from the physical seed of someone else, but it was from our union.

I did have a few worries once I got pregnant that the bank might have mixed up the vials, and I would give birth to a baby of a different race. That would have been hard to explain.

When Jay was born, he looked so much like me I was worried, but he's such a Daddy's boy. Jeffrey, our second, looks more like my husband. . . . My husband's father was very prejudiced about everyone when he was alive, so telling him about using a donor would have been a problem. I know that if we had adopted, he would have had a hard time also, though. My mother felt it was private, but not wrong.

We worried that it would constantly be an issue, but Joe says he doesn't even remember unless it is specifically brought up.

The positive impact of using a donor

Christians open to donor insemination see it as a valid option for Christian infertile couples today and see the main impact from the use of donor gametes (sperm or eggs) on marriage relationships to be positive. Some Christians also base their positive view of using donor gametes on the flexible view of conceiving children as seen in the Old Testament. (See chapter 6 for a further discussion on this.)

A child conceived by one spouse and an *anonymous* donor has an advantage over adoption in that the child legally belongs to the couple *immediately*. This makes conception with a donor more attractive than adoption in some ways because our legal system has incorporated so much red tape and so many laws supporting the biological parents over the adoptive parents during the first months and even years of the adoption process. If a woman becomes pregnant using donated gametes, the parents don't have the worry that a birth-mother will change her mind. With anonymous donor conception, no one can take your child. He or she is legally yours from the start.

Problems with using a donor

DI is not a simple solution for male factor infertility, however, nor is receiving donated eggs a quick fix for female infertility. Sharon said she didn't think about some of the complex issues of using donor sperm before she and her husband used this method to conceive: "I guess I really didn't think through the ethics of our decision. I was a new Christian, and we weren't attending any church at the time. We just decided to do it. I felt adulterous about it to begin with, but my sister said at least it would be half ours."

The psychological difficulties when using donor sperm or eggs are complex, as John Jefferson Davis, a professor of Theology at Gordon-Conwell Theological Seminary in South Hamilton, Massachusetts writes:

> AID [Artificial Insemination by Donor] introduces an imbalance into the relationship between the husband and the wife. Her maternal functions have been fulfilled, but his paternal function has not. The AID child remains as a constant reminder of his biological failure, and the shadow of an anonymous third party clouds the relationship.[6]

Annette Baran and Reuben Pannor wrote the book *Lethal Secrets* about some long-term consequences of DI. They talked with older children and adults who had been conceived by DI, sperm donors, and infertile couples who used DI procedures. They found remorse on the part of some of the men who donated sperm once they had grown older and had their own families. It was then the men realized the implications of what they'd done. The authors also found donor offspring who felt cut off from their genetic father's roots, similar to the way some adopted children feel.

And they found infertile men who struggled years later with their decision to have their wives conceive through DI. The following summary of one couple's experience shows some of the psychological under-currents:

> During the period when Zack's wife was undergoing monthly inseminations of donor sperm, Zack experienced a myriad of feelings, ranging from anger, despair, fear, and anxiety to withdrawal and depression. He had readily agreed to insemination for his wife when it was offered by the doctor as the obvious solution. He wanted and needed a fast solution because of the depth of his pain. . . . [but] he needed to recognize the ramifications of his loss in terms of family name, blood line, genetic continuity, and sense of immortality. Not only did he need to live through that pain and loss, but he needed to recognize how important the shared experience of biological parenting with Carly had been to him. Now not only was he not siring a child, but he and Carly together were not producing the progeny that would have represented their coupling and loving.
>
> In our interviews . . . we became increasingly aware of how tentative [the sterile husbands'] feelings about the use of donor insemination really were . . . [but] to deny their wives the experience of pregnancy was unthinkable for most of them. If they could not provide sperm, they had to let someone else do it for them.
>
> To most of these men, that sperm was emotionally equivalent to infidelity. . . . [The couples'] relationship under-[went] subtle changes, and the balance of power [was] shifted.[7]

Obviously some infertile men (and women) have reservations about using donor sperm (or eggs) even after their child is conceived and born. The further choice of confidentiality or openness about the procedure adds another layer of complexity. The premise of *Lethal Secrets* is that it would be better for the childrens' sakes to do away with the secrecy so that they are allowed to know their genetic heritage. The problem with this openness though, is that it insinuates the third-party donor into an even more prominent place in the couple's marriage.

For those contemplating using donor sperm or eggs, it is extremely important to listen closely to your spouse, voice all hesitations about this procedure, and if the partner who's infertility will not be cured by this procedure has any hesitations, it probably should not be done.

With the potential consequences, is it wise?

Because of the problems just mentioned, some Christians such as Pastor Steve Zeisler see the use of donor sperm or eggs as unwise:

> I think it is much wiser . . . that a couple would be better off adopting a child whose genes are 100 percent unrelated to them rather than attempting to have a child with genes 50 percent related [which would mean] one of them—husband or wife—[would be] excluded from that relationship. I think the emotional tangle between Sarai and Abram that resulted from the situation with Hagar suggests some of the difficulties that a couple would probably have with donor eggs or sperm. Once it becomes clear that God won't allow a child to be born except with third-party help, I think the wiser course then is to ask Him for a child to care for who is already born [as in adoption].

What about a donated embryo?

Embryo adoption, which uses both donor eggs and donor sperm, doesn't raise the concerns about the baby being connected biologically to just the husband or just the wife. If another infertile couple who had extra embryos were going to choose to let them die, would you perhaps be saving lives by adopting the embryos?

In the best and worst case

In the best scenario, using a donor to help you create a baby enables both you and your spouse to have the family you desire with minimal regrets for either of you. You draw closer as husband and wife because of the experience of parenting. Your child may question her heritage at some time, but your love makes her feel so secure that she doesn't give it much thought.

In the worst scenario, the child causes an imbalance and constant tension in your marriage because one or both of you never recovers from the fact that your child is not genetically the infertile spouse's. The child reacts angrily to the knowledge of her lack of genetic connection to one parent.

Personally, using donated sperm or eggs is an option with which neither Michael nor I would feel comfortable. It is not because of biblical absolutes, but because of the relational issues involved. We would also rather be infertile together and adopt (with all of its expense and trauma) than have one spouse cured and the other still struggle with feelings of inadequacy. Of course, this decision is based more on theory for us, since this would not help our particular problem. The option we might consider would be receiving "extra" embryos (created during an IVF procedure) that a couple will not consider trying to implant. This situation seems similar to adoption because we might be saving the life of a child already created who wouldn't have a chance otherwise.

Thinking it through

1. Consider how you both *really* feel about using the sperm or egg of a donor to conceive a child. How would the introduction of a known or unknown donor affect your marriage relationship? Would the spouse whose infertility is not cured see the child as a symbol of his or her failure?

2. Are the testing and controls to prevent donors from passing diseases, such as AIDS or other sexually transmitted diseases, acceptable to you?

3. Have you thought about the possible physical harm to

the egg donor? The hormones and procedure to retrieve the eggs have a small potential to damage her reproductive organs.

4. Would you choose to tell the child of her biological parentage or keep it confidential?

(a) If you choose to tell the child and the donor is anonymous, how might you deal with a child who feels something is missing in her life by not knowing half of her genetic roots?

(b) If you choose to keep the child's genetic parentage confidential, how will you deal with the possibility of the child "accidentally" finding out the truth—either by a medical emergency or by someone who knew of your infertile condition?

5. Have you considered the possibility of donor children growing up to unknowingly marry a half-sibling?

6. Do you feel that it is ethical to pay a donor for sperm, eggs, or embryos?

Surrogacy

Surrogacy is when a woman other than the wife agrees to carry a child for a couple. It can involve: (1) the husband's sperm and wife's eggs fertilized through IVF, (2) the husband's sperm and the surrogate's eggs fertilized either through IVF or DI, or (3) donor eggs and donor sperm fertilized through IVF. If the eggs have been fertilized through IVF, they are transferred into the surrogate's uterus.

The main concern with surrogacy is the involvement of a known third party introduced into the marriage and the resulting changes in the couple's relationship. It can also cause confusing and painful maternal feelings on the part of the surrogate. When the surrogate has no genetic tie to the child, as in the case of using the husband's sperm and wife's egg(s), it is hoped that she would not bond with the child as strongly as if it were genetically 50 percent her child, but no one knows how strongly a surrogate will feel toward the baby she is carrying until she is already carrying the child or even until delivery.

God allowed a form of surrogacy (with concubines) during a certain period of Israel's history, but it was not always beneficial. For instance, it caused pain and rivalry between Sarai and Hagar, depression for Sarai, disharmony within Sarai and Abram's marriage, pain in Ishmael's life, and warring of subsequent generations and nations.

"You need to look at what is God's intention in marriage," said Dr. Vernon Grounds. "If the woman is unable to carry the child, would it be better for her to accept that as a limitation rather than having a child produced by another woman who in fact is the mother?"

The continued legal, relational, and ethical problems with surrogacy concern me personally: the surrogate's grief (and that of her other children, since most surrogates are required to have borne other children to prove fertility) in surrendering the child, the surrogate's potential bonding to the husband while carrying his genetic child, the possible confusion of the child later on, the child's missing genetic heritage in some instances, and the payment made to the surrogate.

The type of surrogacy where the embryo is created through IVF, then carried by a surrogate who has no genetic ties is sometimes done by a sister or mother. This type of surrogacy eliminates many of the concerns about surrogacy. Yet, it still involves a known third party in the marriage/reproductive relationship. The biological parents also still need to legally adopt the baby after delivery because in most situations, the surrogate must be placed on the birth certificate as the legal mother of the baby. In a recent case of a gestational surrogate suing for rights to the child, the court ruled that since the genetic material for the child was from the husband and wife, the child was legally theirs. This was a painful case where the surrogate bonded with the child.

Thinking it through

1. What effect would introducing a (fertile) and known surrogate have on your marriage relationship?

2. What role would the surrogate play in your family's life after the birth of the baby?

3. Have you thought about the possible physical or emotional harm to the surrogate (and possible emotional harm to her spouse and children)?

4. What if the surrogate changed her mind and wanted to keep the baby? How would you handle this?

5. Would using a surrogate cause confusion in the child's life? How would you handle this?

6. What would you do if something was wrong with the baby?

7. What would happen to the child if you were to die before the surrogate gave birth?

8. How would you feel about paying a woman to genetically contribute and/or carry a child for you? Is there an ethical difference between assisting a birth mother with expenses for a child already conceived and paying someone to conceive and birth a child for you?

Your Personal Journey

1. What do you feel is God's desire for your marriage? Do you as a couple feel that pursuing any of the assisted reproductive techniques might be an ethical option for you? Which ones?

2. Even if you are not yet a candidate for these treatments, discuss them ahead of time. With which procedures would you be ethically comfortable or uncomfortable? Why?

3. Would taking the medical, emotional, and financial risks needed for these treatments be acceptable to you?

6

Finding Help for Making Ethical Decisions

If you want to know what God wants you to do, ask Him, and He will gladly tell you, for He is always ready to give a bountiful supply of wisdom to all who ask Him; He will not resent it (James 1:5).

Love does no wrong to anyone (Romans 13:10).

He that always gives way to others will end in having no principles of his own. —Aesop

I progressed through the medical tests and treatments until the next option for me was the fertility drug Pergonal. If things went well, I could fit in two cycles of Pergonal treatment before our insurance changed. (This was important because each Pergonal cycle would cost between $2,000 and $3,000.) Again we hoped that our problem would be fixed.

Everything looked great midway through the first cycle of Pergonal. The latest ultrasound showed that two eggs on my left side (the side with the good fallopian tube) were maturing well. With each ultrasound, I became intimately aware of the earliest stages of my eggs' development. On the way home from one ultrasound appointment I found myself saying to God, "Lord, I pray that one of these two eggs that are growing so well will become our next child." Then I started laughing at myself; I was feeling maternal

71

toward my eggs before they were even fertilized!

I went in the next day—the day the eggs finally should
have been big enough to be released—excited to take the
next step. The ultrasound though, showed that more eggs
had developed. Some had even grown large enough overnight to have a viable chance of being fertilized and producing a baby. There were at least seven potentially viable
eggs. So, if I chose to take the HCG shot to release the
eggs and proceed with the insemination, we could possibly
become pregnant with seven babies.

I was stunned. I was faced with a choice of no baby or
possibly seven. And I'd gone through such effort and pain
on this cycle! I told the doctor that "pregnancy reduction"
was not an option for me. (My belief that life was given by
God and that we didn't have the right to take it away
unless we had just cause, had solidified during my years
of infertility treatment. I had seen the intricacies of the
reproductive process up close, with all the marvelous
changes and development that happen so quickly once an
egg and sperm join. It was because of this awareness of
how early brain waves and heartbeat started in a fetus
that I had developed convictions against abortion.)

The doctor seemed surprised at my decision against
pregnancy reduction, but he told me I had about a 5 percent chance of a multiple pregnancy over three. It was so
hard to have come that far then choose to stop. Part of me
felt like playing the odds, with the hopes that we'd only
have one or two babies. But then I thought about how
excruciating it would be to get pregnant and find out there
were four or five. Medically, I had reason to believe my
body couldn't carry that many to term. So, if I was to
become pregnant with multiples, I would have to decide if
I wanted to end the lives of some of my children with the
hopes that I could carry a few of them to term.

I felt so strongly against abortion that I never dreamed
I'd even consider it as a possibility, much less a realistic
option. It was incredible that wanting a baby so badly

*would make me now consider abortion. My mind rational-
ized: If we abstain from sex and don't let the sperm near
the eggs (the ones I'd already bonded with), they would
never produce life anyway.... But if I gave them a
chance, I might have to take life from some of them....
But that would at least give the chance of life to two. It
was hard for me to deny the possibility of life to the eggs
I'd already thought about as my future children.*

*I was not in the best physical or emotional shape to
think through this enormous decision. I had pelvic aches
and nausea from the Pergonal, bruised arms from the
needles for blood testing, sore hips from the Pergonal injections, a sore throat, laryngitis, and was hobbling
around on crutches with my broken right foot in a cast.
Within five hours I needed to make the choice: take the
HCG shot to release the eggs or miss the opportunity.*

There is a difference between theoretical discussion and
having to make ethical decisions that affect you personally.
When I was right on the brink of another failed cycle or
was feeling emotionally fragile from fertility drugs, I found
that making a good moral choice was more difficult than I
ever dreamed it would be. That was compounded by the
knowledge that my time for having children was limited.
My purpose for including this chapter is not to give final
answers to all the theoretical ethical dilemmas, but to ac-
quaint you with some ethical issues you might encounter
and to allow you the chance to think through your convictions before you're in an upheaval of emotion.

Our dilemmas do not revolve around growing a baby in
a cow's stomach or creating a super race, but as Christians,
we just want to know if it is within our moral bounds to
use the new medical technology to help us have a baby.

A doctor I recently visited told me: "I think religion has
no place in medicine. It should be kept totally separate."
He didn't understand that Christians are unable to shut
down their awareness of God and the spiritual consequences of their actions.

On the other hand, the author of a recently published Christian book stated that all assisted reproductive technology (ART) is improper, implying that the less a couple does medically to have a child, the more spiritual they are. I don't find a biblical basis for this viewpoint either.

I believe Christians can find help in making ethical decisions by (1) knowing what the Bible says on the matter, (2) praying to keep our hearts right with God, and (3) knowing the proper medical information.

The Bible is not definitive on some of the ethical issues of infertility testing and treatment, so there is room for disagreement about some choices. But, the Bible can be used for guidance to explore several of the gray areas.

Biblical Directives and Principles

In looking for direct biblical instructions, I searched in my concordance under "Assisted Reproductive Techniques," but couldn't find it listed. I really wanted something like: 1 Conceptions 28:13 — "Do not participate in using in vitro fertilization to create life unless it is before sundown on the Sabbath. Fertilize no more than three eggs, replace them within 72 hours without tampering with them and it shall be well with your household."

I didn't find that. But I did find biblical principles that apply to bringing life into the world.

- **Who gives life and when?**
God gives life and is ultimately in charge of creating life.
"The Lord God formed a man's body . . . and breathed into it the breath of life. And man became a living person" (Gen. 2:7).

"He Himself gives life and breath to everything" (Acts 17:25).

- **How valuable is a human life?**
Even before birth, God values a human life, knows it, and has a purpose for it.

The verses below show God's connection with a soul and His planned purpose for it before the fetus even grows in the womb or is born.

God said to Jeremiah that He planned and had purpose for his life before he was born: "Before I formed you in the womb I knew you, before you were born I set you apart" (Jer. 1:5, NIV).

David said to God: "All the days ordained for me were written in Your book before one of them came to be" (Ps. 139:16, NIV).

Elizabeth said to Mary: "As soon as the sound of your greeting reached my ears, the baby in my womb leaped for joy" (Luke 1:44, NIV). In verse 1:36, the angel told Mary that Elizabeth was in her sixth month of pregnancy. Mary left right away to visit Elizabeth. Then in verses 1:41-44, when Mary and Elizabeth saw each other, Elizabeth's baby (John the Baptist) was spiritually aware of Mary's baby (Jesus) who was just conceived.

Each human being is created in God's image and so has incalculable value.

"Then God said, 'Let Us make man in Our image, according to Our likeness' " (Gen. 1:26, NASB).

"Not one sparrow . . . can fall to the ground without your Father knowing it. And the very hairs of your head are all numbered. So don't worry! You are more valuable to Him than many sparrows" (Matt. 10:29-31).

"God loved the world so much that He gave His only Son so that anyone who believes in Him shall not perish but have eternal life" (John 3:16).

God created people as eternal beings.

"Jesus told her, ' . . . He is given eternal life for believing in Me and shall never perish' " (John 11:25-26).

"God has given us eternal life" (1 John 5:11).

● *What is the purpose of marriage?*
Marriage is given to us as a picture of God's love for us.

Emotional and physical fidelity is essential to a Christian marriage. Sexual relations outside of marriage are not acceptable.

"God will rejoice over you as a bridegroom with His bride" (Isa. 62:5).

"Honor your marriage and its vows, and be pure; for God will surely punish all those who are immoral or commit adultery" (Heb. 13:4).

God originally linked the act of intimacy, of two becoming one, with procreation.

God created man and woman and immediately told them to procreate. But, the marriage/sexual union is more than a promise to bring genetic material to life. It includes the emotional, spiritual, and relationship bond that transforms a man and a woman into a union so strong they become soulmates.

"This explains why a man leaves his father and mother and is joined to his wife in such a way that the two become one person" (Gen. 2:24).

"God said to them, 'Be fruitful and multiply, and fill the earth' " (Gen. 1:28, NASB). (Some people believe this is a corporate command for mankind that has been fulfilled, since humans now "fill the earth" by living on every continent. Others believe it is an individual command to every married couple to have children or adopt them.)

● *Does the reason or method matter?*
God cares about our motives.

I mentioned this point in chapter 2: "The Desire for a Family." Children are meant to be a natural outcome of marriage, but since children aren't coming to us "naturally," we have the time to examine our motives for having them. Are we pursuing children because God is directing us to do it? Or are we pushing God out of the picture and turning to medicine as an alternative to trusting God? Are we transferring our trust in God to trust in a technique or a doctor? A procedure can be right or wrong depending on our motives.

"But the Lord said to Samuel, ' . . . Men judge by outward appearance, but I look at a man's thoughts and intentions' " (1 Sam. 16:7).
We aren't to hurt others.
We are to think of the other person and let love always govern our actions. We should not *use* others to get what we want if it would harm them. This includes our spouse, anyone who would offer sperm or eggs to enable us to become pregnant, future children we might conceive, and society as a whole. We need to consider the impact of our choices on all those affected.

"Love your neighbor as you love yourself. Love does no wrong to anyone" (Rom. 13:9-10).
God demonstrated a certain flexibility in the Old Testament in the ways He allowed children to be conceived.
I found this third principle surprising and remarkable. In Deuteronomy 25:5-6, as part of the "Levirate Law," God actually required a man to marry (and take responsibility for) his brother's childless widow specifically for the purpose of giving her a child. Some Christians believe that the modern practice of donor insemination allows a man with the characteristics of a brother to donate sperm to ease another's childless state. For further information on the Levirate Law, see Genesis 38:6-8; Ruth 4:1-10; and Matthew 22:23-30.

I was also amazed at the story in Genesis 30. Both Rachel and Leah used their maids Bilhah and Zilpah to produce children with Jacob. God didn't admonish them for the practice of surrogacy, instead He honored the children born of those unions by making the sons—Dan, Naphtali, Gad, and Asher—part of the twelve tribes of Israel. Of course, this was also different than today's surrogate practices because the surrogate lived as part of the family. The jealousy and discord this arrangement caused is also recorded.

The Old Testament also has other examples of concubines used as surrogates. One of these, Hagar, was used specifically to produce a child for an infertile wife, Sarai. But the account illustrates that surrogacy wasn't God's plan for Sarai and Abram. God wanted them to trust Him to make Sarai pregnant. Sarai sought her own alternative to her infertility (Gen. 16:1-3), because of her impatience. In fact, God eventually gave her the biological child she desired (Gen. 21:1-7).

Because these Old Testament situations do not directly relate to the situations and culture of today, they lead to two differing viewpoints. One viewpoint is that because God demonstrated His flexibility in allowing alternate ways of conceiving children in these Old Testament situations, the same flexibility *still* applies. The other viewpoint is that God deviated from the norm only to accomplish specific purposes for those days. Since those specific cultural purposes no longer exist, we should not assume He allows alternate methods of conception for our desires.

Responding to Biblical Directives and Principles

God has given us these biblical principles to guide us. But if we have a choice to make that's not spelled out in the Bible, we are also given the freedom to choose—based on the principles God *has* given us. As Christians, we are in a love relationship with God, but this freedom also gives us a great responsibility to act in love toward Him. If we truly love God, then we won't want to do anything contrary to His desires or anything that would cause Him sorrow. Carefully search for the path God will show you by studying what God tells us in the Bible and by seeking the leading of the Holy Spirit.

Pray for Wisdom and Direction

Another help we have in making ethical decisions in fertility treatment is prayer. Rich found that the decisions he and his wife had to make during treatment were so important that prayer became second nature.

We were aggressive once we started medical tests and treatments, but every time there was a choice, we sat down and asked ourselves if this was a direction God might want us to go. Then we prayed and slept on it. A door either opened or closed in our minds. These are heavy decisions. What you decide in a few seconds, you will have to live with for the rest of your lives.

Before making any major decision, we need to ask God to guide us and give us wisdom in our choices (James 1:5). It's important that we do this together as a couple—to ask the Holy Spirit to guide us in agreement so that we both have peace about the decision. We can feel comforted by the fact that God will not have conflicting plans for a husband and wife.

Gathering Medical Information
The third help in making ethical decisions is learning the specific medical information about fertility treatments. Ask your doctor for information about the tests and treatments: What are the detailed steps of the procedure? Will any of my husband's sperm, my eggs, or our embryos be used in other ways, such as for other couples or experiments? Have any of your other patients had ethical questions about this procedure?

Ask for specific statistics from your doctor or clinic about the success rate for various treatments. It doesn't matter if the clinic or nation has a 15 percent success rate. What matters are the statistics for your particular problem, at your age, with that particular clinic. Be sure to ask what the success rate means because there is a major difference between testing pregnant by a chemical test and actually taking home a baby (called take-home baby rate). You may make a very different decision if the possibility of taking home a baby is 30 percent or 1 percent per treatment. Keep in mind though, that many things can affect the statistics of clinics, such as their screening process, age of patients accepted, number of embryos normally transferred, or the ability of the lab personnel. The American Fertility Society can provide you with statistics for IVF clinics. (See Appendix A: Resources for more information.) Also, consider getting a second opinion.

Talk to others who have had the treatment. (RESOLVE, which has national and local chapters, can refer you to someone who has had the procedure you are considering. See Appendix A: Resources for further information on RESOLVE.)

In addition, go to the library or bookstore. A medical library is best for articles on the most recent studies, but your local library should also have books available on current reproductive techniques. (RESOLVE also sells some books and has an annotated bibliography of books available.)

Your Personal Journey

1. Have you and your spouse prayed for wisdom and direction together?
2. What additional Bible verses can you find that apply to the creation of life or principles that could guide your decisions?
3. Do you feel you need more specific medical information before making a decision?

7

When Ethical Issues Become Personal

Inability to tell good from evil is the greatest worry of man's life. —Cicero[1]

The difficulty in life is the choice. —George Moore[2]

*W*hen I knew I had five hours to decide whether to try to inseminate my multiple eggs, I cried all the way home. Then I knelt down by my bed and prayed. I tried to call Michael at work, but he wasn't at his desk. I didn't want to look at the long-term negative possibilities. I just wanted to think about the fact that I had a good chance to get pregnant that month. To clarify what I was thinking, I started writing in my journal. As I saw in black and white what I was thinking, I began to see what a major compromise in my beliefs I would be making. If I chose to inseminate those eggs, I would always know that I had consciously chosen to open myself up to the possibility of a pregnancy reduction. I know that others have successfully delivered four, five, or more babies. But I also knew that as the number of babies goes up, the odds of survival go down, and that I wasn't a *good candidate for carrying a multiple pregnancy. I didn't feel strong enough to stand up to a doctor who might encourage me to have a pregnancy reduction or probably lose all the babies I would be carrying.*

Pregnancy Reduction or Embryo Reduction

A pregnancy reduction is when a doctor deliberately interferes with one or more of the fetuses, causing them to die. This is usually done between ten-and-a-half weeks and four months gestation, by injecting a solution into the amniotic sac. Deciding which fetus to "reduce" isn't done according to which one is weaker, but by which fetus is easiest to reach with the needle. Then the fetus is either absorbed back into the uterus or is expelled through a partial miscarriage. The procedure is done because the chances of survival for the fetuses go down in inverse proportion to the number of fetuses in the womb at one time. The pregnancy reduction procedure can occasionally cause all of the fetuses to be miscarried.

The reason that pregnancy reduction needs to be addressed by couples pursuing fertility treatment is because using fertility drugs to create more eggs during a cycle to increase the chance of a pregnancy also increases the chance of a multiple pregnancy.

Deanna had been pregnant three times, but had lost all three babies at various stages of the pregnancies. She was apprehensive when she found out she was pregnant again, but this time with triplets!

As she and her husband Richard began to get used to the idea over the next couple of visits, the doctor told them of possible problems, particularly with two of the babies who shared the same gestational sac. Additionally, Deanna hadn't been able to carry one baby to term, much less three. The doctor gave her three choices: (1) to keep all the babies and very probably have a *difficult* pregnancy or miscarriage, (2) to have a a pregnancy reduction (abort one or more of the fetuses to give the others a better chance at survival, or (3) abort the whole pregnancy and start over again.

Richard and Deanna were frightened about what lay ahead for them, but felt strongly that they did not want any abortions. One of the doctors in the practice took them into his office and in Deanna's words "put extreme pressure on us to abort the two babies in the same amniotic sac." He told them the babies had less than a 20 percent chance to live and the only way to significantly raise the odds of survival was to "reduce" the pregnancy. "But we've never seen an ultrasound that looked so good in any of Deanna's other pregnancies. We can even see all of their strong heartbeats and even their arms and legs," Richard told him. The doctor spoke more insistently, saying yes, the ultrasound of the babies looked good, but Deanna and Richard should spend some time in a neonatal intensive-care nursery. He warned them that if the babies lived, they might be attached to tubes for the rest of their lives. He told them that since the pregnancy was now four months along, they only had two days to make the decision, because after that the reduction process would be harder.

Richard and Deanna chose to keep all three babies in spite of the difficulties, but they were unnerved by the pressure that was put upon them.

Deanna eventually gave birth seven weeks early to two girls and a boy, who are now healthy toddlers.

Is pregnancy reduction justifiable to save the lives of the siblings?

Pregnancy reduction in the uterus of a woman carrying too many babies to survive is sometimes compared to an abortion to save the life of the mother because it is done to save the lives of siblings.

Pastor Steve Zeisler had this to say about the pregnancy reduction being compared to an abortion to save a life: "I think there is a significant difference, in that the group of siblings who will be sacrificed were [originally] placed in danger by the choice of the doctor or the couple."

Aren't they just part of the mother's body at the beginning?

In regard to the idea that the fetuses are just a part of the mother's body, John Stott says in his book *Involvement: Social and Sexual Relationships in the Modern World:* "That an embryo, though carried within the mother's body, is nevertheless not a part of it, is not only a theological but a physiological fact. This is partly because the child has a genotype distinct from the mother's. . . . "[3]

How can anyone know more than we, the infertile couples who ache to have a child, how precious the miracle of life is? Personally, I can't think of anything more devastating for a couple who has struggled to become pregnant, than to be told that all of your babies will probably die unless you choose to take the lives of some of them.

Because of this ethical dilemma, some have said that if you believe pregnancy reduction is wrong, then assisted reproductive techniques or even fertility drugs are not ethical options at all. But, rather than closing the door to these treatments altogether, preventative measures can also be taken within the treatments.

What are our options?

With careful ultrasound monitoring, the risk of high multiples can be kept to a minimum. If the number of mature eggs, and thus the number of potential embryos is high during one cycle, the couple has the choice of not trying to become pregnant that cycle. Another choice (which wasn't yet available to me at the time of my decision) is to use the new technique of aspirating (the technique used with IVF of suctioning out with a needle) the extra mature eggs before fertilization, leaving two or three, then proceeding with normal intercourse or insemination.

With GIFT, the couple can choose to place only the number of mature eggs they would be willing to carry to term in with the sperm before it is placed back into the fallopian tube(s).

With IVF, the couple can choose to try to fertilize only the number of eggs that they would transfer and carry to term if fertilization did take place. Or if they feel it is an ethical choice for them, they can choose to freeze some of the "extra" embryos (and commit to having them transferred at a later date) or donate them to a Christian couple.

If you plan to choose one of the options which limits the number of embryos created, it is important to notify your doctor of this and to ask how that choice will affect the success rates you have been quoted for a particular procedure.

Michael and I have come to the conclusion that because of what we've read in the Bible about life in the womb, because of our knowledge of fetal development, and because the need for it is mostly preventable, pregnancy reduction is not an option we could choose without compromising our moral values.

Infertile couples may have a hard time visualizing themselves with one baby, much less five, six, or seven. But we need to pray about this, think about it beforehand, and make preventative choices based on what we believe is right. Of course, there are times when we may end up with more babies than we had planned as can be true with "normal" pregnancies. That's where trust comes in. We do our best and trust God to take care of the rest.

Masturbation

A separate ethical issue related to infertility is the one of masturbation to obtain a semen sample. Masturbation for sexual gratification is considered immoral by a number of conservative Protestant churches, the Roman Catholic church, and the Jewish religion. Masturbation to obtain a sperm sample, for other than the most conservative Christians, is not viewed as an ethical problem. "Masturbation [in this situation] is not being done for erotic pleasure," said Dr. Grounds. "I see no problem with this even if someone felt masturbation for personal erotic pleasure was wrong."

Special seminal collection condoms

Dr. Panayiotis Zavos has done a great deal of research comparing the seminal characteristics of ejaculates collected during masturbation and during intercourse (collected in a special *sterile* condom)[4]. The special seminal collection condoms contain no spermicides and have a coating to let the sperm slide out easily. In studies he has done, the semen obtained through the use of these condoms in intercourse is significantly higher in volume, as is the total number of sperm, percent of normal morphology, and the grade of motility.[5]

If after discussing this issue with your spouse, either of you feel uncomfortable with masturbation to obtain a seminal sample or if you have low sperm parameters, these condoms are available commercially. You will need to coordinate the timing with your doctor in order to deliver the sperm sample to the lab within a short time (two hours) of obtaining it. If your fertility specialist does not have these Seminal Collection Devices (SDCs) available, your doctor can obtain them or a brochure about them by calling the manufacturer: HDC Corporation in San Jose, California at 800-227-8162.

Use of Pornography in Fertility Clinics

Another related ethical problem is that some fertility clinics offer pornographic magazines or even video tapes to assist men in giving a semen specimen. Matthew 5:28 makes it clear that sexually fantasizing about anyone other than your spouse is not acceptable to God.

Pornography is not only wrong for Christians, but I believe that it is devastating to our society and demeaning toward women. And marriages already strained by infertility do not need something as destructive as pornography introduced into their relationship. (For more information on the destructive effects of pornography to our society, contact the National Coalition against Pornography in Cincinnati, Ohio at [513] 521-6227).

While it is a tremendous pressure for a man to have to "deliver" on schedule, other avenues of stimulation need to be explored rather than introducing pornography. Feel free to discuss other options with your doctor, such as producing the sperm at your nearby home, having the wife present in the "collection" room at the clinic, or even using the collection condom at a nearby hotel or your residence. (One IVF clinic provides an apartment above the clinic for out-of-town couples to stay in and which they may also use at collection time.)

Once You Have Decided

After you have developed convictions about which choices in your treatment you feel would honor and respect God, talk to your doctor about them. Is the doctor comfortable with supporting your beliefs? Do you feel comfortable placing your beliefs in the doctor's hands to be conscientiously followed? If we follow our moral convictions and uphold our respect for the miracle of life in our choices within fertility treatment, I believe we can honor God in our choices.

In the end, the decision to use assisted reproductive techniques to try to become pregnant *is* an individual choice, but we are not deciding in an ethical vacuum. Ultimately, we are responsible directly to God for our decisions. Our freedom of choice in the areas in which the Bible is not specific gives us an even greater responsibility not to be ignorant of what God has told us in His Word, but to diligently seek to understand it. If after searching the Scriptures and praying about it, you believe that a particular approach is wrong, then it *is* wrong for you and you shouldn't do it. As Christians, our choices should be based on a right attitude of respect for God, studying what God *does* say in the Bible about His instructions for us, and asking God to lead us as a couple to please Him.

When Michael came home that night, of course he affirmed the choice not to have the insemination that month. Good old rock-solid, go-by-what-is-right-not-by-what-you-feel Michael. Even though we were able to try Pergonal six more times late in the next year, I never got pregnant while using it. Nevertheless, I'm so glad about the decision I made that month. I think that God allowed Michael to be unavailable that day so that I might come to the decision by myself. I came to realize how easy it can be to make a wrong choice in the emotions of the moment, and I am grateful that I don't live with that profound regret today. I am newly aware of my vulnerability, though, and because of this, I have much more compassion for those who *do* live with regret for choices they may have made in the crisis of the moment.

Your Personal Journey

1. What ethical decisions have you had to make (or would you anticipate making) in dealing with your infertility or medical treatment?
2. On what did you (or would you) base your decisions?

Part III

"God, Why Do We Ache So Much?"

8

Feeling Broken

Save me, O my God. The floods have risen. Deeper
and deeper I sink in the mire; the waters rise around
me. I have wept until I am exhausted; my throat is
dry and hoarse; my eyes are swollen with weeping, waiting for
my God to act   (Psalm 69:1-3).

When my spirit was overwhelmed within me,
Thou didst know my path   (Psalm 142:3, NASB).

*I didn't know how long I'd been lying across the
bed. The sun was going down and I knew I should
get up and do something, but I felt like someone
had pulled a plug and drained all the life out of my body. I
had no control over the tears that continued to run down
my cheeks. My body had betrayed me once again. I had
vowed not to get my hopes up any more, but this month
the twinges of nausea and my period being a few days late
had worn away my resolve. I couldn't deny the hope that
had once again exploded in my heart.*

But my period had come again that afternoon.

*It was about my fifth month on Clomid—the wonder
drug that I had been sure would fix whatever hormones
were off-balance. Even with my cycles more regular because of the Clomid, I still wasn't getting pregnant. (I
later realized that with each new treatment, my hopes,*

which had started to level-out, would skyrocket.)

A bothersome thought pushed its way into my brain again, then struck my heart with horror—what if I can never have a baby? Of course, it had been a hypothetical possibility before, but I had never really considered it.

I'd wanted children and loved babies my whole life. I couldn't even imagine not having them. I tried to picture what my life would be like without children. I loved my husband dearly, but knew his life would be full with his career. I had never wanted a career. It seemed like such a sterile existence compared to creating new life and raising little people to be caring adults.

I saw our future home—nice, but devoid of children's giggles, building blocks, and dolls. I thought of never being able to share the joy of discovery with my children: their first steps, their first taste of ice cream, their funny words, their fresh insights about the world, or their first kiss.

I pictured how people would view me: "Oh, there she goes. It's a pity, when she was younger, she desperately wanted children but was never able to have them. I wonder what was wrong with her?" Or they might wonder why it bothered me: "Can you believe she made such a big issue about not being able to have a baby?" Or they might see me as being under God's discipline: "I hope she turns and repents of whatever she's doing wrong so God can bless her with a baby." Our joyous secret of trying to conceive had become a shameful secret. I felt embarrassed, like a child who doesn't want other kids to see him be disciplined by his parents.

I felt I couldn't go on feeling this agony and sense of isolation. The only One who could have helped me through it seemed as though He had turned His back on me. It was excruciating. Because of my anguish-induced tunnel vision, nothing else seemed to matter. I couldn't see myself ever finding anything else worthwhile or even enjoyable in life besides mothering. I thought of ending my life just to end the pain.

The sun had set. I felt drained inside except for the ache at the thought of life without my own child. My arms yearned to hold him or her. I began to writhe from the pain and thrashed from side to side to try to escape it. I felt I was being torn apart. I yelled out: "God, You promised not to test me beyond my endurance! But I'm the one living in this body and I'm letting You know that this has gone beyond what I can bear! Have You forgotten me?! What have I done?! Have I offended You so much that You would keep a child from me? I know You can do miracles, but You're choosing not to do one for me. Why? Aren't I loving You and obeying You to the best of my ability? I'll do anything God, just tell me what it is! If You want one of my limbs, take it. I'll gladly pay that for a child. I'm broken and despairing, and You still won't answer me. You have refused the gift that would give the most meaning to my life. I can't go on like this. I need You to give me a child or take away this crushing ache."

Hours later, something drew me to call Michael, who was working graveyard shift. I was too scared to tell him the depth of my feelings, but I was crying as I told him I had gotten my period again. He offered to come home, but I told him I would make it through the night, and I realized then that I would.

The Paralyzed Limb

Finding out that you are infertile can feel like suddenly discovering a limb is paralyzed. Everything looks normal until you need to use it.

What if for instance, a woman on her way out the door in the morning, reached out to pick up a glass of orange juice and found her arm wouldn't move. Imagine her shock. She thinks, *That's strange, maybe I just need to think about what I'm doing.* She concentrates and tries again. Nothing happens. She's confused because she's never had any reason to doubt that her arm would work. The cold fear of something dreadfully wrong settles on her. She sees a doctor and goes through years of test and treatments. All the doctor can tell her is that she might never regain the use of her arm, but there is always the chance that it might spontaneously heal sometime in the future if she keeps trying to use it.

Each time she thinks of using her arm, a small persistent hope rises in her—maybe this time it will work. But each time it fails her hopes are crushed. Meanwhile, she looks no different to the outside world. People are confused when she stops coming to the volleyball games or won't shake hands.

When she finally ventures to tell some friends about her disability, she hears a lack of understanding: "well at least you have your other arm," or "at least it's not life-threatening." Occasionally she finds someone who seems to understand her hurt, who empathizes without pitying her. She holds on to these friends like a lifeline. Although these friends are priceless, they can't fix the problem. She will have to go through a myriad of feelings on her own as she sorts through and realigns herself to her new reality without the use of her arm. Before she adjusts, the shock and fear will probably turn into questioning, anger, feelings of vulnerability, and deep sadness before she'll be able to reassess and see herself as "normal" without the use of her arm.

With an infertile person, the part of his or her body that would make a baby or hold a baby until it can be born is that part that is disabled. To varying degrees, we go through this same type of grief and reassessment process as we adjust to the reality that part of our body is not working and what that means to our self-image and life plans.

Tasting Grief

Those unable to conceive a child do not experience a clean grief because the loss happens over an extended period of time as a monthly cycle of hope and grief. This cycle includes the losses of: privacy, sense of control, having grandchildren, purpose, time, money, career progress, innocence, giving to another, being needed, and the acquired credibility of being an adult who has raised children. This is why many women view infertility as the most upsetting experience of their lives.

What surprised me about grief was the way it kept blindsiding me when I least expected it. A day at church would start with no great emotional load, but a word or a song would set me off, and I would have to leave because I couldn't control my sobbing—not crying—uncontrollable sobbing. Eventually, I regained my equilibrium.

I felt guilty that I wasn't one who "responded well" to my infertility. I *wanted* to breeze through it. I didn't want children to matter to me so much. At first I felt ashamed because I had failed in having a baby, then on top of that I was embarrassed that I was depressed about my failure. But, I finally realized that feeling the pain so deeply just meant that I had a stronger desire to have a baby. It didn't mean I was less healthy or spiritual. When I realized this, I was able to go to God for comfort and also open up to others, which eventually helped me to face my grief and come out on the other side. I learned there was nothing wrong with the intensity of my feelings, I just had to make the choice to honestly work through the grief process and choose to express my feelings in the right way.

I've been amazed at the compassion and depth of character I see in people who have been willing to do this. The ones who ignore the process often seem to build up walls and become unreachable or bitter. The ones who allow themselves to feel, and make themselves vulnerable to God in the process, are the ones who end up as people of such character that when I'm with them, I want to sit for hours and soak up their wisdom and insights. I trust their wisdom because it has been tested through their journey of pain.

If the grieving process is overwhelming you right now, know that you aren't alone. If you recognize yourself in any of the following emotions, I encourage you to face your feelings honestly and share them with someone you trust. Pray about the cause and ask God to help you work toward whatever solutions are available.

Reeling from Shock and Denial:
"There Must Be Some Mistake!"

Some individuals ease themselves gently into facing their infertility. Vicky and her husband Steve did this:

> Realizing that we were infertile dawned on me slowly. It started as a nagging doubt and grew into an awful reality. I was afraid to say the words *infertile, childless,* or *barren* aloud for fear that speaking the words might make it so.
>
> When I finally admitted to myself something might be wrong, I then had to convince my husband. Here I was, trying to convince him of something I didn't want to be true! He's an optimist, and I was easily talked out of my doubts. Looking back, I think we were both in a state of denial.

My situation was somewhat different because I had the physical proof of a problem with my irregular periods. I didn't deny we had an infertility problem for long, but I was still shocked. After all, my mom had no problem having four kids. One of her pregnancies even happened while she was using birth control! How could I be having problems when I came from those genes?

It was so hard for Michael and I to adjust our thinking. Ever since we were married, we worried about having a baby too soon, so we thought once we stopped using birth control we'd immediately get pregnant. We were stunned to find out it doesn't always happen that way.

For a time, shock and denial are valid responses to our infertility. It gives us a breather before we go into battle. I've had women call me for information about our support group although they don't yet define themselves as infertile, even though they have been trying to get pregnant "for a couple of years." They want to ask a question about a doctor or find out what support is available if they should need it, but they can't quite believe they fall into the infertile category yet. I've learned not to try to intrude on anyone in this stage, but to support and give any information they request, respecting a person's need to go through this stage in the process of grieving.

Searching for a Cause or Reason: "Why?"

I don't know any infertile person (outside the denial stage) who hasn't asked the question, *why?* This question is usually focused in two areas. The first is the overall question: *Why is God allowing this to happen to me?* (Or more simply stated: *Why is this happening?*)

To help you answer this question, seek your answers from God. Pray to Him and ask for the answers to your questions. Study His Word on your own. And get involved in a Bible study (or stay involved in one). Attending a Bible study has helped me so much. Even though I wanted to withdraw from everyone, so many issues became clear during our discussions of the Word. If you can't face people you know, attend a Bible study where you don't know anyone. Don't stop asking the questions until God gives you an answer. He is faithful and will answer.

The second area of questioning is more specific: *Why is my body not working right?* During this process of searching for causes and reasons, you might find yourself wondering if something you did in your past caused your infertility. You may question the air you breathed, the asthma medicine you took, or even something as serious as a previous abortion you had. It's important to remember that if we've confessed to God any wrong we've done and turned back to Him, we start with a clean slate. God doesn't hold a grudge. We also need to remember though, that the fundamental principle of cause and effect still exists in our

world. We may be forgiven while still bearing scars from
the past.

When we're on this questioning search, we should keep
checking the direction of our thinking against what we
know is right. Sometimes we're looking so hard for an
answer that we pounce on anything we find, no matter
how irrational. As Pam said:

> It's amazing how I can go off pursuing a wrong direction in
> my thoughts. Sometimes I really go off on tangents and can
> drive myself crazy. I have to remind myself to reel my
> "what if. . . ?" thoughts back in and start again from what I
> know is true.

A doctor can help you search for the specific medical
causes of your infertility. If you choose to go to a doctor, I
would also encourage you to look for answers by forming
a network with other infertile couples and doing research
on your own.

Frustration and Anger: "This Isn't Fair!"

Throughout my infertility, most of my frustration and anger was directed at God for what I perceived as His rejec-
tion. I was also frustrated that everyone around me
seemed to get pregnant and have babies so easily: my
friends, family members, and even women in the grocery
store. (I was *certain* that all the pregnant women who
bombarded my vision had never even had to take their
temperature.)

There is also the complication of needing to include the
possibility of being pregnant next month/year into all our
decisions: *Should we buy a two-door or four-door car?*
Should I take the promotion or prepare to be a stay-at-
home mom? Should we move into a larger place? Should I
buy this new pair of pants? Take this aspirin? At the beginning, it was fun to wonder. After several years it just
added to the frustration. Because Michael and I were toil-

ing over all these things in the back of our minds, we found we had a low tolerance level for other problems; anger or tears were often close to the surface.

Anger at injustice

I also found myself infuriated at women who abandoned their babies to die after giving birth, mothers who gave birth to cocaine-addicted babies, and mothers who abused their children. I would rant and rave and cry over the news reports. The injustice of it all!

Julie, a high-school counselor felt this too:

> One of the things that really frustrates me is that in my job I end up working with a lot of pregnant, teenage girls. I see this as a test of my spirituality right now, but I don't understand why I'm going through this! I'm newer to this infertility stuff, but I'm having to leave my job because it is just too difficult. Why are those girls getting pregnant and I'm not? I can't tell you how many I've dealt with this year.

For Theresa, a large part of her anger was focused on the doctors who didn't listen to her. For years she had been trying to find the answer to her extremely painful periods. She was understandably angry at the doctors for missing the obvious diagnosis of endometriosis ten years earlier when they might have been able to control it.

Anger at injustice is valid. I've found the important thing about anger is to honestly admit it, then express it appropriately. Pretending you're not angry or "stuffing" the feeling causes other problems, but so does flying off the handle and hurting people with your anger. If we use our anger the right way, it can motivate us positively to look for medical answers, to find out more about God's character, or both. Once we have admitted how we feel, we have a choice in how we respond to it. Am I going to forgive? Am I going to trust God to care for me in this vulnerable position?

Destructive anger

Sometimes we may find we are focusing our anger about our infertility on the ones closest to us: our spouse for not agreeing to a test or procedure, doctors for insensitivity, friends for not understanding, or even on ourselves for any number of reasons. Try to determine if you are just frustrated and lashing out or if there is a specific problem you can address. Try to address the problem, not attack the person. If you find that you are consumed with anger, lovingly confront the person who was insensitive (in person or by writing them a letter) or write in your journal. Ask God to help you forgive the person.

If you find that you are dwelling on past mistakes that contributed to your infertility, you will be inhibited from moving through the grief process. Confess to God that you made wrong choices, then move on. If self-guilt motivates you to change for the better, it is good guilt. If it immobilizes you, it is destructive and is not from God.

Loss of Self-Esteem: "I Feel as If I'm Defective."

In one of the the "Thirty-something" television show episodes, the character Nancy was forced to have a hysterectomy and described some of her feelings of emptiness and worthlessness. She was unable to hold Faith's baby because the child reminded her that she was unable to have any more. She described feeling that time seemed to be passing differently for her, as if she were wearing a broken watch. Then she went on to say she felt as if *she* were broken. She felt that she had lost her wholeness, felt empty, let her husband down, and expected him to look at other women because she was nothing. Her feelings after a hysterectomy closely match those of many infertile women. Infertility can feel like an emotional hysterectomy. Infertile women can feel different, broken.

Just as virility is linked in men's minds with masculinity, being able to become pregnant and bear a child has a strong link with a woman's sense of femininity. When a woman realizes her hormone levels are so off that she can't become pregnant or has a body that betrays her and won't carry a child to term, she may begin to feel unfeminine. She can also become vulnerable to temptations. Whether it is a temptation to feel unlovable to God or to become jealous of someone to whom God has given children, the weakness can often be related to her distorted view of herself.

Beth found that she was tempted in ways related to her femininity:

> I found myself daydreaming about being attractive to other men. I had never been tempted to have an affair before, but suddenly I understood the temptation. I just wanted to escape the sadness in our marriage and feel feminine and desirable again. I really had to watch myself.

Infertility can erode our sense of worth. We can lose our healthy or proper perspective, which is seeing ourselves as God sees us. But how do we get what we know in our heads into our hearts? It takes a lot of work, a lot of tears and sweat. It takes going back again and again to what we know is true: God *loves* each of us, and we have been made in His image. We are valuable just as we are.

Feeling Vulnerable and Fragile: "I Can't Handle Being around People."

As the pain of infertility grows, you may find yourself trying to avoid pregnant friends, baby showers, or Mother's Day gatherings. You will need to find your own balance between doing things and waiting for healing. This balance may be different within each phase of your grief.

I felt so vulnerable and exposed when I was grieving intensely. As hard as I tried, I couldn't seem to function normally. I was confused and forgetful. For a while, when I went to a baby shower, I felt like an alcoholic must feel at a cocktail party, being tempted again and again to take a drink. Attending a baby shower would break through my fragile resolve to trust God and turn my focus again to what I didn't have.

When my anger flared at an intrusive question during a baby shower one day, I knew that I needed to back off from showers until my emotions weren't so raw. Even though I had worked through some of my grief, I still didn't have enough strength to keep from falling back into my negative ways of thinking. I stopped going to baby showers. I thought it might be forever, but gradually I felt strong enough to attend again.

I began healing faster once I stopped isolating myself and found understanding people to talk to. I found I could talk more openly once I shed the stigma of infertility, but I couldn't do that until I realized that *it wasn't my fault.* Armed with that realization I chose to share our condition with a few close friends and family members whom I thought might be supportive. They were, so I began to tell others. If I encountered a hurtful reaction, I drew back and waited a while until I felt secure enough to share again. The most healing came from being able to talk with others in my wonderfully supportive infertility and pregnancy loss group.

The important thing in sharing with others is to take small steps and not isolate yourself forever. Talking to another infertile person or joining an infertility support group are probably the safest ways to start.

Sadness and Depression: "I Can't Seem to Stop the Tears."

Grief is scary. You may fear that if you really allow yourself to feel your loss, you will never make it back out of the depths again. But the strange thing about grief is that if you allow yourself to face it, you are beginning the process of healing. If you focus on it for a time and talk about it, you are building tools to deal with it. This focus, or tunnel vision, is really a concentration which is needed to deal with this enormous problem and upheaval in your world. You may need to spend much of your time and energy trying to incorporate the tragedy into your view of life. Virginia first tried to ignore her grief:

> I didn't know how to grieve. I kept trying to rationalize the situation—to put it in a box so that I could put it on a shelf and forget about it. [I learned that] grieving is a process, and it's not logical or necessarily quick or even finished at a specific time. I also learned that it's OK to grieve, that you need to ask God's help, and make choices to help yourself according to your need.

Your loss is real and valid. An acute feeling of emptiness or hollowness is often felt by women who are unable to conceive or have experienced pregnancy loss. Deanna described this feeling of extreme sadness:

> I felt like I was failing in the most important job that I could ever do. I completely withdrew from the whole world for a while. Right or wrong, that's just the way I handled it. I had a hard time being around anybody. I would pretty much stay at home. I had a hard time going back to work. I was scared to face everybody there. Each day was a challenge. There were many days that I left work crying. My arms literally ached, and I felt so empty. I didn't want to cook or clean. I left the house dark. I wasn't sleeping, so the doctor prescribed sleeping pills. I would take a sleeping pill and end up crying myself to sleep every night. It was a long process to recover.

When I finally realized I was infertile, I felt the most intense negative emotions that I'd ever felt. I was tired, run down, sad, disoriented, and felt helpless to lessen a pain too great to bear. I felt I'd lost my pride, control, strength, and self-esteem. I remember reading a book about a woman who had been infertile for ten years. It was inconceivable to me to live with pain as deep as I was experiencing for that long. What I didn't know, was that the pain of my infertility was the most intense in the first couple of years and gradually lessened to a dull ache. After a few years, I'd worked through some of my misunderstandings with God, developed some coping tools, and started a support network of infertile friends.

The song "Strength of My Life" by Leslie Phillips, hit the mark with me about how intense grief can feel and how we need to depend on God for each day's strength. Some of the words are:

"Strength of My Life"

I open my eyes to the sound of morning news.
I wish for ten more minutes left to sleep.
And as I get into the shower,
The thoughts of facing one more day
Overwhelm me and I begin to weep.

And I've never felt
Like I've needed Your help
So bad.

Well, my tears are pushed away now
For the sake of morning rush
Till the Bible on the table catches my eye.
And I read that You are near to
The hearts that break with grief
And I realize that I don't have to try
To live life myself
Because You're ready to help me live.

And everyday I look to You to be the strength of my life.
You're the hope I hold on to. . . .
Be the strength of my life today. . . .[1]

If you are despairing, I urge you to keep struggling with Him to answer your hard questions. Talk to others. Pray and/or ask others to pray for you. Join a Bible-study group to focus on what is true about God. Remember Deuteronomy 30:20: "that you may love the Lord your God, listen to His voice, and hold fast to Him" (NIV).

There is nothing in the Bible about an appropriate length of time for mourning, just about staying open and soft to God. Don't base your decisions on what others say about you; however, if you have severe depression longer than about two weeks, or recurring thoughts about suicide, find someone to talk to. Perhaps you could talk to your pastor, or maybe he or your doctor can refer you to a good Christian counselor, psychologist, or psychiatrist. While it is normal to feel depressed, don't neglect to ask for help if you need it. If you *aren't* overwhelmed by grief, that's also an appropriate reaction. People have a wide variety of responses; no level of grief is better or worse than another.

I found that a major portion of my grief was because my image of a caring God was damaged. If He allowed me to go through this grief without answering me, was He trustworthy? If I couldn't depend on God and I couldn't even have children, what reason did I have to continue? Infertility had such an impact on my view of God that I've committed the next chapter to exploring our relationship with God during infertility.

Regaining a Sense of Balance: "I'm Finally Beginning to Get My Legs back under Me."

I had no dramatic miracle happen to me after my low point of crying out to God. I still had nights of crying and frustration, but after the night I described at the beginning of this chapter, I had a foundation that kept me from reaching that rock-bottom point of despair again. In hindsight, that time of laying myself bare to God was a turning point in my life. I opened myself up to feel His comfort and in the process, my tunnel vision began to open up. I started to see God working in other areas of my life and began to feel hope that I would experience joy again. The pain didn't go away entirely, but with God by my side to comfort me, the healing began.

I no longer feel the despair that I did during that first deep grieving process or again when I later miscarried. While I was in the depths of the grief, I feared I would never recover. I realize now that my grieving was a normal, common process and although I couldn't imagine it at the time, hope and joy did come again.

My healing began after I was honest with God. I still found myself responding to my infertility with frustration or deep sadness sometimes, but these intense emotions usually lasted for days rather than for months. I began to feel hope for my future, that I could live even if I never had children, that much of that life would be enjoyable, and that I could make choices in other areas of my life.

Your Personal Journey

1. Were you shocked when you found out you were infertile? Do/did you struggle to find a reason for your infertility? Have you found any answers yet?
2. Do/did you feel angry and frustrated? Why? How have you expressed these emotions?
3. Have your feelings of self-worth or self-esteem been damaged by infertility? Do you feel vulnerable? How?
4. Have you felt any times of healing from your grief over infertility? What were they?
5. Which feeling, related to your infertility, is the strongest for you right now? Why?

9

"Where Are You, God?"

Lord, I ask more questions
Than You ask.
The ratio, I would suppose
Is ten to one.
I ask:
Why do You permit this anguish?
How long can I endure it? . . .
Do You see my utter despair?
You ask:
Are you trusting Me?[1]

For the eyes of the Lord move to and fro
throughout the earth that He may strongly
support those whose heart is completely His
(2 Chronicles 16:9, NASB).

I have trusted God my whole life to care for me. But when infertility dragged on and on, I began to question my relationship with God and His care for me.

David, who was called "a man after God's own heart," was refreshingly honest and intimate when he talked with God in the Book of Psalms. When I discovered this, it gave me the freedom to be honest with God also. I decided to follow David's pattern and write my own psalm to express some of my feelings to God.

10/5 Journal Entry: A Psalm of the Childless
How long Lord? How long will my tears drench my pillow? How long will You keep silent when I pray to You? I cry out to You day and night from the very depths of my soul, but You don't answer. Don't You care about

this anguish that touches every aspect of my life? With one word You could breathe life into me. Why do You hold back? Where is Your compassion?

I search the Scriptures for answers, but there are no promises of a child for me. Have I committed a great sin against You that made You turn Your back on me? Just show me what it is. I'm willing to change anything.

I have confessed every sin You have brought to my mind. I still struggle to do right, but it is because of my love for You, not my fear of You. I have searched my heart and stand open to You. I watch people who don't even want children reproduce with ease, then abuse the children You've given them. Why?

Is it because I'm not sincere enough in my asking? Am I not praying hard enough or long enough or fasting? Lord, I know You hear when we pray. Why won't You answer? (Based on Psalms 69:3; 77:1-4; 88:1-3; 92:7.)

Spiritual Questioning

When people experience difficulties having children, they often go through not only a physical and emotional struggle, but also through a time of spiritual questioning. I love the Book of Job because it deals with spiritual questioning resulting from Job's physical pain and emotional loss, and with "helpful friends" who make his pain worse.

Dr. James Dobson once commented about Job:

What impressed me most about Job was that the most severe suffering he experienced was not from the loss of possessions or even the loss of his family; it was from the fact that he couldn't find God. He said, "I looked for Him in the north country, the south. If I could just go find His throne and plead my case to Him, I could make Him understand." For a period of time God sealed the heavens and cut him off. He couldn't communicate with God for a time. Not only does Job go through that, but sometimes we pray to brass heavens too, yet God is there, just as He was with Job.[2]

Why, God?

My first reaction toward God was confusion. This didn't make sense! I had believed that if I committed myself to God and followed my sincere desire to obey Him, then He would bless me. I wasn't asking for something outlandish such as being able to eat anything I wanted and not gain any weight or something materialistic such as obtaining great riches. I was just asking for my body to work as He'd originally planned. Yet, here I was, overwhelmed with longing for a child, my body broken, and God seemed detached and motionless.

I also realized though, that I was the half of the relationship who was not all-knowing. I knew that I had to investigate and see if my beliefs were based on misconceptions of what God had promised for my relationship with Him.

Don't You understand the depth of my pain?

I knew that if I ever was given a child, and I saw him or her hurting as much as I was now, I would be moved to do something to help. Why then wasn't God moved by my pain? I wondered if God thought I was "making a big deal out of nothing" as some of my acquaintances implied.

Then I found Isaiah 54:1 which says:

> Shout for joy, O barren one, you who have borne no child;
> Break forth into joyful shouting and cry aloud, you who have not travailed;
> For the sons of the desolate one will be more numerous
> Than the sons of the married woman," says the Lord
> (NASB).

Isaiah is using the picture of a barren woman here to show how Israel will eventually be spiritually fertile through Christ. Brian Morgan, a pastor at Peninsula Bible Church in Cupertino, California once taught about the three different terms in this passage that described barrenness and how they indicate an intensification of the pain. He said the last term "desolate one" was "a desolation so appalling it leaves the onlooker speechless." That sounded to me like God, as revealed in Isaiah's words, understood the depth of pain that barrenness can produce.

Other verses also show God's understanding of the distress that accompanies our inability to bear a child. In Proverbs 30:15-16, (NIV) the longing and desolation that barrenness can bring are clearly understood:

> There are three things that are never satisfied,
> four that never say, "Enough!":
> the grave, the barren womb,
> land, which is never satisfied with water, and fire, which
> never says, "Enough!"

So through these verses, I learned that God did understand my pain. I didn't understand why He still wasn't doing anything to fix my pain though. The next possibility I examined was that He was punishing me.

Am I being punished?

I grappled with this question constantly during the first few years of our infertility. I thought our difficulties must be the result of personal sin. I confessed everything I could think of, but it never seemed enough. After much prayer and study, I grasped the concept of corporate sin.

Even if I confess my sins and am right with God, I still live in this corrupt and fallen world with the residual effects of sin. There is a difference between the corporate sin of mankind and personal sin. It is this continuing effect of sin in our world that has resulted in handicaps like infertility and death as in miscarried or stillborn babies. I still don't fully understand why God left the effects of sin in the world; but I do understand that for some reason He did, and I am affected by it. (I later found a partial answer for this question in the book, *Disappointment with God* by Philip Yancey.)

There are other instances in the Bible which make clear

that some problems are in no way related to an individual's sin. Job's friends kept telling him that he must have done something wrong to cause his suffering, but we get a glimpse into what is happening in heaven and find that God is not punishing Job because of sin. God allowed Satan the freedom to exercise limited power for a specific period of time in order to confirm that Job didn't love God just because of the blessings.

Elizabeth and Zacharias are another example. The Bible says they were blameless, but they were childless until late in life. God was timing the birth of their child (John the Baptist) to accomplish something great (Luke 1:6).

Of course, God doesn't give blessings only to couples who are sinless. He has also withheld things from people in order to draw their attention to their sin. In Genesis 20:17-18 (NASB) we read, "And Abraham prayed to God; and God healed Abimelech and his wife and his maids, so that they bore children. For the Lord had closed fast all the wombs of the household of Abimelech, because of Sarah, Abraham's wife." (Abraham, fearing Abimelech, had told Abimelech that his wife Sarah was really his sister. Abimelech had unwittingly become involved in sin by taking Sarah as his wife.)

This shows that God has control over all of His creation—including wombs—and may do what He wills in order to accomplish His purposes. Because God ultimately wants us to develop our relationship with Him and learn to trust Him, He may use something as important as our infertility to reach us and draw us to Himself.

Sometimes there *can* be a direct relationship between our past choices to disobey God's directives and our infertility, such as the results of sex outside of marriage that caused a Pelvic Inflammatory Disease (PID), which in turn caused scarring that blocked a woman's fallopian tubes. In this case, the response should be the same. God gladly, upon our request, forgives us. Once we've done that, the sin is gone (Ps. 103:11-13). (We may still have to live with some of the consequences of our choices.) Our response should be to confess any sin, then believe that God has forgiven us as He said He would (1 John 1:9).

Do I lack faith?

Some churches believe that because sickness and disability weren't part of God's original plan, people are sick only because they don't have enough faith to be healed. This heaps an additional burden of guilt on the person who is sick or disabled. Now, not only are they hurting, but they are made to feel that they are at fault.

Personally, I didn't spend long on this question. I *knew* that God could heal me in a second and make me pregnant. That was what was so frustrating! I just wanted to know *why* He wasn't doing it.

Do I have a major character flaw?

Did God know something about me that would make me a cruel mother? Would I raise a child who would become an ax-murderer? I saw no signs of this in myself. I knew I wouldn't be a perfect parent, but I was raised in a loving Christian home and thought I had the skills and love to do the job. In answer to this question, I found I just had to look around at people who abuse or even kill their children. I *knew* I could do a much better job than that.

Debbie S. found an answer to this question by seeing other infertile couples who would make wonderful parents:

> I couldn't understand why God was doing this to me. I fluctuated between feeling unloved and guilty of some unknown sin. Why was God causing me so much sorrow?
>
> It wasn't until I joined an infertility support group that I turned around in my thinking. I realized that some women, even some beautiful, godly women, can't have children. It doesn't mean God doesn't love them or that they've sinned. They just can't have children.

Just as we don't *deserve* grace from God, we don't *deserve* to have children either, but then neither does anyone else. They are gifts given to the undeserving. Of course we can still wonder why we didn't get a gift when others did, but it helps to know it wasn't because we would be such bad parents.

If my relationship with God is real, how could I be angry at Him?

I wanted to soar through my trials knowing I had such a strong relationship with God that nothing would affect me. I expected that if I were strong spiritually and trusted God, I would not experience deep pain or anger. My relationship with God had sustained me throughout my life. When I let myself be honest and realized that I was confused, frustrated, and angry at God, I felt guilty.

Philip Yancey's book, *Disappointment with God,* was especially helpful to me in dealing with the guilt I felt at being angry at God. I felt that if I was angry at God, that meant I didn't love or trust Him. I found myself relating to the man Richard, whom Yancey wrote about:

> Richard was feeling a pain as great as any that a human being experiences: the pain of betrayal. The pain of a lover who wakes up and realizes it's all over. He had staked his life on God, and God had let him down. . . . True atheists do not, I presume, feel disappointed in God. They expect nothing and receive nothing. But those who commit their lives to God, no matter what, instinctively expect something in return.[3]

When I realized it was *because* I presumed an intimate relationship with God that I could feel betrayed (when I hurt and He did nothing to fix it), I stopped feeling guilty about not being close enough to God. I was able to change my focus from what I was doing wrong in my relationship with God to dealing with the rest of the grief emotions.

Do You really love me, God?

I slowly recognized that childlessness wasn't a punishment, but I still couldn't understand why God wouldn't "fix" me. I began to think that if God weren't punishing me, maybe He was playing some cruel game with me. The game went like this. I was doing something dreadfully wrong, but didn't know what it was. God knew, but He wasn't going to tell me. I had to figure it out on my own, then He would show His love for me again. My job was to find out what would earn His love again.

I probably memorized John 3:16, the classic verse about God's love, when I was five or six years old. I grew up in churches that emphasized you shouldn't base your relationship with God on feelings, but on truth alone. While I still believe this, somewhere I also interpreted it to mean that I don't need to feel anything for God, just obey Him. Likewise, since emotions were to be distrusted, then what God feels for us must be more of a sense of duty. If we obey, He is obligated to hold up His end of the bargain.

God used my infertility to break through my intellectual beliefs to reach my heart, my emotions. I finally grasped that this was what God wanted. A true relationship has emotions, and a truly intimate relationship has the strongest emotion—love. The light dawned on me that the Bible would have used the words *duty* or *obligation* if that is what God meant. Instead the Bible uses the word *love:* a pure *emotion* of *caring* so strong that He sent His Son to die for me.

Ephesians 2:4 says that God is "rich in mercy" (NASB). This is translated from a Greek word meaning womb and relates to a mother who has love for a child just born. Think about how much love you would have for a baby you were finally able to have. How much do you long for a relationship with a child that might be born to you in the future? Know that God feels that same intense love and desire for a relationship with you.

Sometimes God goes out of His way to show us some of

the many ways He cares for us. We just have to open our eyes. One night at our support-group meeting, Sara shared this story of how God pointed out His care for her.

I saw an ad for a new shade of nail polish a while ago which was not pink and not peach, but in-between so that it went with anything. The color was called 'shrimp.' I was so excited about this silly color. It was just what I had been looking for. I went everywhere trying to find it, but no one had it. The "makeup specialist" at one store said it had been a special promotional item and wasn't available anymore. I kept looking, but could never find it.

One day my husband and I were having a disagreement about a job he had applied for in Colorado. He didn't get the job. He said, "I guess God showed us direction on that one," but I was angry.

It was in this frame of mind that we went to the drugstore to pick up a prescription. While I was waiting, I voiced some of my anger to God. I said, "Why couldn't You have given us that job in Colorado? Don't You know how much we wanted it? And don't You know how much we want a baby too? You just don't care. I couldn't even get that stupid 'shrimp' nail polish! Well, I looked up then and right in front of me was the makeup display. I thought, *Should I go look? No, I'll be struck by lightning by the time I walk down the aisle. Should I or shouldn't I?*

Finally, I got up and walked over . . . and right there in front of me were three bottles of 'shrimp' nail polish. This was the same store where I'd been told, "No we don't have anymore and we won't be getting it in." I laughed out loud and picked up the nail polish. I realized that God was letting me know in no uncertain terms that He's in control of our lives and cares about everything about me, even down to 'shrimp' nail polish. Later, while in prayer, I just felt Him say, *"Sara, I would never use you. I love you. I suffered and died for you. I care for your anguish. If you never did anything but know how much I love you, it would be enough."*

God *loves* us. This is not just an intellectual idea. It's an emotion that God feels for us. He loves us deeply, tenderly, and passionately. I now am unshakably certain of that.

Why do I have to wait?

But even knowing that God loved me didn't make the waiting any easier. Was He making me wait because I was wanting the wrong thing? Was God telling me to forget children altogether? I used to think that if God told me I had to wait four more years, and then I would have children, that would be fine. I could go on with my life and make decisions based on that knowledge. The real kicker to all of this waiting was that I didn't know if any children would ever come from it. I found that learning to wait on the Lord doesn't mean giving up. I can actively wait while leaning on God for courage and direction.

Anyone can be spiritually strong during a short crisis, but a long-term sorrow requires deep spiritual roots. Waiting reveals what we are made of as our defenses give way and the core of our soul becomes exposed. To keep us from totally focusing on what we don't have, we need to remember to thank God for what He has already given and continues to give us while we're waiting.

I remember when the revelation came to me that God was answering my prayers and blessing me in other areas of my life. When Michael and I had just completed our first year at Denver seminary and our first 18 months of infertility, because of unexpected circumstances, we didn't have enough money for the next two years of seminary. While God didn't answer our prayer for a baby, He did provide a way for Michael to be accepted into a less expensive seminary, provided a scholarship which would pay all the tuition at this new school for the next two years until he graduated, and, out of the blue, money for moving expenses. When I realized that this series of miracles was happening to move us to another place, I finally was able to comprehend that God was actively involved in caring for us. He wasn't withholding a baby from us because He didn't like us. He was showing His love for us in other ways, but just saying no right now about a baby.

If I had not had to wait, if I had felt God's comfort right away, I would never have gone through the effort to press God for meaning to my situation. My relationship with Him would have been weaker for it was based on false assumptions. I wouldn't have gained clearer perspective on God and His relationship to me. Romans 5:3-5 states:

> We can rejoice too when we run into problems and trials for we know that they are good for us—they help us learn to be patient. And patience develops strength of character in us and helps us trust God more each time we use it until finally our hope and faith are strong and steady. Then, when that happens, we are able to hold our heads high no matter what happens and know that all is well, for we know how dearly God loves us, and we feel this warm love everywhere within us because God has given us the Holy Spirit to fill our hearts with His love.

Jeannie, who experienced years of infertility before adopting two boys, learned that waiting on God wasn't easy, but it had hidden benefits. Here is a portion of a letter that she sent to her sister-in-law and brother-in-law when she heard of her sister-in-law's second consecutive miscarriage:

> The sad news of your miscarriage left me feeling empty and without words. I know that I really have no idea what your grief and sorrow are for you. You know the cost of life; at best I can only estimate it.
>
> [But] I do know grief and I do know the feeling of emptiness. I know that these valleys are dark and deep, but that I never walked them alone. For all the long, lonely hours, for all those tears shed on my pillow, for all the unanswered "why's," I would not trade any of these for the intimacy I gained with God. My faith, my confidence and [my] reality of God are SO BIG now that it is even unbelievable to me!

In the midst of my grief no one could really comfort me,
very few have experienced what I experienced, it seems
only One knows pain, grief, and sorrow deeper than I. And
so to God I'd go and have wonderful talks with [Him];
sometimes He'd answer, sometimes He was silent. But my
faith grew, without me even knowing it.

... God is *real* ... God does love you ... [and] God is
interested in [a] bigger picture than we can see. He is
more interested in us, calling us to a ... higher place in
His love ... than just answering our prayers. This is a hard
one ... waiting for God's plan. [But He is] equipping and
moving circumstances and lives and events around until
His timing lines [everything] up together just *exactly* right.
So you walk through this long, dark valley (or are carried)
and the burden is heavy, but God is equipping, building
your faith and calling you ever so sweetly, ever so quietly,
so lovingly. . . .

And in the waiting there is hope. . . . Rest in the arms of
the One who gives hope ... who comforts the weary. . . .
So rest; Rest in your grief, because right next door is
hope. . . . Don't waste the experience; let your intimacy
with God grow. Your wait is purposeful, the soaring is up
to you (Isaiah 40:31).

I love you both,
Jeannie[4]

Our Response

If your first reaction to God about your infertility is fear,
resentment, or anger, I encourage you to wrestle with God
and cling to Him like Jacob wrestled with the Angel of the
Lord. God initiated that event in Jacob's life because He
had something to teach him. Jacob was blessed because he
didn't let go of God (Gen. 32:24-30). Understanding probably won't come overnight; it took me years and I still
don't understand everything. I urge you though, not to
give up the struggle until you have experienced God in a
new way. When you are broken, you can choose to turn
away from God and become bitter, or you can cling to
Him until you get the answers you need. Be honest with

God. Honestly wrestling with Him will bring you closer to Him.

In a published sermon, Gary Vanderet, a pastor at Peninsula Bible Church, Cupertino, once explained what we should look for when we feel the pressure is too much and want to give up on staying open to God:

> Paul [in 1 Corinthians 10:13] doesn't say God will not allow us to be tempted beyond what we *think* we are able. God often takes us beyond that point. In fact, He must if growth is to be accomplished. . . . God must push us beyond what we think we can withstand by confronting us with more pressure than we think we can handle. But it is a controlled pressure, it will not be more than we can handle.
>
> " . . .But with the temptation [God] will provide the way of escape also, that you may be able to endure it" (NASB). When the pressure is active in the Christian's life, there is a counteractive power available from God.
>
> It is interesting that the word for "escape" is almost exactly the same word as "exodus," a way out of the wilderness. When we are in the midst of the wilderness and we think we cannot take any more of the pressure, then we must remember that God is right there with us. David wasn't resting in a green pasture when he wrote Psalm 23. He was in a wilderness—a desert.[5]

If you feel there is no way out of your wilderness (or barrenness) and are tempted to become bitter, keep looking for the escape. God promises it will be there.

Choosing to be honest and trust

I was confused about the rewards of following God. Yes, there are often positive consequences to following God and choosing His values, but our ultimate reward is intimacy with Him. We can have no true intimacy without trust. When I went through the struggles that came with infertility, I questioned why God allowed those struggles in my life. I still don't understand all the reasons why God chooses to do things the way He does, but I'm more open to the fact that my perception of something being unjust might be because of my ignorance, not because God is acting maliciously.

Even Christ asked not to go through the suffering of the Cross, but God knew that Christ's suffering had to continue because the Cross was the only way our relationship with Him would be restored. God didn't "fix" Christ's suffering because it served an important purpose. Romans 8:32 says, "He who did not hesitate to spare His own Son, but gave Him up for us all—can we not trust such a God to give us . . . everything else that we can need?" (PH)

James 5:11 tells of Job's continued trust: "Job is an example of a man who continued to trust the Lord in sorrow; from his experiences we can see how the Lord's plan finally ended in good, for He is full of tenderness and mercy."

God's Response: Comfort

The turning point in my grief came when I discovered that God was not my enemy. Instead of God sitting in heaven glaring at me for some indiscretion on my part, I realized it was more likely that He was crying with me over the hurt caused by the effects of sin. One night while I was praying, I felt God's presence and knew He was grieving with me. I could almost tangibly feel His hand reaching out to me and holding mine. I knew He would hold me up. For the first time since the beginning of my infertility, I began to feel a sense of God's caring for me. I also felt a sense of peace as pictured in this poem.

> Sometimes the Lord calms the storm,
> Sometimes He lets the storm rage . . .
> and calms the child.[6]

Going through infertility has caused me to change my whole concept of God. I know my understanding is still extremely limited, but I feel I've been reintroduced to the God of love and comfort. His comfort didn't feel like happiness to me, but like peace of mind and contentment. My confusion and turmoil dissipated. A quiet trusting took its place as I realized God's love and blessing to me.

Ruth is a woman who also found she was seeing God from a new perspective. She is facing her infertility as a single woman because she had both of her ovaries removed due to ovarian cancer. She found she related to Helen Keller in trying to find meaning for her circumstances:

> [When] Helen Keller was awakened by hands "spelling" into hers persistently, at first the movement was like a game, just another stimulus, and no more significant than the rest of the darkness around her. Then one day the movement against her palm burst with meaning. She learned.
>
> I feel like that with God. Maybe He's "finger-spelling" into my hands, and for long periods of time it's just another stimulus, no more significant than the chair that's under me. I'm still in the dark, but maybe this movement under my fingers has meaning. Maybe God is trying to communicate.

Another way that God has shown His loving care for us is that He gave us the Holy Spirit specifically to comfort us. He has not abandoned us in our hour of need. God anticipated that there would be times we would feel abandoned by Him "as orphans in the storm" (John 14:16-18), so He left us the Holy Spirit. We need to thank God for the presence of His Spirit and rest in His comfort.

If I Know God Loves Me, Why Do I Still Hurt?
Does knowing God's comfort remove the pain? Virginia, who had gone through two miscarriages said, "There have been a lot of insights regarding struggle in my life because of this experience, but it still hurts too much to say I'm

more grateful for those blessings than the babies I could have had."

I'd felt so guilty because I felt so much grief over the inability to have a child. I felt it wasn't godly. But I learned that sorrow is a natural part of this life. When I kept myself soft to God, I experienced His presence and felt the affirmation of His love for me. My comfort and courage now come from knowing God waits with open arms for me whenever I'm ready to take my pain to Him.

When Christ died on the cross, He wasn't singing. He was crying out to God in anguish. Yet, who knew God more intimately than Christ? When we look at His suffering though, we are able to see the wonderful results that came later. We can see why He had to go through it. This gives me hope that in time something really *wonderful* will come out of our pain if we trust God to give us strength and, in time, to heal our broken hearts (Ps. 147:3).

Grieving is a process. Yes, we all want to be "done" with it (and everyone else wants us to be done with it too), but it isn't instantaneous. We can't simply "decide" that it is all better without experiencing the process. While you are in the process you aren't a failure. You aren't a "bad" Christian. You're simply redefining some of the things you've taken for granted in life. If you hang onto God, whether you crawl up into His lap for comfort or you wrestle with Him for answers, He will bless you with a deeper relationship with Him.

Here is the end of the psalm I wrote to God.

Help me to remember that You have compassion and cry along with me when I mourn the loss of a baby that will never live, just like You expressed Your sorrow by crying at the death of Lazarus. Restore my heart to You. Let us be intimate once more. Replace my anger with knowledge of Your love and an unshakable trust in You.

Lord, help me to walk so close to You that I will not fear my monthly failure. Help my mind and emotions know that You are taking care of me. Turn me away from wanting any other plan but Yours.

I recall the many miracles that You have done for me in other areas of my life. Bring them to mind when I forget them and feel that You have forgotten me.

I believe Your Word when You say, "Delight yourself in the Lord and He will give you the desires of your heart" (Ps. 37:4, NIV). If a child is not in Your plan for my life Lord, then take away the intense desire that breaks my heart. Replace it with a desire for whatever is in Your special purpose for my life.

In the midst of this turmoil that I wrestle with in my heart and mind, while I am still waiting for answers to my questions, while I still don't understand why, while I continue to quake under this refining process, help me not to cause another to stumble. Help me to reach out through my pain to comfort someone going through a similar experience. And the hardest of all Lord (because it reminds me that You haven't chosen this miracle for me yet), help me to rejoice with someone who has just been given the miracle of a baby. Also, please help me to react with love when others say things that are hurtful about this, my softest spot.

You have promised to hear and listen to my prayers. Lord, I am choosing to trust You with my life and dreams. You are trustworthy! I know I will again have reason to praise You when I have traveled far enough to look back on this sorrow through Your eyes instead of mine. (Based on Psalms 37:4; 40:1-3; 56:8; 77:11; 112:7; 119:37.)

Your Personal Journey

1. Write your own psalm to God telling Him your feelings about your infertility and your relationship with Him.
2. If you can't pray, ask others to pray for you. List two people who will *really* uphold you in prayer. Ask them to do that.
3. Think of ways that God has been faithful to you in the past. Write them down to help you when you don't feel loved by Him.
4. Look for ways that God is actively participating in your life now. What is He currently giving you? A loving marriage? A caring doctor?
5. Look up the following verses and write down what they mean to you: Psalm 84:11; Psalm 103:5; Psalm 139; Psalm 142:3; Psalm 145:14; Isaiah 43:1-4; Jeremiah 29:11; Matthew 10:30; and James 5:11.

Part IV

"Is There Anyone Who Understands?"

10

Learning to Cope

He gives power to the tired and worn out, and
strength to the weak   (Isaiah 40:29).

For Jehovah God is our light and our protector. He
gives us grace and glory. No good thing will He
withhold from those who walk along His paths
(Psalm 84:11).

*I tried to keep up a brave front as I ate my piece of
pink and blue frosted cake at the third baby shower I attended that summer. I chose to go, steeling
myself for the battle of emotions, because I really wanted
to celebrate my friend's happiness. I tried to blend in with
the furniture as much as possible, hoping that no one
would touch my hurting wound. "Insider" pregnancy
birth stories and jokes flowed freely. I found myself praying again: Why, God? Why have you singled me out for
this pain of infertility? Will I always be an outsider to*
motherhood? You know how important children are to
Michael and me. Couldn't You have chosen this struggle
for a couple who didn't care as much?

*During a lull in the conversation, a woman across the
table cornered me with her eyes and loudly asked the
question I'd been dreading: "So Debbie, the question that*

*always comes up at these gatherings is (pregnant pause)
when are you going to start a family?" I felt a wrenching
pain inside as I started to sweat. I glared at her and
retorted: "I know that question always comes up. That's
why I try to avoid these things." She raised her eyebrows
at my response, then turned to the woman to her left and
asked, "How about you?"*

*I was as shocked at my response as she was. I thought
my defenses were up. I thought I could respond patiently
when she asked that question again. I left the shower as
soon as politely possible and cried all the way home. I
realized after that shower, that I was in such pain that I
couldn't trust my emotions any longer. I decided that I
needed to avoid some of the situations that were encouraging me to sin in my anger and become jealous of others — until I worked through some of my grief and shame.
I stopped going to baby showers, going to church on
Mother's Day and Father's Day, working in the church
nursery, and other circumstances that tempted me to focus on my inability to become pregnant or have babies.
The Bible didn't say I needed to go to baby showers, but it
did say I shouldn't hurt someone with my anger.*

*This was just one situation, on one day, in many years
of infertility.*

Day-by-day Stress

The stress of infertility can be enormous. Along with the
general grieving process, there is the emotional stress of
the constant cycle of hope and despair. One infertile woman dealt with this by never accepting an invitation to a
child-oriented function until she checked her calendar. If
the event were scheduled for day 16 of her cycle, when
she would have just ovulated, she would accept, but if it
were scheduled for day 2, after her period might have
started, she declined.

On the good days, there is just a mild tug at your heart;
then there are the bad days when the pain is uncontrolla-

ble, and it's hard to function at all. In dealing with this roller coaster of stress and also the physical stress of medical testing and treatment, we may find we don't have much energy left over to deal with the rest of life. "With the exception of a life-threatening illness," write the authors of *Overcoming Infertility,* "infertility is probably the most difficult and protracted medical problem a couple will have to face."[1]

Infertility brings day-to-day stresses that are similar to living with a chronic illness: dealing with the schedule of doctor's appointments and medication, operations and uncomfortable medical procedures, the side effects of drugs, the emotional energy spent in working through fears and grief, and needing to adjust to a different reality than we had planned. As in the case of chronic illness, we keep hoping for a miracle turnaround, and that may happen, but it isn't something we can count on. All of this can eventually lead to exhaustion.

The continued stress of infertility has also been expressed as being similar to having a family member missing in action because of a war. Hope is always around the corner, but grieving is happening simultaneously.

It's easy to say that you should try to compartmentalize your infertility and keep your life balanced, but infertility affects so many areas of life. It's one thing to anticipate a problem going to a baby shower, but the pain can also come out of the blue and blindside you.

I recently broke my toe. But, when I went in to have it x-rayed, the technician asked, "Is there any chance you might be pregnant?" I couldn't believe it. I'd broken my *toe,* but I had to explain my infertility history now. What made it worse was that a man in his fifties was standing next to the nurse, obviously waiting to talk to her. I glanced at him to see if he would go away, but he didn't. So, I gathered my courage and explained to her that even though I didn't know for sure, it was unlikely that I was pregnant, then explained about my infertility.

She said I needed to get a pregnancy test before they could take the x-ray. I told her that I had just ovulated, so a pregnancy test wouldn't be accurate yet. (I avoided glancing at the man who was *still* standing two feet away). I ended up waiting for three days to have a pregnancy test before they would take an x-ray. No, I wasn't pregnant. Yes, my toe was broken. I couldn't believe that even a broken toe would expose my infertility.

Emotional Exhaustion

One of the inconceivable things about infertility is how it wears us down emotionally month after month because the stress isn't being alleviated. For two weeks after ovulation of every month we have to follow the rules for pregnant women because we hope we might be sharing our body with a baby. We are constantly hearing about or reading of the dangers of eating or drinking specific things during pregnancy. Some things pregnant women are told to avoid or use sparingly are: tobacco, alcohol, coffee, black tea, cocoa, and chocolate because they contain caffeine; x-rays; all medications unless checked by a doctor; vaccinations; and excessive heat from hot tubs, saunas, hot baths, fevers, or excessive exercise.[2] I've even read some books that you should avoid pesticides, certain household cleaners, and shell fish. No wonder we feel a little crazy at times if we have to act like we're pregnant while being infertile.

Trying to avoid the stress by ignoring thoughts of pregnancy might work until someone brings up the question of pregnancy when you have your teeth x-rayed, attend any social gathering, refuse an alcoholic beverage, or are tired or sick. You are also reminded by warnings for pregnant women on medications or at amusement parks, childproof caps, home pregnancy test commercials, or by financial forms that ask about your children.

Then there are the ubiquitous pregnant women seeming to surround you or the sweet-faced child who asks,

"Where are your babies?" It takes strong emotional resources to navigate through these stumbling blocks in the typical day of an infertile person.

Because of the time involved, going through medical testing and treatment for infertility is like taking on a part-time job. Because of the tests, appointments, drugs, and operations, you may feel as if you've donated your body to science.

Ways of Coping

Coping means maintaining, not going under while undergoing the grief process. While there are no easy answers, good coping strategies help. Here are some suggestions:

- Keep a journal. One of my journals started as a pregnancy journal, but when the pregnancy ended in miscarriage, it became a place to write about the pain.

- Research. Finding out information about your particular problem or about infertility in general can give you some sense of control. Write down questions as they come up, then research the answers.

- Exercise. Get outside. Walk if you don't have the energy to do anything else. Do something you enjoy or used to enjoy. When your period comes, do something that is "dangerous" for a pregnant woman to do, such as skiing, roller-skating, ice-skating, biking, water-skiing, or even hang gliding.

- Eat nutritious food. Don't do this just because you might get pregnant but because you are worth taking care of.

- Be nice to yourself. Give yourself small consolation prizes when your period comes. Take a long, hot bubble bath or spend time in a hot tub (which pregnant women shouldn't do). Eat one thing you've been denying yourself because you "might be pregnant," such as a diet soda or something else with no nutritional value. Buy a new pair of pants but don't wear them until your period comes.

- Allow yourself to laugh. If you can learn to see the funny side of your horrible experiences and laugh at yourself or your situation, you have a wonderful coping skill. Laughter can be a great stress reliever, even if it is from macabre humor. At one RESOLVE conference a speaker joked, "With all the time I've spent with my feet in stirrups, you'd think I'd be an accomplished horsewoman by now." If it is ovulation day and you only have 15 minutes to have sex during a lunch hour before your husband leaves on a business trip, you've got two choices. Either you become uptight, or you learn to laugh.

- Don't let others determine what you need or make them guess your needs. Tell your doctor, husband, family, or friends what you need, but also be aware that they may not be able to give you everything you would like. They're only human too.

- Remove yourself from stress when needed. Your high-stress times are not the times to be hard on yourself if you're not meeting everyone's high expectations.

- Find someone to talk to who can gently support you. It may be your husband, or a good friend, or a counselor. It may also be a group of infertile women or couples who get together for the reason of supporting each other. If you can't find anyone, look for books to read about infertility, your relationship with God, or your particular area of struggle.

- Ask for prayer from your friends, family, or pastor.

- Meditate on Bible truths that show God cares about you.

- Try to notice God working in other areas of your life. This is not advice to "look on the bright side," but an invitation to truly discover where God is caring for you in other ways while you're on hold in the child-bearing area.

- Change what you can. Looking back at our first few years of infertility, I see that we had a lot of other stresses at the same time. I had a very difficult job; Michael was struggling through school; we moved five times in one year; we had crazy landlords, bug infestation, and water from broken pipes flooding our living room. Some of those stresses couldn't be changed, but some of them, like my job, could have. Eventually I did choose to work part-time.

Coping with Holidays and Special Events

Holidays are often described by infertile couples as: nosy relatives, comparisons, unfulfilled expectations, a symbol of another year gone by, and drawn out child/family focused celebrations. Whether the strain grows each year with infertility or whether you've experienced the loss of a baby, holidays can be especially trying.

First Samuel 1:1-18 describes how painful family celebrations can be. Year after year Hannah went to the Jewish feast where her infertility was exposed. She was teased to the point of tears and wasn't able to eat. The feasting was a part of the celebration, but Hannah just couldn't do it. Her husband Elkanah didn't understand. He asked her: "Why do you weep and why do you not eat and why is your heart sad? Am I not better to you than ten sons?" (v. 8, NASB) It sounds as if he was basically saying, "Buck up Hannah, and eat something! You still have me!" Did this make Hannah forget her pain? No, in verse 10 we read that she is "greatly distressed" and weeping bitterly. Eli the priest didn't understand either. Eli thought she was drunk.

Hannah was honest with Eli about her great concern and how she was provoked by her infertility to the point of shaking and tears. It was not until Eli prayed that God would answer her prayer for a child that her sorrow lessened and peace came to her. Then Hannah "went her way and ate, and her face was no longer sad" (v. 18). She was able to move on once she knew her pain was understood and was given hope, but this came after *years* of suffering through celebrations.

Mother's Day

I sat about four rows from the back of the church trying to regain control of my tears. I wondered if it would be less distracting to the other worshipers to open my purse and rustle around for another tissue or get up and go to the rest room. Rustling for the tissue won out this time because I realized I would have to walk past the people sitting behind me who would see my tear-streaked face; I was so ashamed that once again I was crying over not having a baby.

Mother's Day at church was an especially hard day. To hear about what a gift and blessing children are, that the children of a woman who fears the Lord will rise up and call her blessed (Proverbs 31), and be reminded of the great mothers in the Bible was difficult.

I thought back to one church we attended. Ushers gave carnations to all the mothers, who were then asked to stand up during the service to acknowledge the great work they were doing for the Lord in raising their children well. During another service young couples were even admonished from the pulpit for following society's wrong values, of making money before having children. I wanted to take part in motherhood with all my heart. Everything that was done and said just seemed to isolate me and brand me as inferior or as having wrong values.

Visiting after the service was just as brutal. Either I felt the sting of someone's insensitivity or saw pity in people's eyes. I resolved to stay away from church on Mother's Day for the next few years. This was a hard decision for me. It usually meant that I stayed home by myself because Michael was involved in teaching or running the services. I even stayed home one year when he preached the morning sermon. I knew he wasn't even going to touch on motherhood, but I didn't know what to expect from the other parts of the service he didn't control.

I worried that I would look like a failure as a Christian for staying home. I imagined that people would say, "It's too bad that she isn't able to get past her selfish desires to rejoice with the rest of us. If only she were more mature spiritually."

Is avoiding the situation a valid way to cope?
Mother's Day is one of the hardest holidays for infertile women or women who have lost a baby during pregnancy. I did not choose to stay home from church on Mother's Day because I wanted to diminish the recognition of other mothers. (I owe my life to my mother!) I chose to stay home for other reasons.

First, I realized that listening to the virtues of motherhood extolled encouraged me to sin. It caused me to take my eyes off what God was doing in my life right now and shift them back to my barrenness. If I had gained some peace in the last couple of months about God's love for me in spite of not giving me a child, on Mother's Day that went right out the window again. I sank back into depression.

The second reason was that I felt I was a distraction. My ache for a child was so great that I had to build up strong walls around the pain just to function through the week. Church, though, was normally a difficult place to keep up my resolve because part of the act of worship is to let down our barriers in order to become intimate with God. Singing has always been a part of worship that touches my emotions. So when I sang in church my love for God welled up, along with my conflicting struggle to understand why He was abandoning me. My feelings were so intense that when I let down the walls, my raw insides were exposed. I would cry, then worry that my crying would be a distraction to the celebration of the other worshipers. I felt they deserved a day to truly celebrate, but I couldn't do that right then.

The last reason I stayed home was that if I'd succeeded in strengthening my protective walls enough to withstand the inevitable insensitive comments or the revering of motherhood, I had a hard time letting my guard down to actually listen to the sermon or the words of the song. I was always worried that if I really started to listen, an emotion would creep into my brain that would crumble my defenses.

If we're in pain, so are others
Feeling pain on Mother's Day, though, opened up my eyes to others for whom this holiday was not especially joyful: the woman who's mother died the previous year, the single woman who desperately wondered if she would ever have the chance to become a wife and mother, the mother whose child was in rebellion, the mother who gave her baby up for adoption, the mother who had an abortion, or the person who grew up with an abusive mother.

These people don't fit the "joyful celebration of Mother's Day" picture. If you know women like this, it might help to send a card to them on Mother's Day to let them know you care. Or, you might want to send a card to another infertile friend, encouraging her that she is not alone in her struggle.

Christmas
People often feel stressed from the complex events, traditions, and family interactions that normally surround Christmas. Adding infertility or a recent loss can be overwhelming. I had always been a person who *loved* Christmas and everything surrounding it. (I even had to have a "fix" of Christmas music in July because I couldn't seem to live without it for the 11 months between Decembers.) I loved getting the tree, having Christmas stockings, making fudge, and pausing to wonder at the miracle of God coming to live among us.

But it became depressing to deal with the focus on children and on family in the midst of hurting from infertility. I tried to focus strictly on the spiritual celebration, but so much of it focused on a *pregnant* Mary and on the *Baby*

Jesus. I felt guilty and sad to be unable to celebrate and worship wholeheartedly in the traditional way. As an infertile friend once said, "I *know* God could make me pregnant if He chose to. He didn't even need a husband for Mary!"

Christmas was also harder for me to avoid because it was intertwined with celebrating God's gift. Because Christ came as a baby, I couldn't seem to get past the baby focus in carols about "the newborn King," "Holy Infant so tender and mild," "this is the night of our dear Savior's birth," and "for unto us a Child is born" to feel worshipful or positive.

It took years, but I learned to refocus my worship of God during Christmas so that I could celebrate again. Just as in most other areas of my life, I had to rethink Christmas.

Is Christmas only about pregnant Mary and Baby Jesus?

Christmas is about God showing His love for us. Here are some ways I learned to focus on other areas of God's many-faceted love for us during Christmastime:

- I concentrated on Christmas enabling us to become adopted children of God. This turned my attention away from the birth process and more toward the redemptive possibilities of adoption.
- Instead of focusing on Christ as a baby, I learned to focus on the rest of His life as an adult and His teaching. The whole reason that Christ came was to give us hope and a way to escape the results of sin in this world.
- I just wanted one worshipful Christmas carol that I could sing without stumbling over the baby themes. I found two Christmas carols that had a spiritual emphasis that didn't focus on Jesus as a baby, "Joy to the World" and "O Come, O Come Emmanuel." I was relieved to know I could sing these carols wholeheart-

edly and actually allow myself to feel what I was singing without worrying that the image of a baby would
pop up in the words.

- An advent wreath helped me to focus on the time that
the people of Israel waited for their Messiah to come.
Lighting one candle each of the four weeks before
Christmas helped me to realize that the Israelites
waited for many years without any sign of fulfillment.
They waited and wondered just like me.

Christmas traditions

Christmas can be a great time to celebrate as a couple and
create traditions that make the two of you feel like a family. Traditions should show you care for each other. Children are a great excuse to enjoy certain things, but you
can give yourself permission to enjoy them without the
excuse of a child. Talk with your spouse about what you
enjoy about Christmas and what hurts. Be creative in
thinking of nontraditional things to do that you both
would enjoy. Don't put off starting these traditions until
you have children.

What if an old family tradition is painful? Are you obligated to continue it? If you anticipate that a family tradition will be painful for you this year, try to see if family
members would be willing to try something new. In doing
this, you may find yourself offending family members because family history and meaning is often tied in with traditions. If the tradition is still meaningful to the others in
your family, then encourage them to continue it, but minimize your participation. Show your care for the family in
other ways: by sending letters, or going out of your way to
visit them at times other than the holidays.

If the time of opening gifts is hard for you because there
are too many nieces and nephews around, arrange to
open presents by yourselves, then get together just for
Christmas dinner rather than spending all morning immersed in exchanging gifts. Another possibility is to try

scheduling most of your time with your extended family in the afternoon (during naptime) or the evening if the babies will be asleep.

If lessening your time with family doesn't help enough, don't be afraid to say no to painful events. Sometimes, by passing up one it is easier to cope with the next one.

For those who have lost a baby, know that it is all right to skip the traditions and rituals and just take some time to grieve. Later, holidays can be a special time of remembering rather than celebrating. This is difficult because others will probably feel more comfortable ignoring your loss. It's also acceptable to choose to be by yourself or with other people. But don't expect the holiday to be the same as in the past.

With your new sensitivity, also look for other people who are lonely or hurting at Christmas. Maybe there is another childless couple, a child who needs extra attention, a single person, a college student away from home, or an elderly person who is also feeling left out. Take time to send a note or ask them over. Buying clothes for a needy family's children one year also helped remind me that having children doesn't mean the end of all problems.

Whatever you do to cope with the holidays, reassure your family and friends that you care about them as you let them know what you can handle.

Your Journey

1. Which area of your infertility is causing you the most stress right now? What other stresses do you have in your life right now? Which ones could you change?
2. What triggers your anger, depression, or sadness?
3. What holiday traditions would you like to start with your spouse? How would you modify existing holiday rituals?

11

Husband and Wife—
Supporting Each Other

Many men grow up to see a conversation as a contest—either to achieve the upper hand or to protect themselves from other people pushing them around. For many women, however, a conversation is a way to seek and give confirmation and support.[1]

A key lesson I've learned in living through six years of infertility and two adoption processes, is that my wife is really different from me. . . . We have very different personalities and comfort levels with situations. All of that produces the likelihood that we're going to respond differently to things that are important to us. —Mike S.

ichael and I have always enjoyed each other and our marriage. I would even say we've had a relatively easy marriage in regard to our relationship. We've encountered many difficulties from outside sources, but we've been united in dealing with them. The hardest periods in our marriage though, have been directly related to our infertility. During these times, we were frustrated to find that we were separated by a great chasm that neither of us could seem to cross.

One time was about three years into our infertility when we were deciding when to move on to adoption. I was ready to adopt, but Michael still wanted to try more infertility testing. I was so wrung-out emotionally, that I would cry at the thought of going back to the doctor. (We had taken a break from testing for a few months.) I'd had enough and was ready to stop the merry-go-round of office visits. Taking my temperature and going to the doctor's office seemed like constant reminders of failure. I was ready to be a parent through adoption and feared that once we got on an adoption agency's list, we still would have years to wait.

Michael, on the other hand, still felt very strongly about exhausting the possibilities offered through medicine first. Part of his reluctance to adopt stemmed from the legal system and the horror stories we'd heard about adoptive parents having their baby taken away when a birth parent changed his or her mind. He didn't feel he could bear that. He also didn't want to "compete" with forty other couples in the adoption game for the same baby.

This difference in our thinking was so difficult because it was no longer "us" against the infertility. Now, I saw Michael blocking my chance to become a mother through adoption and he saw me blocking the chance to find out if we could have a biological child through medical treatment. We were at a crossroads in our journey through infertility, and we each wanted to go a different direction.

I felt alone in the struggle for the first time. I couldn't go to Michael for comfort as I usually did. I thought, Can't he see how desperately I want a child? How can he deny me this? *He wondered,* Why is she pushing so hard for adoption? Can't she see that there are other medical options? *It took hours, days, weeks, and months of talking to work out this problem. I realized that Michael wasn't against adoption, it just felt safer to him to go the medical route. Michael realized how afraid I was that I would never be a mom. When we finally understood the depth of each other's feelings, we agreed to compromise. Michael agreed to put our name on an adoption agency's waiting list (an estimated 3–5 year wait). I agreed to continue the infertility testing while we waited for an adoption to come through. Because we worked to understand each other's deep feelings, not just the initial objections, and then each gave a little, we were able to fulfill both of our goals: Michael's for a definite answer on the possibility of a biological child and mine to have a child to raise as soon as possible.*

Different Reactions of Men and Women

While it's not fair to generalize because everyone is unique, there is some benefit in realizing that men and women often react differently to infertility.[2] It can bring great trauma to a marriage before a couple sees the growth it can bring to their relationship. Not only is each spouse affected by infertility, but the marriage relationship itself is redefined.

Even in the best marriage relationships, the number of life-changing decisions infertility can bring is stressful. Do both of you have an equally strong desire to have children? Do you agree on the way to build a family? Do you cope with stress the same way? Understanding and becoming unified in these areas often takes intense communication.

Most spouses have personalities that differ from their partner's (surprise!), in addition to different ways of dealing with stress and conflict. One spouse wants to research the problem and talk it out for months on end; the other wants to just wait. One is pessimistic about the ultimate outcome, the other perpetually hopeful. Discovering and accepting your differences, then learning to function together in spite of them is a lot of the relationship work involved in dealing with infertility.

My husband Michael once described his feelings about our differences to our infertility group:

> On the freeway, I'm more emotional than Debbie, but not in the area of infertility. I just figured it was timing. We just had to hit the right moment and it would work.
>
> Then we started realizing there were other problems. Debbie began to hurt and get frustrated. All the while, I was focusing on school and my career. I hurt with her, but what I remember most was the nuisance of sex being scheduled for us. All the while, I was confident that we

would get pregnant, but it was OK if it didn't happen right away.

I really wasn't despairing; Debbie was despairing. There were times when I saw her hurting and I would just break down in tears. I'd ask her, *"What do you want me to do? I just can't do anything to help."* It is such a helpless feeling to see your wife hurting.

I think I maintained a high confidence level about having children because I didn't have the same emotional investment as Debbie. A lot of men don't seem to get the same level of satisfaction from having babies. I was also more detached from the whole process. It was easier for me to say we'll just keep going because I wasn't doing the tests or treatments. Also, until I had gone through every single test the doctors had, I wasn't going to admit defeat.

Whether by conditioning or genetics, men and women generally approach problems from different viewpoints. Based on research and interviews, the following responses are a sampling of how men generally react to problem situations.[3]

- I discuss problems with few people other than my wife.
- I try to approach problems rationally.
- I was raised not to discuss my feelings or cry easily.
- I was raised to find self-worth through my job.
- If I share a problem, my intent is to find a solution.
- If my wife is hurting, I feel my job is to fix the problem to protect her.

Many women on the other hand, tended to respond to problems (and specifically infertility) this way:

- I usually discuss problems with my close relatives or friends along with my husband.
- I'm the only emotional support for my husband in discussing our infertility.
- I don't like that my body is the main focus of most infertility tests and treatments (unless the doctor determines early on that the cause of infertility is in the man's body only).

- When I want to discuss a problem, I'm not necessarily looking for an answer, just support to help me deal with it.

Know the Foe

What often happens when we don't understand differences in our spouse, is that we try to win the spouse over to our "right" way of thinking. Communication is good, but the way it is done is critical to its success. It's natural to have many talks and even "intense discussion" (arguments) while we try to figure out each other, God, medical treatments, adoption, and our place in society. We need to remember when we're working out these issues though, not to confuse attacking the infertility and attacking our spouse.

The Bible helps us to do this. Try to focus on what the other person is saying and meaning, as James 1:19 says: "Let everyone be quick to hear, slow to speaking, and slow to anger" (NASB).

Deal with the issues, resolving them rather than withdrawing from each other, as Ephesians 4:26 says: "If you are angry, don't sin by nursing your grudge. Don't let the sun go down with you still angry—get over it quickly."

As we talk things out, it is so important to remember not to say anything abusive toward each other that we will regret later. Avoid blaming, name calling, or loaded words, as Colossians 3:8 warns us: "Put them all aside: anger, wrath . . . and abusive speech" (NASB).

Working through the grief of infertility is hard for a couple to endure, but continuing to reach out, learning more about each other, and caring for each other will bring deeper intimacy to our marriages.

From the Male Perspective

When the problem is sperm

If the problem lies with the wife, men tend to be more pragmatic about infertility. But when the medical problem lies with the husband, the man's response is often more emotional. He is then the one who may be taking fertility drugs, having a variococele procedure, or wearing a "cooling device" to cool the scrotum for better sperm production. These actions affect the private areas of his body as well as his psyche. Because the ability to father a child is sometimes wrongly connected with sexual performance, he may feel that his masculinity and sexuality are being questioned.

Ted felt this when doctors found problems with his sperm:

> When I was thirteen, I had one of my testicles removed. It was up in my abdomen and the doctor had to remove it because he thought it was cancerous. It was hard on my pride and ego. My wife felt uncomfortable even bringing it up to me, but we wondered if that was possibly causing our problem. We wanted to find out, so I took every test I could.
>
> We found out that half of my sperm were dysfunctional. I wondered, did defective ones get into the eggs and cause our children to miscarry? Maybe I didn't produce the right chromosomes. Maybe I didn't have the right mechanical parts within myself to give [my wife] a child. I felt like a failure. I struggled with feeling that I was to blame for our problems and with my sexuality at the same time.

Handling embarrassment

Men also have the embarrassment of having to "deliver" sperm on a schedule. Delivering sperm samples makes most men uncomfortable because of its connection to sexual stimulation. Something very private is suddenly public. As Michael attests, delivering sperm samples definitely has its embarrassing side:

> Once, as I was taking a sperm sample to the hospital, I walked outside, and of course I ran into someone I knew. There I was holding my little bag as my friend kept talking.

It was so cold outside. I was so tense thinking *these little guys are going to freeze.* I had to quickly think of a believable reason to leave before he asked what I had in my lunch bag.

Men also grieve

Some husbands feel the grief of infertility deeply and want to talk about it, but feel restricted in expressing it. Some of the differences in the ways husbands and wives react are triggered by the way our society views men's and women's roles. Women are given more permission in our society to cry and talk. Sometimes husbands may feel forced into playing the role of the strong protector when they don't feel strong, as Richard discovered after his wife's second miscarriage:

> The instant I knew that we were pregnant, it was like a big explosion of excitement and joy. Instantly, I loved our baby. It is an instantaneous, forever love.
>
> I'll always love the ones we lost. Every time we had a miscarriage, I thought it would be easier if somebody would just take [my] arm or leg so I could have a child. Here was something I loved, that was living just a short while ago, and the [procedure] pulled it all apart.
>
> My wife became very withdrawn and hid herself from her family and friends, but I had to go back to work. The sadness hit so deep [I] couldn't sleep. It was blacker than black. When you're that low, there's not much anybody can do or say. [But] I had learned from past experiences how to hide some of that emotion and continue to operate. My wife needed me to be the strong statue of love and tenderness, faith, and hope. But, I wanted someone to lean on also.

Dealing with infertility indirectly

One study found that when men were affected by infertility, they tended to respond indirectly to it. The men chose objects or activities to fill the void of childlessness. Some chose to "lavish parental affection and pride" on a non-human object (such as improving a house); others became immersed in body building, personal health, or macho sexuality; while still others got involved in activities which included other people's children (such as coaching a Little League team or leading a church youth group).

The study also found that the men who reached out to other children were much more likely to eventually have a child or adopt, and to rate their marital happiness higher later on. So, it is important to recognize that there are indirect ways of dealing with infertility.[4]

What's a Husband to Do?

Steve learned to understand his wife's grief about childlessness by relating it to other grief in his life:

> I have a sperm motility problem and my wife has endometriosis, which is a killer combination for fertilizing things. It wasn't a huge, emotional thing for me to not be able to replicate my particular gene pool because adoption was always an option for me. Because It wasn't such a big problem for me, I think that set up and intensified the conflict between my wife and myself.
>
> We both agreed about [wanting kids], but my wife *needs* children much more than I do. I mean, sure, I think children are a great concept, but I don't need them to fill an emotional need. She has about 15,000 pounds of concern about kids and I've got maybe 25 pounds.
>
> The year that changed my attitude, helped me recognize, accept, and even value Vicky's difference was the year we found out that the cancer my father had was terminal. He literally wasted away before my eyes and died. [Also that year], I was laid off from work; Vicky lost her job; and we found out that we absolutely, positively could not have babies.
>
> I was grieving for my father. . . . I had a real intense love for him. I cried almost every day for 16 months. Vicky loved my dad and felt concerned about me, but she didn't feel it as intensely as I did. It finally occurred to me that there was a good reason for that. It was simply a matter of

relation. She didn't stand in the same relation I did with my father.

That's really the difference between me and my wife. I don't stand in the same place in infertility that she does. I don't have the capacity to bear life in my body. I don't have a monthly reminder of that capacity. I haven't lived with the expectation from the time that I was a small child that I would someday bear life and rear children. Our different reactions to infertility doesn't mean I don't care enough about her, it simply means I don't share in the same experience she does. That was a real turning point. It took some bitter, bitter life experiences to teach me that. But it was a valuable lesson that cemented our relationship and marriage.

Some specific suggestions for husbands
- Ask your wife how she would like you to support her.
- Share your pain and other feelings about infertility with your wife.
- Pray with your wife and for your wife (Gen. 25:21).
- Listen, then hold and hug your wife.
- Get involved in the process. Read about infertility. Go together to the doctor's appointments. Record the temperature chart for awhile.
- Give your wife room to grieve or feel the pain of infertility more deeply or for a longer time. It can be difficult to watch someone you love hurt intensely, but she will heal more quickly if you acknowledge her pain and let her know it is OK for her to feel what she does.
- Discuss with her ways that you can work as a team and protect each other when the subject of babies is brought up at gatherings.
- Tell your wife you love her and also tell her the specific things you appreciate about her. Choose another day of the year to celebrate your wife, such as the Saturday before Mother's Day.
- If you feel frustrated about the way or amount that

you talk about infertility, try the 20 minute rule. Set aside a certain amount of time each day when you talk about infertility and promise to listen to each other carefully. Then agree not to mention it again that day (unless something big like a medical procedure has happened).

● Talk with your wife about additional losses you've both felt because of your inability to have children now.

● If, as a man, you find yourself struggling with the emotional effects of male or female infertility, you might be helped by talking to other men who have been in the same situation. If you don't know anyone to contact, the organization RESOLVE can connect you with someone. (See Appendix A.)

What's a Wife to Do?

Debbie S. thought her husband's easier acceptance of their infertility meant he didn't care:

> My husband was very sweet and supportive of me and my sorrow over our being infertile. He cried with me when the doctor gave us the discouraging news. But he wasn't devastated. He could live without children and go on with his life. I had a hard time with his ability "to get over it" when I felt I'd *never* get over it. My desire for children was such a part of me it reached to my soul.
>
> He was afraid I was being consumed by my desire for a family. I thought he didn't care enough. We had many conversations, discussions, and arguments over having children and have come to understand our differences. Our marriage is stronger after going through infertility and adoption together, but only because of God's grace and our perseverance at communication.

Other specific suggestions for wives

● Ask your husband how he would like you to support him.

- Share your hurt with your husband, but let him know you aren't asking him for an answer or to fix it.
- Pray for and with your husband.
- Husbands sometimes complain that they feel their wife only sees them as a sperm delivery service. Respect your husband's feelings and physical well-being in scheduling sex.
- If you need to talk about infertility more than your husband wants to, discuss it with other infertile women, a counselor, or a pastor.
- If the side effects of taking fertility drugs or other medical treatments are taking their toll on your marriage, be willing to take a break from treatment.
- Learn to laugh together at the ridiculous side of some infertility tests and treatments.
- See the section, "Some Specific Suggestions for Husbands" earlier in this chapter for the 20-minute rule.
- Tell your husband you love him and tell him specific things you appreciate about him. Choose a day to celebrate him, such as the Saturday before Father's Day.
- Let your husband know specifically what would help you, but don't expect him to do all of it.

Keeping Intimacy Alive

The feeling of being out of control of your sex life is often stressful. Mary and her husband had the usual resentment toward scheduled sex:

> After a while, I resented telling my husband I was ovulating and it was the right time to have sex. He always seemed surprised. I took this as a lack of caring. Although he also wanted children, I guess he thought I was asking for a command performance. We decided to post the temperature chart on our headboard where we both could see it and anticipate the "big O" day.

Some husbands can also find that the pressure to perform sexually is a hindrance to their sexual arousal. Being intimate means sharing your innermost self with another, being closely personal, and private. What happens during infertility is that the sexual part of intimacy is inspected, analyzed, scheduled, and discussed. Perhaps it is only discussed and analyzed between spouses or you may be given "helpful" suggestions by friends and relatives. In the case of medical testing and treatment, it may be inspected, analyzed, and scheduled in meetings with medical professionals. Sex can also become difficult because something once so full of joy can now become linked with sorrow or failure. Infertility can change your sex life dramatically if you don't take precautions to balance the functional part of trying to procreate with the intimate part of sharing yourselves.

This is not to say that you need to wait until the optimally romantic moment to have sex. It's fine to have sex at ovulation time even if you both agree that it isn't the best timing (for example, because of the sunburn you just got or the cold you're developing). Sex is one area where humor is imperative during infertility. But if you sense an unequal desire to have sex around ovulation time, be sensitive to the underlying reasons. Talk about them before you get into the bedroom so that sex doesn't become a major point of conflict.

To refocus your sex life on the intimacy it is meant to convey, try to remember what sex was like before infertility. The emotional feelings and physical feelings are intertwined. Try to recapture those feelings. Put creative energy toward focusing on a variety of ways to be affectionate, such as holding hands, hugging, and other intimate contact. While intercourse is needed to conceive, remember that sex is a gift you give to each other. Your relationship can be damaged if the gift is demanded without regard for your spouse's feelings.

In building intimacy, pastor Gary Vanderet suggests focusing on this joy of giving to each other:

God has given us the ability to give the gift of love to another person, and it is the joy of that giving that creates the ecstasy of sexual love. Now to do this, to ensure your mate's sexual fulfillment, you need to talk, to understand, to listen, to care about another's needs.[5]

Along with talking, making the choice to love will eventually bring greater feelings of love and intimacy. Consciously making the effort to do one thing each day to show each other your love will help you focus on your marriage and reaffirm your importance to each other.

Specific ways to compensate for lost intimacy
Some other specific ways to compensate for lost intimacy, especially during medical testing are:
- Plan for the husband to be present during procedures such as intrauterine insemination (IUI). Plan a romantic time to be together afterward.
- Plan for a special time together after a particularly stressful cycle or procedure—either to grieve or to celebrate together.
- Take time to remember to really look at your spouse and be thankful for the good qualities you see.
- Plan dates with your spouse to have fun and keep your relationship balanced.
- Take a vacation from treatment to focus on each other.
- Vary who does the initiating and how you initiate sex around ovulation time.

For some couples, although infertility scheduling has been an unwelcome intruder on their sex life, they have also found it has given them an added incentive to keep their sex life strong, consistent, and a priority.

Not Feeling the Same, but Understanding
Michael and I definitely don't react to problems the same way, but I've grown in my appreciation for this man who

never stopped loving me through all these years with all this pain. What Michael did for me during this time was give me a safe place to share my innermost feelings. I appreciate the way he has worked through the sorrow with me. When I look back now, I see that it would have been a catastrophe if both of us felt and reacted the same way at the same time. We've learned to listen to each other, have compassion for each other, and trust each other with our lives, so real intimacy grew. I know without a doubt that he's committed to me and I to him.

Michael didn't have the same level of pain that I did, but he worked at understanding my pain and accepting me through it. He didn't make me feel inferior for feeling more deeply. Because of that I learned to accept that he didn't have to suffer the depth of despair that I felt in order to really want children. As Michael put it, "I finally understood that she didn't want me to cry all the time, but to tell her that it was OK if she needed to." Neither grieving deeply nor not grieving deeply is less "spiritual."

When we have that understanding, instead of standing with our hands on our hips and saying, *you should feel the way I feel,* we can work on coming to agreement with our spouse on major infertility decisions. Then periodically, we need to ask our spouse again how he or she is doing and take the time to listen to the answer. This won't make the pain go away, but it will be easier to deal with because we will be united.

Infertility puts pressure on individuals and marriages. Marriage must be top priority during infertility. If we're never able to have our dream children, we'll still have a soul mate and the strong, supportive relationship we've cultivated. If we are able to have children, they will be able to grow up with the security that their mom and dad deeply love not only them, but also each other.

Your Personal Journey

1. Read Philippians 2:1-4. Write down specific ways you
   can do the following for your mate:
   ● encourage,
   ● console,
   ● show affection for,
   ● show compassion for,
   ● be united with,
   ● maintain love with,
   ● regard as more important than yourself,
   ● and look out for his or her interests.

12

Support from Friends, the Family, and the Church

Each man can interpret another's experience
only by his own. — Thoreau

I hope that among those of us who may have
never known such pain, failure, or grief,
an enlargement of heart may occur.[1]

After staying home from church one Mother's Day because it was too painful to go, Michael and I went to dinner at my parent's house. When we came in, my mom and dad hugged us, knowing what a difficult day this was for us. After praying for God to bless our mothers, we gathered in the kitchen for the buffet. A family friend (who didn't know about our difficulties in having children) announced, "Since this is Mother's Day, all the mothers should help themselves first." I was the only female who wasn't a mother. I stood where I was, feeling two feet tall. My failure was exposed, and I felt relegated to the status of a child. My mom tried to cover, knowing the pain that statement had caused me. She whispered, "Come on Honey, you too." The family friend then reached over and barred my way to the table. He accused, "Oh no, not you there! I said mothers only."

I caught my breath because the pain was so intense, it scorched right through me. Michael quickly navigated me toward the back bedroom, where I sobbed. I was tired of living on the edge of tears for so long. I felt like a quivering, open wound.

Rationally, I knew our family friend was being insensitive but wasn't deliberately trying to hurt me. But I also knew he could have honored the mothers in another way without having to exclude me. I wanted to rise above the situation, shrug it off, and go on with the dinner, but I couldn't.

It was hard to know who and when to tell. If I hadn't previously told my mother, I wouldn't have had her support in this situation. But, I wasn't ready to tell our family friend because our relationship wasn't close enough to share intimacies. I also didn't know if he would be supportive or still wouldn't understand. I was dealing with enough emotions right then without taking the chance that I might have to defend myself to someone who didn't understand the pain of infertility. I finally got myself under control and went out to join the others, hoping they wouldn't ask about my swollen, red eyes.

A Couple May Not Be Childless by Choice
People who are infertile or who have lost a baby during pregnancy often have the same need for understanding and support as those who have lost an older family member or close friend to death. Their grief is less public though, so sometimes friends and family don't know how to help. This chapter is written to help grieving people clarify what might help. It is also written to be shared with family, friends, and church.

Friends and family members need to realize that married couples without children may not be that way by choice. Just this simple awareness can go far in helping them reduce their insensitive comments. Sometimes friends and family members don't realize that what they are saying can be hurtful to an infertile couple.

Paul's grandfather unintentionally causes him and his wife a stab of pain every time they visit him: "My 91-year-old grandfather asks when we're going to have children every time we see him, which is once a week. He has no concept [of our problem] whatsoever. Subconsciously that's pressure."

Vicky felt the same hurt from her mom:

> My mother's hobby is grandbabies. My sisters were having babies, so I didn't tell her about our problem for a long time. She'd just pick up her cat and remark sometimes: "Well, this is my grandbaby until I get one." I'm not the type of person to speak up and say, "That hurt my feelings." I just fall apart in the car on the way home. Finally, I told her what we were going through and how hard it was. She said, "Oh Honey, just pray about it." I'd [already] been praying so hard and for so long! Finally she's come around to see how much it hurts. But it was so difficult for my mother of all people not to understand.

Philip Yancey, author of *Where Is God When It Hurts?* once said the following when asked about how well-meaning Christians could add an emotional burden to those already suffering:

> Many Christians talk a lot about healing, and they're doing it from a positive basis . . . they're wanting to provide hope. But, if the person who is suffering does not find healing, if God does not choose to heal that person, then very often that person feels like a second class citizen, that there is something wrong with [me] spiritually. [I] don't have enough faith. God has passed [me] by.[2]

The choice to heal a person of a disability is God's alone. There are many times He chooses not to heal people in order to fulfill His plan. (See chapter 9 for more information on this.)

Comments and Questions That Hurt

When the couple has not shared their status

- *"Did I tell you about how cute so-and-so's baby is?"* (for the fifth time) *"Well, you all know what labor feels like . . ."* Talking about pregnancy or baby news all the time can make an infertile person feel isolated.

- *"When are you going to have kids?"* or even worse, *"Don't you have kids yet?"* Or for those with secondary infertility (couples who struggle to have another child): "Don't you think your child needs a baby brother or sister?" These questions imply that the couple is remiss in not having children. These questions are most often asked casually, but they can cause deep pain to those whose attempts to bear children have failed.

When the couple has shared their struggle to have children

- *"Are you pregnant yet?"* After individuals confide their infertile status, this question can make them feel they've failed all over again. Try asking instead how their medical tests are going or just how they're feeling. Be assured they will shout it from the rooftops if they become pregnant. (The other version of this is to look at a woman's stomach and ask, *"Are you pregnant?"* This is an awful question to ask anyone who is not pregnant, and it is hard to recover if the answer is no.)

- *"It will happen. Don't worry." "Kids aren't all they're cracked up to be." "Here, take mine." "At least you have the fun of practicing." "Look on the bright side . . ."* These remarks ignore or minimize the couple's grief. As Proverbs 25:20 says: "Being happy-go-lucky around a person whose heart is heavy is as bad as stealing his jacket in cold weather, or rubbing salt in his wounds."

- *"Maybe you just weren't meant to have children." "You can always adopt." "Just relax or take a vacation." "You're still young." "Maybe it's just not God's will."*

These are the type of pat answers which can make a couple feel you don't understand the problem. Some of them imply that the infertility is the couple's fault (for example, if they were less stressed, they would be pregnant by now). If someone told you he had a broken arm, responses similar to these would seem silly. The above responses to the medical problems which cause infertility, such as uterine fibroids, hormonal imbalances, blocked fallopian tubes, or low sperm count don't make sense either.

• *"Are you sure you understand how babies are made?" "Do you need some help?"* Don't make jokes about or assume something is wrong with an infertile couple's sex life.

• *"Maybe you'll get pregnant if you adopt."* Be careful offering medical advice. Many people believe the old wives' tale that if a couple adopts a baby, they will relax and have an increased chance of getting pregnant. According to a large study done by Stanford University Infertility Clinic, fertility is *not* enhanced by adoption.[3] In fact, those who adopt may have a slightly *lower* statistical chance of becoming pregnant than those who do not. (You may know of people to whom this happened, but the infertility of couples who conceive after adopting is just more visible than that of childless infertile couples who finally become pregnant.)

Also understand that adoption isn't a *cure* for infertility. It alleviates childlessness, but the couple will still need to address other issues: living with a dysfunctional body and losing the chance to create life, experience pregnancy, and pass on genetic traits.

• *"Maybe God isn't giving you a child until you change." "You shouldn't be angry."* The Bible doesn't say anger at injustice is wrong, but that we shouldn't sin in our anger (Eph. 4:26). Anger at injustice is a natural stage of the grieving process as a person works out how his or her struggles fit into a relationship with God. Encouraging honest and respectful communication with God will allow the person's relationship with God to grow. If someone expresses anger in an inappropriate or destructive way, then intervention is needed.

Be careful about offering "spiritual" advice. It is easy to quote Romans 8:28 "all things work together for good," but remember that Romans 8:26 comes first: "The Spirit also helps our weakness; for we do not know how to pray as we should, but the Spirit Himself intercedes for us with *groanings too deep for words*" (NASB, emphasis mine). Try to identify with and communicate your understanding of the infertile person's pain as stated in verse 26 before offering verse 28.

When the couple has lost a baby during pregnancy
As with general infertility, it is difficult for those who haven't experienced pregnancy loss to understand the pain it can bring.

• *"It was for the best."* This is painful because malformed babies and death are tragedies that were not in God's original plan. Because of God's love for us, He will turn death around and use it for good, but it is not in itself a "blessing."

• *"I hope you feel better soon." "Don't you think you should be over this by now?"* Couples need to take time to grieve. These comments can make them feel they should ignore their grief to make others feel better.

• *"Aren't you thankful for the child(ren) you already have?" "You can always have another."* Other children do not take the place of a baby who has died.

• *"At least you never knew the baby."* This is not seen as a blessing to couples who ached to know their baby.

Comments and Questions that Help
Infertility is a loss worthy of mourning. Sending a note to say you are praying for infertile friends or family members is very appropriate. It will mean a lot to them that you appreciate their loss. I've listened to enough hurting peo-

ple, though, to know that it can mean a great deal to them when someone lets them know they care.

Deanna was devastated after her miscarriage, but she prayed for the first time in a long time after receiving the letter below. Her friend helped her back to God by acknowledging her pain, her need to grieve, and by sharing her own circumstances and what had helped her. She offered to be available to talk, but didn't push.

> As I sit here in my kitchen thinking of you, your husband, and your child, I find myself in tears as I remember my similar experience three years ago. I understand your deep woundedness, and I am *sorry* that your baby died. I know the loss and emptiness and the questions that are raised by such an experience. I would not presume to say that I have all the answers for you and Tom, but I can tell you that because I confronted God with all of my hurt and anger, He was able to bring answers and deep healing, even for issues deeper than my son's death.
>
> ... Be *tenacious* and *truthful* in your pursuit of God and His healing words. Know that He wants to reveal Himself to you. Give yourself the freedom to express your hurt and frustration. *He's not looking for a perfect performance* to come out of your reaction, but He wants to dig out and reveal deeper truths to you as you respond to Him openly and truthfully.
>
> I hurt with you and rejoice with you all in the same breath because I know that the Lord will be faithful to you and Tom. Pursue God and He will meet you. If it would be helpful to chat, please call.
>
> Much love and prayers for healing, Lorry.[4]

One problem for couples who have never been able to conceive is the lack of an event or specific time to send a similar note. But if you listen closely to your friend and to what the Lord nudges you to do, a note of caring can be a wonderful comfort. The perfect time might be after a bad medical test/treatment or other negative news, such as an adoption possibility that has fallen through, or just when you think the couple is having a tough time with their infertility.

If you have trouble relating to the struggle of an infertile friend or family member, think of how you might feel if the life of your child were taken away. Infertile people can have those same intense feelings.

Here are some suggestions of comments that might be helpful.

When the couple has not shared their status

Often couples feel questions about starting a family are too personal to come from strangers. If you have developed a relationship though, perhaps you might broach the subject by asking, *"Would you like to have children someday?"* This can be an open-ended way to bring up the subject of children, allowing the couple to be as vague as they want to be in their reply. Be sensitive if they don't seem to want to open up at all.

When the couple has shared their struggle to have children

- *"Is there anything I can do to help you?"*
- *"I have no idea what it must be like for you. I've never been infertile. Can you tell me what it feels like?"* *"It must have been hard to have been connected to the life of your baby when you lost it."* If you feel comfortable with listening to the responses, these questions can give an infertile friend an invitation to talk.
- *"I wish I could give you reasons why things like this happen, but all I can tell you is that I am hurting with you, and I know that God is hurting with you."* Don't feel you have to give your infertile friend all (or any) answers. What she is looking for is caring, not logic.
- *"I'm sad for you."* *"How are you doing through all this?"* *"What can I do for you?"* *"I'm sorry."* *"I'm here and want to listen if you want to talk about it."*[5] These suggestions are offered in the book, *When a Baby Dies: A*

Handbook for Healing and Helping, as open-ended ways to respond which also acknowledge a couple's grief.
- *"I hurt for you." "I will pray for you."* (Then really do it.) For couples with secondary infertility: *"It must be hard to not be able to have another child. I'm sorry."*
- *"Would you like me to ask about how your testing/treatment/adoption is coming or would you prefer to let me know when something changes?"*
- *"I think you would/will make wonderful parents."* Many infertile people wonder if children are being withheld from them because they would make bad parents.

Also, unless you disagree with a choice that an infertile couple makes on a clear moral issue, try to offer uncritical support. Even if you have a moral disagreement, do some biblical or medical research before gently sharing your concern to ensure that it is a real moral issue, not just a personal choice.

- If you aren't able to offer personal support, help your infertile friend or family member find others to support them. Do the research and offer them information about a support group, supportive pastor, counselor, or just the name of another infertile person. It isn't true that allowing your infertile friend or family member to talk about his or her sadness, hopelessness, or anger will make it worse.

When the couple has lost a baby during pregnancy
- *"It is tragic your baby died."* Acknowledge the couple's loss and share your own feelings of grief about the loss of their child. Ask if they named the child. Talk to them about "your baby" or use the name the couple chose.

Supportive Deeds
Expressions of caring are also wonderful ways to show support.
- Don't avoid infertile friends or family. Let them know you care and want to listen to their feelings if they want to share them.

• Give a hug, make a meal, offer to drive to doctor's appointments. Read about infertility or pregnancy loss.

• Dedicate yourself to pray for and *with* your hurting friend. Let the infertile person hear you pray for him or her. If you pray for and *with* a person, you are actually taking her into God's presence. This may not be the time to share biblical "truth," but let her hear you pray for her comfort from God.

• Include the infertile woman in your circle of mothers, but give her an out when she's had enough. Get together with the childless person without your children sometimes. When you are with her, try to limit your conversations about how wonderful/terrible children or pregnancies are.

• Support an infertility or pregnancy loss support group. One friend made dessert for our infertility support group meeting and another offered money for postage and supplies to show she cared. Other infertility or pregnancy loss support groups take donations "in memory of" miscarried babies.

• Understand if your friend doesn't attend a baby shower, family gathering focusing on children, or Mother's Day church service.

• Offer to write a letter of recommendation, take pictures, or help financially for an adoption. The adoption process takes a great deal of paperwork and expense which is rarely returned if the adoption falls through. This can leave the couple financially unable to try again.

• The book, *When a Baby Dies,* also suggests the following ways friends and families can help someone who has lost a baby: attend the memorial service; call or send a card on the baby's due date, birthday, or death day anniversaries; give remembrances—a baby ring, a plant, tree, or flowers in a baby vase, a poem.[6]

Family and friends may feel they need to walk on eggshells for a while around someone who is infertile or has experienced a pregnancy loss, but remember it won't be forever. Infertile people will usually be appreciative if you realize that right now most of their energy is taken up in just surviving. (For additional resources to help you relate to couples experiencing infertility or pregnancy loss, see Appendix A: Resources.)

The Church and the Infertile Couple

While it's important for the church to value families, church members can go to the extreme of making people without children feel they are not part of the church family. Couples trying unsuccessfully to have children can feel like outcasts at church. Paul felt isolated because of his church's emphasis on children:

> Being at our church became such a painful, painful time, that we dropped out altogether for about six months. Everyone was having babies. Sunday mornings became a baby-fest where they would talk about their babies and children for half the Bible class time. They'd introduce and have the newly pregnant mothers stand. In the Bible class bulletin they had a little chart that said how many people had two-year-old babies, how many had one-year-old babies, how many had babies on the way, and how many wanted to have babies.

What can the pastor or church leaders do?

While the church can be a source of pain for infertile couples because of its family focus, it can also be a source of compassion, wisdom, support, and strength. My husband, Michael, felt this support from our church pastor:

> One of the most encouraging things that happened to me was when I was the associate pastor at a little church in Milpitas. We started telling people in the congregation that we were infertile and were in the process of trying to adopt twins. During the prayer portion of the service, we asked the pastor to pray that the adoption would go through. He prayed that we would be able to adopt, and

also included that if it was the Lord's will, we would become pregnant too.

He didn't say that we had a spiritual problem or we should just pray about it. He prayed fervently for us. He very devoutly believed in prayer and would sometimes be in tears as he prayed. His understanding caught me completely by surprise.

● Emphasize the value of each individual in God's eyes. Some of the current emphasis on children in the church is a reaction to our society where children are undervalued. It is important to teach against thinking of children as "a leave of absence" from a career at best and an "obstacle to our career" at worst. Yet, we can value children and speak highly of them without talking about them constantly or inferring that having them is the only way to please God. Families are important, but they aren't the main emphasis of the Bible. The two most important things God wants us to do are love Him and love others.

● Be careful that the young couples/young families classes don't become so centered on babies that they make an infertile couple uncomfortable attending. By the end of two years in the Sunday School class of 23 young couples that Michael and I attended, we were one of only two couples who had no children. We were so relieved when Michael was asked to teach in the college group. (It was great for us at the time because no one was having babies! We could also relate to the college student's questions about the future: Will I ever find someone to love? Does God have a plan for me? This might be a good option for an infertile couple at church, but they should also feel free to attend a class with their peers.

● Be sensitive to someone wanting a memorial service. Perhaps a couple who has miscarried a baby or who has decided to end their infertility treatment would like a time of closure for their loss. An intimate memorial service is appropriate. (The organization SHARE, listed in Appendix

A: Resources offers a sample ceremony for those who have suffered a pregnancy loss.)

• Ask a childless couple to write something for your church newsletter or as an insert to your church bulletin to raise awareness of infertility (not only after they have adopted). Before Mother's Day or Father's Day can be a good time for this.

• Show support if someone is interested in starting an infertility support group at your church. Also, become aware of other support groups offered in your area. Look for resources on infertility or grief and have them available to share.

• Take the time to read a book on infertility to gain compassion for the people in your congregation who are struggling in this area. *The Infertile Couple* (listed in the Appendix B) is a good, concise book for pastors or counselors.

• Become aware of the ethical issues involved with infertility treatment so that when a couple asks you for counseling on these issues, you are aware of the specifics of the medical treatments offered and what the Bible says on the subject.

• Be prepared to contrast a couple's infertility today with the concept of barrenness in the Old Testament. Couples might question whether their barrenness is a sign of God's anger, as in parts of the Old Testament. Help them to understand that God's specific plan for Israel was different in many ways than His plan for Christians today. Ray S. Anderson, a professor of theology and ministry at Fuller Theological Seminary, once explained it this way:

> In the Old Testament, childbearing is considered crucial to the development of Israel as the people of God.
> The messianic hope of Israel is grounded in the birth of a child, the Messiah. . . . [A consequence of this was that] conception was interpreted as a mark of divine favor, and infertility as a sign of divine displeasure or indifference. . . .

With the birth of Jesus, however, we see a radical trans-
formation of this emphasis on childbearing. . . . The primary metaphor is no longer conception, but adoption. . . .
The value of each person is centered on being a child of
God, not in having children.

All this does not, of course, remove the frustrations and
grief of the infertile couple. But it does remove the stigma
and the feeling that infertility is a failure of prayer or a
form of divine displeasure.[7]

• Make room in your church's program for non family-
oriented ministries.

• Specifically remember childless couples on Mother's
Day, Christmas, and other holidays which are focused on
children. Sometimes if you simply mention that there are
hurting couples who want to become parents (not by
name!), it can make them feel included on the holidays.

The Infertile Couple's Response

If and when you choose to share your struggle to have
children, will you receive support? Telling your family or
friends about your infertility can be frightening. Infertility
is such an intimate subject to talk about, because it is
related to self-image, sexuality, and life dreams.

It would be nice to know how someone will respond
before you tell them, but it's a gamble. If a friend can't
relate to your struggle with infertility or understand it to a
degree, your pain and sense of isolation can feel worse.
But, sharing can be a wonderful way to stop the unintentionally hurtful questions and deepen relationships. If you
receive a negative reaction when you first share with
someone, try to remember that this is usually because of
their inexperience with infertility, not malice.

Sharing is easier when the shame is gone

For a while I didn't want to share about my inability to
have children because I thought my infertility was a punishment. Once I figured out it wasn't, I was more confi-

dent in sharing about it with others. It was still an intimate subject though, so I shared selectively with those I felt genuinely cared and could keep the information confidential. I found the pain lessened once I was able to talk about it with others.

Gracious answers to insensitive questions

What do you do if you're caught off guard by questions about your "family" plans? First, try to decide how well you know the person asking. Then determine the intent of his or her question. Is she just being polite and trying to make conversation? Is he curious? Or does he truly care about you? Then, based on your perception of the person's intent, feel free to vary your answers. You don't need to tell your life story to an acquaintance. You don't even have to tell it to a family member if he or she will probably not understand. But if you're feeling strong that day, you can try to educate the person about your struggle.

When you aren't up to sharing

Returning a question with another question is one way to turn the focus from yourself in an uncomfortable situation. For instance, if a stranger at a party asks, "Do you have any children?" You could reply, "No, we don't, how about you?" If it's a person at church who is pressuring you by asking, "When are you two going to start a family?" You could respond with: "It's in God's hands, but how do you like this weather?" The trick is to have a brief response ready, then take control of the conversation by quickly changing the subject. If you really don't want to share and someone continues to be intrusive, a simple, "Oh, excuse me, please," and heading off to the bathroom works well.

Forgiveness and understanding

Sometimes the pain of infertility is so intense that we have a difficult time being forgiving of the fertile world's insensitivities. but our goal should be to follow Colossians 3:13 which says: "Be gentle and ready to forgive; never hold grudges. Remember, the Lord forgave you, so you must forgive others." We need to overlook other's mistakes as Proverbs 19:11 says: "A wise man restrains his anger and overlooks insults. This is to his credit." (Just think of all the credit we're building up!)

Just as we ask for understanding during our infertility, we also need to try to read behind fumbling words to the caring intent of our family and friends. Even if we expect that the intent was to hurt us, we can still try to respond truthfully, but kindly. If something that was said still bothers you after a few days, call the person up or drop them a note saying, "I appreciate your concern, but I don't feel that way about it." Or "I used to feel that way before I was infertile, but now I don't any longer and this is why." Instead of taking it personally, try to gently educate the person if you are close to her. Some people may just not care to be educated about infertility. If this is the case, feel free to limit your time together until you are stronger.

Thank you for your support
Above all, if your family, friends, or pastor are supporting you and making your infertility easier to bear, thank God for them, and let them know you are grateful.

Your Personal Journey

1. What are some of the hurtful comments or questions you have received about your infertility or fear you might receive? Anticipate any other uncomfortable situations or comments that might happen in the future.
2. Write down responses to each of these situations or questions.
3. Which people have been supportive of you in your infertility? What specifically have they done? How can you thank them?

13

Starting or Joining a Support Group

What a wonderful God we have . . . who so wonderfully comforts and strengthens us in our hardships and trials. And why does He do this? So that when others are troubled, needing our sympathy and encouragement, we can pass on to them this same help and comfort God has given us   (2 Corinthians 1:3-4).

Only those who are experiencing a similar situation can understand. . . . Secular organizations can only go so far in ministering to hurting hearts yet many churches have been slow to respond to the anguish of infertile couples. Providing appropriate avenues to express this pain and grief with other believers is vital. — Debra Evans[1]

*B*eing part of a supportive group of women has been such a positive part of my infertility. A friend and I wanted to start a group to talk about infertility and miscarriage with others who would understand. We knew that our hope was because of God, so it made sense to have a support group that encompassed our relationships to God and our hope in Him. Sharing with others who understood and cared, praying for each other, and hoping for each other when hope was low was a wonderful experience.

Traumatic events even became humorous when shared with others. For instance, the first time Michael and I tried intrauterine insemination, I got lost while driving the washed sperm sample from the hospital to the doctor's office. It was only about two miles away, but I didn't know the area well and kept taking wrong turns. As I

careened back and forth down the streets, I became frantic
that the little sperm in the vial I was trying to keep warm
were going to die. By the time I got to the office, I was
near tears. If anyone had told me to relax at that point, I
think I would have bitten his head off. I was stressed!
Later though, in describing my panic to the group, we all
saw the funny side of my mad rush and valiant efforts to
"save the sperm." Two women even shared similar stories
of their "sperm excursions" which made us laugh even
harder.

"I am so thankful for this group. Before I came, I
thought I was just going crazy, but now I see that I'm not
the only one affected this strongly," said Sara when she
first attended our support group.

Vicky, who had been infertile for more than ten years
and had adopted a daughter seven years ago, also expressed that being part of a support group helped bring
healing to her relationship with God:

> I came to this group mainly to give support, but it has
> really helped me too. I didn't realize that there was still a
> part of me that was feeling unloved by God because I
> wasn't ever able to get pregnant. But when I sit here and
> look at you guys, I have no trouble at all believing God
> loves you. I know He does. That has helped me to realize
> He loves me too.

What Would We Do in a Group?

When Virginia first came into our support group, she had
just experienced her fourth miscarriage. She said, "I was
in so much pain when I came to this group. I wondered
what I would do in a group with six other women in pain,
but then I saw the joy that you shared because of your
understanding of each other."

We had worked to create a positive tone because we
didn't want our meetings to deteriorate into complaining
sessions. In addition to informal sharing and offering re-

freshments, we set up the following basic agenda for each meeting to help keep us on track.

1. *Introductions.* If a new person is present, we each take two minutes to give our infertility or pregnancy-loss back-ground.

2. *Information exchange.* Various members share information about articles, books, newsletters, other groups, films, speakers, or upcoming seminars, related to infertility.

3. *Devotions.* One person shares a Bible passage or insight that has helped in her struggle, then prays.

4. *Topic.* One member of the group plans ahead to lead a discussion on a topic chosen by the group or on a book we've been reading together. Sometimes we arrange for a speaker or film, or one of the members takes an hour or so to share her infertility or pregnancy-loss experience from beginning to end.

5. *Struggles and Victories.* Each person takes about ten minutes to share how she has struggled and/or been victorious in dealing with infertility since the last meeting and shares specific prayer requests.

6. *Prayer.* We pray as a group for individual needs or victories.

During the first few months we met, we scheduled one woman at each meeting to share the story of what she had experienced with her infertility or loss(es). We each shared the chronological details and how the experience affected the other areas of our lives. This time was tremendously healing.

After we had each had a chance to tell our story, we scheduled speakers, had discussion topics, invited new members to share their stories, or just spent more time sharing. Some of the topics we've discussed are: dealing with the medical work-up, self-esteem, making the decision to adopt, myths and methods of adoption, secondary infertility and only children, how marriages are affected, the option of remaining a family of two, dealing with grief, how to deal with the fertile world, studies on infertile women in the Bible, the moral/ethical issues of infertility testing and treatment, dealing with anger, and how God fits into all of this. One of the best meetings our support group had was when we discussed the topic. "How has your relationship with God changed, and how has He shown you comfort through this time?" I was amazed at the growth in the lives of the women around me; God's love shone through as we saw His positive help in other areas of our lives.

Asking speakers to come can also be helpful. One particularly helpful speaker we had speak to our group was a Christian counselor who had also experienced infertility and miscarriage. She discussed the grieving process and the validity of grief over infertility or miscarriage.

Some other speakers you might invite are: a panel of adoptive parents, adult adopted children, an older childless couple, an infertility specialist to discuss medical options, an attorney who deals in private adoption, a social worker who works with county adoptions, a representative from a private adoption agency, a minister to address some spiritual issues, or husbands to discuss the male side of infertility.

How Do We Begin?
My friend and I met before the first meeting and tentatively set up an agenda. Neither of us had done this before so we were both nervous. What if nobody came? What if nobody talked? We overcame these fears by focusing on our desire to help other women who were hurting.

As it turned out, six women came that first night, and we had *no* problem with them being too quiet. In the last three years, we have averaged about nine women and have formed some deep and lasting friendships.

Because part of our hesitancy to start the group stemmed from not knowing how to start, I want to share with you what worked for us.

Our goals

We started by setting goals to define what we wanted to accomplish and later to help evaluate our progress.

- To let others know they weren't alone in the struggle. (The women in our group cared and God cared about each of us.)
- To provide sensitive understanding during the grief process.
- To encourage and build each other up in love.
- To provide a way to share information related to infertility, miscarriage, stillbirth, and adoption.
- To pray for each other, and look to the Bible for answers to our questions.

Whom should we invite?

We include women in our group who are experiencing primary infertility (who are childless), secondary infertility (who have a birth child, but are having difficulty having more), or have experienced any type of pregnancy loss. We chose this focus for our group because, although the struggles were different, we have enough in common to relate to each other.

Because the husbands of the women who started our group don't feel the same need to talk about infertility, we chose to have our support group just for women. This also gives the women the freedom to share about things that are personal which they might be uncomfortable sharing in front of men (i.e., menstrual cycles or embarrassing medical procedures).

Occasionally, we've invited the husbands to attend to share the male viewpoint or just to socialize. In our group, many of the husbands feel reluctant to be "put on the spot" to share their feelings. So when we planned our meeting called "The Husband's View," we asked two husbands who felt comfortable being open, to think through a few things they wanted to share and be prepared to answer some questions. We invited the other husbands to come and listen, with the understanding that they could participate if they felt comfortable. This worked well. If the husbands of the women in your group are interested in coming more frequently, then you might want to choose to have a couples' support group.

We don't restrict our group to Christians, but invite anyone to come who is comfortable meeting in a group where we pray for each other and relate our struggles to God and passages in the Bible.

How can we find others who are hurting?

We began by praying that God would lead us to other infertile women who would benefit from a group. Then we let women know by word-of-mouth. At the first meeting, we decided on a name for our group: WE CARE (Women Encouraging, Caring, and Regaining Esteem). We asked participants to place notices in their church's bulletins. We also made a flyer to hand out to doctors, hospital chaplains, counselors, or friends of friends. Later, we sent out a letter like this to local churches:

> We are enclosing some information about our inter-church support group for women experiencing difficulty having children or who have lost a baby during pregnancy. Infertility, miscarriage, or stillbirth can be especially devastating to Christian women. The Christian community is so supportive of families, but women in the church who are struggling to achieve their dream of a family often feel isolated and confused. We started our Christian infertility and pregnancy-loss support group because as Christians, we felt the need to address our experiences as they related to the Bible and our relationships with God.
>
> The purpose of our peer-support group is to help women through this difficult time by sharing with and supporting each other. We are an inter-church group because often there may not be enough infertile women in one church to form their own support group. If you would like to ask any more questions about WE CARE, please call.

We found that some churches we contacted were cautious about placing a notice. They wanted to know more about us before connecting us with hurting, vulnerable people in their congregation. I commend them for their cautious concern. We found that it was important to explain our group well, give references (the names of our pastors or group members), and be open to questions. It was worth the effort. Sometimes we reached women who felt they were the only ones at their church who were infertile.

Where and how often would we meet?

Although a home is cozy, we found new visitors felt more comfortable coming to a neutral place like a community center, office, or church. From our list of possible meeting places, we eliminated meeting in someone's home who had a child or in a children's Sunday School room at a church. We chose to meet twice a month, which we based on our need for support and time constraints.

But I can't lead a group!

One benefit of a peer-support group is that no one has to have her act totally together, not even the coordinators. Members take turns organizing the meetings, and all are encouraged to contribute their talents to meet the group's needs.

We have found that having three coordinators has worked well for us. This ensures that one person does not get overloaded with all the work or feel the need to always be "up." It's also important to plan for attrition in this type of group—one month two of our coordinators became pregnant. The group made the transition to new coordinators more smoothly because they weren't all replaced at once.

If you don't feel emotionally strong enough to start a group, you might consider asking a woman who has already adopted or had a child after a term of infertility. She might have the emotional energy to make the initial investment to start a group.

Avoiding pitfalls
Consider setting guidelines for the group to avoid potential pitfalls.

- *Comparing struggles.* Everyone should be careful not to compare and view someone else's loss of fertility or baby as minor. Misery should not be a competitive sport.
- *Confidentiality.* What is said in the group should be kept confidential within the group. A certain amount of sharing will be done later with husbands, but should be done with sensitivity toward the individuals in the group. Husbands also should be told of the necessity for confidentiality.
- *Getting stuck.* We offer the name of a recommended counselor to anyone who might seem stuck in one phase of grief or who is very depressed. Some problems may be so deep, the person needs the professional help of a counselor or pastor.
- *Evaluate.* The coordinators evaluate the direction of the group occasionally. We ask: Are we meeting the needs of the people who come? Are the members of the group still motivated to deal with their own anger, depression, guilt, jealousy, sadness, and so on? After sharing the pain, progress *out* of the suffering should be the focus of the group.

Established Support Groups Available
In Appendix A: Resources, at the back of this book, I've listed several organizations that offer support groups. Specifically supporting a Christian's spiritual struggle is not the focus of these organizations (with the exception of Stepping Stones), but they offer vital help in giving emotional support, sharing medical information and serving as advocates. I encourage you to contact them.

Secular support groups can be helpful, but because they are so diverse, they cannot deeply address the spiritual issue without offending someone. If you can only attend one of these secular groups, I encourage you also to meet with a caring pastor, Christian counselor, or someone with a strong Christian background to help you with some of your spiritual questions.

Putting Pain into Perspective

In attending a support group, you can be helped by the other members who may be further along in some areas of the healing process. But, you may also realize that you are beyond other members in some areas and can help them along. The verse at the beginning of this chapter doesn't say God gives us trials (or makes us infertile or makes us lose a baby) to force us to help others, but that God strengthens us *in* our trials, so we can pass that strength and comfort on to others.

Becoming part of a good support group doesn't take away the pain, but it should put our pain into perspective, so that we can experience understanding support and live with a new and deeper appreciation for God, ourselves, and each other.

Pregnant Members

Some women in the group may eventually become pregnant or adopt. Despite the closeness that develops among group members during their infertility, when one member becomes pregnant or adopts, it can be hard on those continuing to wait and struggle. On the other hand, just because someone becomes pregnant, doesn't mean she no longer needs support. This is especially true for those who have had pregnancy losses.

Our group decided that women who become pregnant while attending the group are welcome to come until they start "showing" or until they pass beyond the point in their last pregnancy when they miscarried. We also agreed to restrict any talking about current pregnancies to the specific time of sharing struggles and victories.

Your Personal Journey

1. Do you feel the need to share your story and struggles with someone who has had a similar experience?
2. Do you know someone who might be interested in starting a support group with you? (Perhaps you know someone who is further along in her infertility journey or perhaps your pastor could suggest someone.)
3. Do you know someone who is struggling with infertility and could use your support?

Part V

"Will We Ever Be Parents?"

14

The Hoped-for Pregnancy — A Nervous Joy

Hope deferred makes the heart sick; but
when dreams come true at last, there is
life and joy   (Proverbs 13:12).

Even those who give birth after prolonged infertility
sometimes feel hesitant to celebrate their new family unit
because they have been conditioned to expect loss.
—Ellen Glazer[1]

I have included this chapter because a large percentage of women who experience infertility and in most cases women who have experienced a miscarriage or stillbirth, will go on to have a baby. At first, I hesitated to include this chapter because I didn't want to add to the pain of those still waiting. But I included it because many women are surprised when the uncertainty, expectations of loss, and other emotions of infertility often don't disappear when a pregnancy occurs. If you aren't ready to read this chapter now, feel free to skip it and return to it at a later time.

Michael and I continued with tests and treatments, but by now we'd been earnestly praying and trying for over five years and nothing was working. One month, while taking a break from Clomid, I again thought I might be pregnant. When my temperature stayed up for two days

183

past the date my period was due, I went to the doctor and had (yet another) pregnancy test.

I was speechless when the words, "You are pregnant" were spoken to me. Miracle of miracles. The feeling of shock and surprise lasted for months. Our sense of awe and thankfulness to God overwhelmed us. Since we'd learned so much about the conception process and knew the number of things that could go wrong, we were doubly thankful for each test that showed the pregnancy was progressing normally.

Then at ten weeks, I started bleeding. Frightened, I called the doctor, who told me to go home from work and rest. By 10 that night the blood had turned bright red and was as heavy as a regular period. Michael and I kept in touch with the doctor, but he said if the miscarriage was inevitable, there was nothing else we could do but rest and let it run its course. We knew we had lost the baby we'd waited for so long. That night we didn't sleep much. We just cried, prayed, and held each other through the night.

The next morning we dragged ourselves to the doctor's office to see if the miscarriage had been complete. As the doctor moved the ultrasound wand, I could barely bring myself to look at the screen. Suddenly Michael said, "What's that?" The doctor grinned and pointed to something flickering on the screen. Then we saw the most beautiful sight ever. For the first time, we saw the beating of our baby's heart. How the baby survived was another miracle.

I stayed in bed for a couple of weeks as the bleeding gradually tapered off and stopped. I reluctantly left the support of my infertility doctor's office and went to an obstetrician. At my first appointment at the obstetrician's office, I felt as if I were masquerading as a pregnant woman. Me? Going to an obstetrician? How absurd. Surely everyone knew that I was infertile and would find out I was only faking a pregnancy because I wanted it so much. I kept expecting the doctor to expose my "game." I still resented seeing pregnant women in the waiting room. Even though I was carrying a baby, I still felt infertile. It wasn't until five months into the pregnancy that I finally began to hope that a baby might result from it.

Then suddenly at six months, I had what felt like gas pains on and off all night which kept me awake. I went to the doctor the next morning for what I thought was bad indigestion, but was actually preterm labor.

I was immediately put into the hospital. At six months, the baby did not have a good chance of survival. The doctors tried to stop the labor with rest, then intravenous fluids, but it wouldn't stop. Finally, with drugs, the labor slowed and stopped. I spent the rest of the pregnancy in bed, taking medication every four hours around the clock to control the labor. Whenever I did anything other than get up to use the bathroom or if I was late taking the medication, the contractions would start again. I don't know if I would have been able to survive that time without the trust in God I'd developed through infertility. Finally, only eleven days early, and over six years after we started trying, our healthy son Justin was born. We were relieved and in awe.

Isn't Pregnancy the Cure for Infertility?

For many who have experienced long-term infertility, it has become a part their identity. Yet, when they become pregnant, they suddenly feel separated from their infertile friends, the ones from whom they've finally found support. They fear telling their infertile friends or even seeing them because they know the hurt that can cause.

Infertile women usually hope that once they get pregnant, they'll be home free. They hope infertility and all the accompanying struggles will suddenly evaporate into thin air. For most though, although pregnancy does ease the feelings of inadequacy, infertility has left its permanent mark. The innocence of a "normal" pregnancy is gone. They have learned enough about the reproductive process to realize it doesn't always work smoothly.

On the other hand, they may expect an easy pregnancy because they've already "paid their dues." Thankfully, the majority of pregnancies for previously infertile couples are uncomplicated. The focus of this chapter is on the ones who might have more difficulty.

Continuing Apprehensions

Women who become pregnant after years of being child-less or who have experienced previous pregnancy losses try to avoid hoping and planning because they fear another loss. One study that looked at how previously infertile couples felt after giving birth showed that "Many previously infertile couples use denial of pregnancy as a way to cope with their fears about potential pregnancy loss."[2] But, using the denial method of dealing with the fear of loss at this point can cause difficulty with bonding and not wanting to invest in caring for the pregnancy. The fears can be especially strong when the pregnancy follows one or more miscarriages or stillbirths. So, using other coping mechanisms, such as sharing your fears, is better at this time.

For those who have had one or more pregnancy losses, a new pregnancy may make a previous loss more vivid again. Carole experienced this when she found out she was pregnant again after three previous pregnancy losses:

> I feel like crying all the time. I thought I had put the pain of my last miscarriage behind me, but getting pregnant has brought all the sadness back. I personally don't feel any hope for [this] pregnancy.

Even though having another baby will, over time, ease the pain, it should not be expected to erase the pain of losing a child.

Coping with a High-risk Pregnancy

Those who have had previous fertility problems do have an increased risk for problem pregnancies. One reason for this is that in addition to the same exposure to risk factors as the "normal" pregnant woman, "sometimes the same problems that caused infertility such as fibroids, malformations of the uterus, or DES exposure can increase the risks during pregnancy," write the authors of *Intensive Caring*. "In addition, IVF or GIFT . . . multiply the odds of conceiving multiples [which increases the odds of miscarriage or preterm labor]. Surgery on the uterus to remove fibroids or to correct a malformation can cause scarring that increases the risk of miscarriage or preterm labor."[3]

There might also be a hormonal problem which contributed to infertility that can affect a subsequent pregnancy. In addition to these, a woman will also be identified as high risk if she has previously had two or three miscarriages, a stillbirth (if there is reason to believe it could happen again), or a preterm birth.

Choose a supportive and knowledgeable doctor

When Virginia found out she was pregnant again, her first concern was to find a caring obstetrician who would give her extra "TLC" and who would have up-to-date information on treating miscarriages and not just call them "bad luck" as her last doctor had done.

When Deanna discovered she was having triplets, she looked for a maternal-fetal specialist who would take her risk seriously and put extra effort into maintaining her pregnancy. As Deanna recalled:

> I had a home monitoring machine to monitor for contractions, [and] took lots of vitamins and gelatin capsules to strengthen the amniotic sac. Later, when I went into preterm labor, I took medication to control that too. When the medication stopped working, I had to spend some time in the hospital.

If you've been identified as having a high-risk pregnancy, you may be able to find an obstetrician who has experience with high-risk pregnancies or a perinatologist (a doctor who specializes in maternal/fetal medicine). Look for a doctor who wants you to share your concerns and fears and who will take the time to give you extra reassurance if you need it.

Ask for prayer

It may be difficult to share the news of your pregnancy with anyone, but share it with those you feel will support you and pray for you.

One of the women in my church asked the Sunday School children to be my prayer support group while I was on bedrest. I've saved a number of crayon drawings and letters from these children who prayed to show my son. One of the letters is from the mother of a seven-year-old boy who said: "My son has been praying desperately for weeks to be able to have a puppy. But after hearing about your baby who might come too early, last night he changed his prayer. He prayed, 'God, you know that puppy I really, really want? Well, I don't need it if you would please just let Debbie's baby be born OK instead.' " My heart melted when I read that.

I'm convinced that it was a combination of the sincere prayers of those children, and of our family, friends, and church, combined with God's timing, that resulted in our son's healthy birth.

Dealing with the fears

Discuss your fears and feelings with your spouse, your doctor, or a support group. Don't feel you have to be all things to all people during this time. Read about what is proper for pregnancy and call your doctor if you have questions about how your pregnancy is going. Also find the ways you can best take care of yourself and the baby during the pregnancy, nutritionally and otherwise.

If you are confined to bed by your pregnancy, a number of groups will connect you with other women also stuck in bed. Ask your doctor, midwife, or contact High Risk Moms,

Inc., The Triplet Connection (for multiple births), or RESOLVE for referrals. (See appendix A: resources for further information on these organizations.)

Your Personal Journey

1. What problems do you think getting pregnant will solve?
2. What fears do you have about pregnancy?
3. What promises from God can you hold on to during this time?

15

The Empty Cradle: Miscarriage and Stillbirth

Those we love are with the Lord, and the Lord
has promised to be with us: we believe, "Behold,
I am with you always." —Peter Marshall[1]

When young children, some newly minted, are recalled
by their maker, away from the coziness of home,
does heaven bewilder them? Where are the teddy bears?
Are there puppies and kittens? Will an angel sing them to sleep?

Comfort, dear Lord, those who have lost little ones,
and hold them in the hollow of your hand.
—Margaret B. Spiess[2]

I had no idea that anything was wrong when the nurse called. After two long years of trying to get pregnant again, I was finally pregnant; other than a little spotting, everything looked fine. Sure, I'd been in that day to have an ultrasound and they couldn't find the baby's heartbeat, but I was only nine weeks along. The nurse assured me that it was probably just too early to detect the heartbeat yet. I felt confident everything was fine. With one phone call my world titled crazily: "I'm afraid I have bad news for you. Your blood test results show that the baby stopped growing. I'm sorry."

The shock held me together until I hung up the phone, but then overwhelming, wracking sobs came from deep within me.

My baby had died.

Just then my son, Justin, who was two-and-a-half by

then, pushed open the bedroom door, his eyes wide with fright: "What's wrong Mommy?" Since I couldn't hide my grief, I decided to tell him. I helped him climb up into my lap and held him tightly (as much for me as for him). It took me a while to get it out because I remembered his joy—dancing around the bedroom when Michael and I first told him we were going to have a baby. Tearfully, I choked out, "You know our baby that's inside Mommy's tummy? Well, the nurse just called and told me that the baby got very sick and died." He looked away and let out a woeful "Ohhhhh."

He was confused and I needed to hold him for a while, so I rocked with him in our big rocker and asked him to sing "Jesus Loves Me" with me. Listening to Justin sing, "Little ones to Him belong; they are weak, but He is strong" touched me deeply. In the midst of my world crashing around me, I realized anew what a miracle it was that he was ever born.

But I still had to grieve.

I thought the lessons I had learned through my many years of infertility would protect me from the grief. I was wrong. The pain was different. It took me by surprise. Although I realized my loss and was sad about it, for a few weeks after the miscarriage I was still able to function normally. Then the numbness wore off and the pain set in. I tried to handle my feelings of grief by myself. I was tired of hurting from infertility, of being the one who struggled. I wanted to be strong. And no one else, not even Michael, was grieving like I was. I decided that I'd try to act as if it didn't hurt. If I tried to just think positively, maybe the sadness would be diminished and eventually go away altogether.

Meanwhile, Michael was thinking: Good, Debbie's recovering. I didn't know if she could handle this. The baby is with God, so it's OK. Let's have hope for the future.

When a friend found that the baby she had miscarried

was a girl, I told Michael, "I wish we had known what the sex of our baby was." He didn't see the pain behind the statement and was frustrated that I'd brought it up out of what he thought was morbid curiosity. He thought it would be better not to rehash the details again.

Two months after the miscarriage we went on a vacation as we had planned. I thought I'd been doing a good job of ignoring the negative feelings, but without the distraction of our busy schedules, Michael was soon frustrated at my distance. I later realized that I'd built up a wall to hold in my emotions, but that wall also distanced me from him. It was as if I knew how a person should act, so I was eating meals and looking at scenery by rote, but my heart was locked up tight to guard the pain. Keeping the pain buried took a lot of effort, so I found myself becoming easily irritated. As I began to acknowledge the pain I'd buried, I also acknowledged that I'd begun to harbor hurt feelings against Michael: Why wasn't he suffering like me? I finally couldn't avoid or hide my heartache any longer, and the walls collapsed. I ended up crying in the car the whole way up the coast of California. What we both came to realize was that I was still intensely grieving and needed to express it.

The grief of miscarriage or stillbirth is different in some ways than infertility in general because the grief of a pregnancy loss is focused on an event in time—the death of a particular child. The heartbreaking fact is that pregnancy loss is not a rare occurrence, since as many as one in six pregnancies miscarry.[3]

Women who get pregnant, but miscarry are sometimes seen as more fortunate by those who have never been able to conceive. Vicky once expressed this feeling to our infertility group: "I would never want to experience the losses that you [who have miscarried] have gone through, but I feel like less of a woman because I never have been able to get pregnant." But those who have lost a wanted baby during pregnancy don't perceive themselves as fortunate.

Women who have been infertile also have a higher than normal miscarriage rate and a higher rate of tubal pregnancies.[4] Also, women who go through IVF or ZIFT treatment can know their eggs have fertilized, but when the embryos are transferred back to their uterus yet don't implant, they too can suffer the grief of early miscarriages. Each one grieves differently, but for those who have struggled to have a family before becoming pregnant, losing a child can take on an even greater sadness.

The Physical Side of Pregnancy Loss

The physical symptoms preceding and accompanying the loss can be frightening. The details of this type of loss aren't discussed much, especially with someone who is pregnant, so this can add to the fear.

A miscarriage is the death of a baby before the twentieth week in pregnancy; most pregnancy losses happen during this time. The physical symptoms can range from moderate to severe cramping that dilates the cervix and attempts to expel the fetus, moderate to heavy bleeding, passing large blood clots, and the passing of the fetus. In many miscarriages the baby will not pass or will not pass completely and a Dilation and Curettage (D&C) will need to be done. If your physical symptoms are not severe and you are strong enough emotionally, some infertility specialists advise waiting a little while to see if your body will miscarry the baby on its own. This is because adhesions or a weakened cervix from a D&C can possibly contribute to future infertility.[5] (Yet, waiting too long can also raise the risk of infection or other problems.)

A stillbirth is the death of a baby after the twentieth week of pregnancy. By this time the pregnancy has begun to "show" and the mother can often feel the baby's kicks. A stillbirth is much more public and harder to hide. So it can involve more explaining to outsiders. Many women also speak of the horror of still having to go through with a "normal" delivery, knowing their baby is already dead. Thankfully, many hospitals and professional medical organizations are now providing training to their medical staff to deal more sensitively with women who have pregnancy losses. Carole's account illustrates some of the physical experiences of both miscarriage and a stillbirth:

> The first time I got pregnant, I was pregnant for three months. That's a long time to bond and plan. I spotted, then started cramping and bleeding. I went to the hospital emergency room where the doctor did a suction D&C. It was very painful and traumatic. I was depressed for about a year afterward.
>
> Two years later we got pregnant again. This time I didn't allow myself to bond or believe. During the fourth month, I actually stated to believe the baby would live. After all, most miscarriages [happen] in the first three months. I remember feeling the wonder of it all—that a baby was growing inside me. I saw an ultrasound of the baby and started feeling her kicking. I had to wear maternity clothes, so people at work started noticing.
>
> At six months, while my husband, and I were taking our last vacation alone together, my body started feeling different. The pressure seemed lower down. I denied that anything could be wrong because I'd had no problems, no spotting, the ultrasound was fine, and I could feel the baby kicking. But soon I couldn't suppress my anxiety any longer. We called the nurse, then started for home. I started timing my contractions in the truck, then we had to stop [because of] bleeding and diarrhea.
>
> By the time we got to the hospital, I was past the point of no return. The doctor broke my water. [As the baby was being delivered], I remember the doctor telling me that the baby was no longer alive. A nurse asked me if I wanted to see the baby. I said no, but later changed my mind and asked to see her. She was beautiful. Little fingers, little toes, all perfectly formed. A beautiful face with eyelashes. It was so unreal, like a bad dream. When I went home, I was afraid to be left alone.
>
> [Three weeks later], the morning of my first day back to work, my milk came in. I'd taken the pills to dry up my

milk, but they didn't work. I had to buy nursing pads. [My leaking breasts were] a constant reminder of my loss.

Then two years later, we finally had my son. I'm so thankful for the gift he is to us.

When my son was four, I got pregnant again. At my first checkup the doctor said the baby's size was one to two weeks behind, [based on] the conception date I had told him. I asked for an ultrasound that afternoon. The [growth of the] fetus was four weeks behind [schedule], but I *knew* when I'd gotten pregnant.

I felt very sad knowing I was pregnant, but that the baby inside me wasn't alive. One week later I started cramping and bleeding. I miscarried at 10 weeks. I kept cramping and bleeding, so I had to go in for a D&C. They assured me it wouldn't be as painful as the first one, but it was. [Carole's doctor didn't use any anesthetic with her D&C's.] As I lay on the table alone, [I felt] the pain, fear, and loss welling up. The D&C did turn the bleeding off like a switch. I was grateful for the care of a doctor and modern medicine. I thought that a hundred years ago I might have bled to death from this.

I felt as if I'd fallen in a black hole. I cried for the child I wouldn't have, for the uncertainty of whether I would ever have another child and for having to live through the pain. I [still] yearn to hold a baby in my arms and call it mine. Yet there is no assurance there will ever be another. We haven't decided whether we will try again.

[Carole eventually did become pregnant again and carried a healthy baby girl to term.]

Some of the physical symptoms that women experience after a pregnancy loss are aching arms and aching breasts with lactation (milk coming in). They may also experience headaches and postpartum depression as hormone levels drastically change, difficulty sleeping, profound tiredness or fatigue and a still rounded body which can't fit into normal clothes. They may even experience "phantom" kicking and movement (similar to the feelings some people experience at the loss of a limb), as Beth did:

I've read about people who lose a leg or arm and still feel the phantom limb itching. I feel phantom kicking. I feel a bump from the inside and suddenly think, *oh, that was the baby.* Then I realize again that my womb is empty.

What causes pregnancy loss?

Shockingly little is known about why babies die in the womb. This can be especially agonizing if you experience repeated losses. Doctors used to believe that miscarriages were the body's way of expelling a baby that had something wrong with it already. This is no longer believed to be true in many cases.

Some of the causes of miscarriages for which tests can be done are: hormonal imbalance, genetic problems, infections and diseases, structural abnormalities of the uterus, antibodies (immunological problems), blood-clotting factors, and other medical disorders such as diabetes or thyroid disease. Doctors currently recommend that women who have had two or three successive miscarriages should have preliminary testing done by an obstetrician/gynecologist, an infertility specialist, or a perinatologist (a doctor who specializes in maternal/fetal medicine).[6] Tests can also be done on the fetus. If the doctor asks you to save the expelled fetus for testing, ask specifically what the testing might reveal.

Some of the reasons for lowered fertility can also be linked to miscarriages, such as cigarette smoking, alcohol, and radiation. In addition, studies are showing some environmental hazards can affect miscarriage rates, such as exposure to two of the chemicals used in making semiconductor chips.[7] There is currently some controversy about whether elecromagnetic fields (from computer terminals, copiers, printers, electric typewriters, electric blankets, or other appliances) can affect pregnancy outcome. Although the studies offer conflicting results, one study showed an increased risk of miscarriages from prolonged exposure (over 20 hours a week) to video display terminals (VDTs) such as those used with computers. Until the results are more certain, Dr. Stefan Semchyshyn, author of *How to Prevent Miscarriage*, advises his pregnant patients "who must work on VDTs to limit their exposure to twenty hours a week or less if possible."[8]

What can be done?

There are some things that *can* be done for future pregnancies. In the book *Preventing Miscarriage: The Good News*, Dr. Jonathan Scher, a pioneer in the field of miscarriage prevention, clearly explains some things you can do before or during your next pregnancy, such as hormone therapy, resting, using a condom during intercourse (to prohibit the prostaglandins in seminal fluid from triggering uterine contractions), avoiding pesticides, and avoiding heavy lifting or unnecessary stress.[9]

A stitch can be made in an incompetent cervix to hold it closed until time for delivery. Natural progesterone is sometimes prescribed to correct a hormonal imbalance. Clomid is sometimes also prescribed with the hope that it will produce a better egg and better support for it, but as of yet, the evidence of its usefulness is unclear.

Many women have voiced that next time they would trust their instincts if they felt something was wrong. They wouldn't be as hesitant to call their doctor to ask if what they were feeling was normal. They would feel more comfortable asking for an ultrasound to check on the baby or for access to a machine that monitors uterine contractions.

The Emotions of Pregnancy Loss

"I felt like I was living on a different plane of reality," explained Jackie. "I'm sure some of the emotions were hormone related, but I was a basket case." In the loss of a baby, we may not only feel our loss—the loss of our dreams for our child, but as a mother, we can also feel our child's loss. We may mourn that our child never heard our love songs to him, felt the enfolding hug of her father's arms, or saw our celebration of himself in our eyes. He never had the chance to find love and marry. We've lost a part of ourselves and an irreplaceable person's life at the same time. Even some of the medical terms used to discuss pregnancy loss can cause emotional pain, such as referring to a miscarriage as a "spontaneous abortion" or the baby as "fetal tissue."

Often the tragedy of pregnancy loss comes as a shock. Other people experience this same shock later in life at the death of a parent, sibling, or spouse, but since miscarriage happens to a couple in their relatively young, childbearing years, it is often their first encounter with death. If you were lucky enough to have had a fairly uneventful childhood, you often haven't formed coping mechanisms to deal with disastrous circumstances. Your perceived reality, which was blended with the eternal optimism of youth, is now replaced with the knowledge that you will not always be protected from devastating circumstances.

If a couple has invested themselves emotionally (and financially), in an adoption attempt which falls through, they can experience much of this same emotional grief of losing a particular child.

Obviously, many grief emotions overlap those of infertility which I've addressed in chapter 8. These can be compounded by the physical symptoms discussed earlier. In addition, those with a pregnancy loss often experience preoccupation with the baby, fantasies about the baby, and a feeling of responsibility for the baby's death.

Guilt

Even when the facts say that the loss had nothing to do with the actions of the mother, women often have to work through a feeling that they are responsible for their baby's death. After her miscarriage, Beth had terrible nightmares which reflected her internal struggle:

I keep waking up sobbing from horrible, devastating,

dreams of babies dying and blood everywhere. I've also dreamed of stabbing my husband and daughter, that I have to kill them in order to stay alive. The dream ends with my friends reassuring me that it was something I had to do and that it was for the best.

I figure that this dream must have something to do with accepting the miscarriage, but still wanting to fight against it with every ounce of my being. I guess I'm also still feeling responsible for my baby's death and fear that if my baby could die, so could the rest of my family. Maybe I'm working out the inconceivable knowledge that neither my brain or heart had any control over my body. It betrayed me by not protecting my baby. If I couldn't trust my own body to take care of a baby I wanted so badly, what would stop it from harming more of the family I loved? I'm pretty calm on the outside, but I have this raging battle going on in my mind.

Need for validation of the baby

Many people don't understand the need to grieve for the loss of a baby who wasn't known outside the mother's body. The book *Overcoming Infertility,* explains that when a pregnancy finally happens, and then loss occurs, the swing of emotions is enormous, "You have gone from feeling empty to feeling full of life. The bounce back to barren is too excruciating to describe."[10]

The depth of grieving is not respective to the gestational age of the baby. With planned pregnancies, parents will have dreamed about the baby even before conception. They will have spent hours thinking about what color hair the baby will have, if it will be a boy or girl, quiet or outgoing, or how old the baby will be on the first Christmas. Dr. Jonathan Scher also writes: "Mothers undergo huge hormonal fluctuations, and we tend to think this grows along with her swelling belly. But, in fact, the greatest impact of maternal feeling occurs *early* in the pregnancy . . . There is scientific (hormonal) proof that these feelings occur!"[11]

Dr. Kochelle Friedman and Bonnie Gradstein agree with this:

> Attachment begins at different times in the pregnancy for different women. . . . Commonly women who have already had a successful pregnancy form an attachment to their future child earlier in the next pregnancy than does an inexperienced mother: they trust that being pregnant will lead to having a child.[12]

If others don't understand your need to grieve, try to realize that this is probably just because of their lack of experience with this type of death.

How long does grieving take?

I didn't fully understand the subtle pressure I felt about still grieving until my infertility support group read through the book *Life after Loss*. The author, Bob Deits, writes of the naiveté of many people who have not yet experienced grief: "Many polls and studies have asked the public, 'How long should it take to mourn the death of a loved one?' The most common answer was we should be finished grieving between 48 hours and two weeks after the death!"[13] But those who had actually experienced grief didn't feel this way. Sister Jane Marie Lamb also wrote specifically about the grief for stillbirth, miscarriage, and infant death: "Normal *intense* grieving, with many ups and downs, may be expected to last 18 months to 2 years. Beyond that time is [also] within normal limits."[14]

Even though during my struggle with infertility I had resolved my anger at God and *knew* that He *loved* me now, I found I still intensely grieved over my baby that had died. At the same time though, I felt the reality of heaven and the hope that my answers awaited there. If you find yourself in the same position, know that is natural. Your time and intensity of grief will be unique, but hold on to the knowledge that hope and joy will come again.

Again, music seemed to reach my grieving soul. I was

touched when I heard the following song by Wayne Watson because it expressed not only the grief and confusion I felt, but also the hope of anticipating heaven when we'll find the answers:

"Home Free"

I'm trying hard not to think You unkind
But Heavenly Father, if You know my heart
Surely You can read my mind
Good people underneath a sea of grief
Some get up and walk away
Some will find ultimate relief

Out in the corridors we pray for life
A mother for her baby
A husband for his wife
Sometimes the good die young
It's sad but true
And while we pray for one more heartbeat
The real comfort is with You

Home free—eventually
At the ultimate healing
We will be home free. . . . [15]

Remembrances and Ceremonies

I needed to have closure to my grief for our baby who had died. Michael suggested we name the baby. Then we decided to take one afternoon, go up to the hills in back of our home and have a private memorial service. I read a letter I wrote to the baby, then we picked a spot next to the creek and with small shovels we buried a small box containing a little blue and white sleeping outfit, the baby's first ultrasound picture, and my letter. We sat on a nearby log and prayed together in this peaceful, quiet place for our baby and the healing of our grief. As we listened to the wind rustling the leaves, the soft music of the creek, and felt the warm sun on our faces, I finally began to feel my emotions calm. The grief didn't seem as raw as it did before. Because of that wonderful afternoon, I am able to think of that peaceful place when I remember our baby, rather than the pain, blood, and horror of the miscarriage itself. This is the letter I wrote to our child:

Dear Aaron (or Erin),

I want you to know that I loved you from the moment I first knew about you. I began to love you even earlier than with your older brother because the first time I was pregnant, I couldn't allow myself to believe that I would actually have a baby. With you, I let myself relax and actually believe that I would hold you in just a few months. Because of your brother, I also had an idea of what you would look like, so when I daydreamed, your image was clearer to me.

I'm sorry. I don't know why you died. I wish I did. There is no way that my finite mind can make sense of this. All I know is that it had something to do with this world being imperfect. I'm looking forward to the day when I'll see you again in heaven. Will you be a little baby then or full grown? You were too small for us to know if you were a girl or boy. If I don't recognize you, will you look for me? I hope your great-grandma is gently rocking you and singing you her favorite Scottish lullaby.

You'll always be part of our family. When people ask me how many children we have, I'll answer "one," but will silently think about you and want to say, "We have another one waiting in heaven."

I'll always love you, little one, but hope this incredible pain of missing you eases. I feel so torn between wanting to go to heaven to see you and staying here. It isn't that I want to die, I'd just like to visit you and check that you are all right. My arms ache to hold you, to rock you, to kiss your soft head, to smell your sweet scent, and to tell you that I love you. But I can't. So I'll hold on to God and you do the same until I get there.

Love,
your mommy

When our deep sadness returned on the baby's actual due date, we went back to this beautiful place to remember. Since the baby was due close to Christmas, we also bought a little tree ornament of an angel and wrote the baby's due date on it. Each year we are comforted by this remembrance of the child who spent such a short time with us.

Other ways of saying good-bye
Ceremonies and rituals have always been an important way to help us celebrate life or mourn its passing. Don't worry that your baby wasn't "big enough" to warrant a farewell ritual. Regardless of gestational age, your baby was someone whom God thought was important enough to call into existence.

If you experienced your pregnancy loss at a hospital, and would like to attend the baby's actual burial, ask the hospital staff about their miscarriage or stillbirth burial policies. They may have a mass burial which you can attend or other options available under your local and state regulations. (Burial cradles are available for the dignified burial of even those babies under 20 weeks gestation.[16]) Or some mortuaries also offer cremation. Sometimes families choose to bury the ashes with a tree or flowers they plant.

A memorial service doesn't have to be connected with the burial of the baby. If you would feel comforted by a private or pubic memorial service, you can plan one that will help you say good-bye to your baby. You can use it to express how you feel about your baby and what he or she meant to you. If you would like to include close family and friends, do so. Sister Jane Marie Lamb, the founder of SHARE, an organization that offers support after pregnancy loss, writes that having family and friends present at the ceremony can be helpful because: "those present are less likely to forget the baby and more likely to be available to the parents throughout the bereavement period."[17]

In the book, *When a Baby Dies: A Handbook for Healing and Helping*, the authors also suggest the following ways to say good-bye: write a letter, poem, or story about and for the baby expressing your hopes and love, disbelief, anger, disillusionment and despair; save momentos of the pregnancy such as a favorite maternity top, ultrasound pictures, pictures of the mother while she was pregnant; save momentos of the birth, such as the baby's hospital identification bands, footprints, crib card, lock of hair, or blanket or clothing the baby was dressed in; or plant a tree.[18] Or perhaps you might want to frame a poem or special scripture to hang on the wall in memory of your child.

Some people suggest putting your sorrow behind you and moving on. Others suggest building remembrances of the baby into your lives. I would suggest that you remain honest with yourself and do what you feel is right for you. Discuss it with your spouse. Feel free to say, "I need a special remembrance day for the baby every year. I'd like to remember him by a picnic at a special spot, giving to a charity, going out to dinner to talk about it, or visiting the baby's grave. . . ." You may want to change what you do from year to year, but you'll know the day is set aside as special. (See appendix A: resources for organizations that deal with grieving and pregnancy loss.)

Husbands and Others

I've discussed some examples of husbands responding to infertility or pregnancy loss in chapter 11. I've also discussed in chapter 12 some of the unique aspects for pregnancy loss. I must admit that before my miscarriage, when I knew a woman had miscarried, I thought about her hurting physically. I didn't think about her grieving. Not until I experienced it.

Was the baby real?

Another thing that can be hard is trying to convince others of the baby's reality, even in the Christian community.

Christians who strongly protest abortion because they believe a baby's life begins at conception can sometimes fail to carry that belief over to help a woman grieving over the life she lost through pregnancy or miscarriage. Platitudes of "Maybe there was something wrong with the baby, so it was better that it died" are hard to hear. See the section "Biblical Directives and Principles" in chapter 6 for comfort on the baby's reality in the womb.

Unstable emotions

Virginia realized that one of the reasons she had a difficult time communicating with people after her miscarriage was her constantly changing emotions:

> The way people treat me varies from perfect to appalling, but then how does anyone know what the "right" thing to say is? Even two months later, my mood can change at the drop of a hat so that something said this morning which was fine will make me cry this afternoon. The best support I've had comes from those more willing to listen than to talk, who just hug and don't offer platitudes. I'm so ashamed of some of the dumb things I've said and done to others in their down times, but for this reason, I don't blame anyone for what they say or do to me.

Spring Will Come

Eventually, you may become so involved in life that you forget to remember at times. Don't feel guilty for forgetting or not being able to feel the emotions as deeply. This is not forgetting your child. It is just that the scales have tipped back again in the direction of celebrating life, such as it is. Know that joy will come again—eventually. And this is good. Out of the winter of your grief, will come spring.

Your Personal Journey

1. Read the words or sing the hymn "It Is Well with My Soul" which was written by Horatio G. Spafford. (It is

in most church hymnals.) Mr. Spafford was a successful attorney and the father of five when a series of disasters struck. His only son died and his ample real estate investments burned down. Then while the rest of his family was on a ship crossing the Atlantic, the ship sank and all four of his daughters drowned. Only his wife survived. As he traveled on another ship to join his wife, he passed over the place where his daughters had died, and wrote the song which begins:

When peace, like a river attendeth my way,
when sorrows like sea billows roll
Whatever my lot, Thou hast taught me to say,
It is well with my soul.

2. Reread the section "Other Ways of Saying Good-bye," and write a letter to the child you lost or consider if one of the other ways would help you express your grief. If yes, discuss this with your spouse. (This doesn't have to be done right away, but can even be done years later.)

16

Adoption

When one door of happiness closes, another opens;
but we often look so long at the closed door that
we do not see the one which has been opened for us.
—Helen Keller[1]

I waited patiently for God to help me; then He
listened and heard my cry. He lifted me . . . and
set my feet on a hard, firm path and steadied me. . . .
He has given me a new song to sing   (Psalm 40:1-3).

In adoption the labor is longer, but less intense.
It is an emotional labor, not physical.—Vicky

*When a woman at church heard we were infertile,
she flippantly said to me: "Well, you can always
adopt." I was hurt by her lack of understanding
of the frustration of infertility. I also knew she didn't have
any idea about the amount of work and the cost that
adoptions involved.*

*Before Michael and I were married, we "decided" we
would have two children, then adopt a third. So, adoption
was always in the back of our minds. About three years
into our infertility, we decided to put our names on an
adoption waiting list, while we continued with medical
treatment. We checked out a private agency in our area,
but they wanted $3,000 up front with no guarantee of a
child ever being placed. So we signed with the County
Department of Social Services, even though they estimated that the wait would be three to five years.*

Instead of years, the social worker called us six weeks later. Because part of Michael's heritage was Japanese, our ethnic background happened to match a Caucasian/ Japanese baby who would be born "soon" and placed for adoption. The social worker wanted to know if we would like to start the home-study process. We jumped at the chance and began filling out heaps of paperwork. Then they analyzed our childhoods, marriage, family relationships, income, housing, and prospective parenting skills. We passed! After just two months, we were set.

We became more excited as the possibility became more certain. We were the only couple in the county who fit the ethnic background of this baby, a fact which was very important to the county and to the birth mother. The social worker just wasn't sure when the baby was due, but she said she would give us 24 hours notice. When we found out the birth mother was carrying twins, we were overjoyed. We prayed for the birth mom and babies every day. Since we couldn't bear to keep car seats, bassinets, and clothes in our home, we arranged to borrow them from friends at a moment's notice. We couldn't stop ourselves from choosing names and buying sets of outfits, though, for every conceivable combination—two boys, two girls, or a boy and a girl. We waited and jumped every time the phone rang for five long months. (We later found out that the birth mom was only two months along when she first contacted the county.)

Finally the call came. The birth mother had given birth at a nearby hospital. A girl and a boy. We were given permission to go peek at them, but nothing would be final for a day or two. The waiting was finally over ... or so we thought. We continued to wait for word that we could pick up the babies.

After several days and many phone calls, I got another call. The birth mother had changed her mind. Our dreams and hearts were crushed again. When I gathered the strength to return the baby outfits, I was taken off guard when the saleswoman asked smiling, "Reason for re-turn?" I don't even recall what I choked out in response.

I still pray for God's protection and guidance for those babies and pray they'll grow up with people who love them.

A year or so later, we signed up with two lawyers to move things along. We filled out more forms, paid additional fees, and wrote "Dear Birth Mother" letters to see if we could find a baby to adopt through independent adoption. Nothing happened for another full year. Then I became pregnant with our son.

Since giving birth to our son, we have also tried to adopt a baby from Romania. We signed up with an international agency, paid the initial payment, then learned that instead of the cost we were originally told to expect of $4,000–$5,000, the cost would be closer to three times that. That was far beyond our means. At the same time, we learned that couples were having problems bringing their Romanian babies back into the country. Although we prayed for the finances, the way just didn't open up for us, so we took that as God closing the door.

Is Adoption the Easy Way?

I've included our experience of unfulfilled attempts at adoption not to discourage those of you pursuing adoption, but to suggest that adoption is not the easy fix for infertility that some people portray it to be. The blood, sweat, and tears of the emotional labor of adoption is hard work. This is not understood by many in our society, which leads to some insensitive comments, such as, "Oh, you adopted. You got a baby the easy way." If they only knew. While I do believe that couples who are willing to make sacrifices of cost, effort, or choices will end up with a baby, it takes perseverance and may have its own heartache along the way.

Adoption is one of the most beautiful and loving ways to build a family. A couple with love in their hearts finds a child who needs that love, and they become a family. This mirrors the picture of what God has done in adopting us so that He becomes our Father and we become His children. It's also a positive answer to the problem of abortion or children unable to be cared for by their birth parents.

The current laws are making the process more and more difficult for the adoptive parents and the birth mother though. In order to protect the birth mother's rights, our country and individual states have created laws that make the process very complicated and more costly than it needs to be. But, if you're willing to investigate which type of adoption to pursue, try to locate a child, complete the home study, possibly travel to the baby's birth site, possibly attend counseling, and complete and file the legal paperwork, adoption is a rewarding way to build your family and just as much a miracle as giving birth.

The strong desire for a child has motivated many, many couples to build beautiful families through adoption. These families see adoption as a special blessing and a gift to all involved, as this poem shows. It was written by a twelve-year-old son to his adoptive mother:

"Real Women"

I've been blessed with two real women in my life.
They never knew each other.
    One I don't remember, the other I call "mother."

One chose life for me and not abortion.
    The other teaches me the Christian way.

One gave me my heritage,
    the other gave me my name.

One planted the seed of life
    and the other will walk me through it.

One provided me with talents,
    the other teaches and encourages me to use them.

One gave me up for adoption
  because she loved me.
The other had been praying for a child
  and God led her straight to me.

One I know as Amy, the other I know as Mom.[2]

What Adoption Is Not

Adoption, though, is not a psychological or physical cure for infertility. People have told adoptive parents: "If you adopt, then you'll probably relax and get pregnant." This is not only incorrect, but it can be harmful to the adoptive child if the child is not seen as a unique and special human being, different from your dream biological child, but equally as precious in God's sight.

Vicky learned that adoption doesn't erase all the old emotions of infertility:

> I had expected that adopting would take away all the sadness I felt from infertility. But, it still hurts when women share their birth stories even though I have a precious, beautiful daughter. It hurts when my daughter says, "Mommy, why didn't I grow in your tummy?" I have to say it makes me sad too. I wouldn't want to have a different child, but I would have liked Nicole to have come from me.

Infertility brings many losses: the loss of the experience of conceiving a child together who is a combination of both husband and wife; missing out on the experience of pregnancy and giving birth, the loss of control; the loss of self-esteem; and the loss of being a parent and having a child. Adoption only "cures" one of these losses—becoming a parent and having a child. Before moving on to adoption, it is important to face and resolve some of your sadness about infertility. This doesn't mean you have to exhaust all medical avenues before applying, but you should realize an adopted child is not an exact replacement for the birth child you can't have.

Making the Decision

Sometimes the decision to adopt is made more abruptly because a major medical problem is discovered fairly early in the infertility testing. Although the grief can be more intense at discovering the door to a biological child firmly closed, it may make the decision to adopt easier.

Rosie and Gordon knew Gordon might have trouble becoming a father because he'd had chemotherapy for cancer earlier in his adulthood. When his sperm count tested low, Rosie thought the doctor would simply give Gordon something to raise it. But instead, the doctor told Gordon that his sperm count was so low, he should think of adopting if he wanted children and sent him home with an adoption agency's name scrawled on a slip of paper. The shock was hard on both Rosie and Gordon. Since using donor sperm wasn't an option with which they felt comfortable, especially Gordon, they started looking for a child to adopt.

More often, the decision to adopt is made gradually as the door to a biological child slowly closes, but never shuts altogether. When Vicky and Steve realized the thing they wanted most was to be able to raise a child, they turned their focus toward adopting.

> There comes a time as you're going through infertility that the clock starts ticking, and you realize you don't have much time left, and your medical options start running out, or you can't afford them, or you don't feel morally that you can go that one more step medically to get a baby.
>
> Adoption usually isn't a decision where people wake up in the morning and say, OK, let's adopt. It's more of a gradual awakening to "Well, maybe we could do that. Do we really want to be childless forever? Is this an option we want to pursue?"
>
> We decided we wanted to have a child more than Vicky wanted to be pregnant. We'd been emotionally and physically wrung out by two years of infertility tests and surgeries. We decided we were ready for children, not more

tests. So, we quit all the medical procedures and sought a child through adoption.

Because adoption usually takes a great deal of effort, both husband and wife need to be motivated and committed to it. If you are having trouble deciding if adoption is for you, consider the following with your spouse: Are we ready to love a child who wasn't born to us? Do we have the emotional energy, finances, and other resources to adopt a child? What appeals to us about building our family this way? (For example, we would help a child who needs a home, or would be able to stop medical treatments.) What doesn't? (For example, we wouldn't have control of the baby's health during the pregnancy or whether the birthmother would change her mind.) Are we still young enough to parent? Is now the right time to pursue it? How will our friends and family react? How will we deal with that? (Just as with infertility, some families will be very supportive of your desire to adopt, while others will not.)

The decision basically comes down to: Do we want to be parents—to raise and nurture and contribute to the physical, emotional, and spiritual growth of a child? Do we want this even if we can't experience a pregnancy, the baby doesn't carry our genes, and might not look like us? After discussing these questions, you'll know better if you're ready to adopt.

Adoption Options

Once you make the decision to adopt, one option is just to wait and see if a baby falls in your lap. Sometimes this does happen, as it did to Julie and Russell:

> Family was so important to us because, through various circumstances, we had both lost ours. Off and on for four long years the disappointment of the unfulfilled dream began to chip away at our faith. Amazingly though, after each month's letdown, we would somehow manage to hold

onto a glimmer of hope [through] faith. This past October, the night we returned from vacation, our friend told us that her aunt knew of a 34-year-old woman who was pregnant and wanted to give up her baby for adoption. Oh, and by the way, she's due *anytime!* Are you interested? On faith, we went for it!

We [found] out that this baby about to be born was *truly* a miracle. Last March—at the same time one of our pastors prayed for God to bless us with a child—the birth mother was frantically trying to borrow money for an abortion, but to no avail. A few weeks later, she started bleeding and nearly miscarried. Then the bleeding stopped. God had spared [our baby's] life for a special purpose.

[One month later], after a four-hour midnight ride to the birth mother's city, our precious little boy was born. Miracles truly can happen.

Although it gives us hope to hear of these babies who practically knock on couple's doors, most people will need to be more active in their search for a child to adopt. If you choose adoption as a route to build your family, I would suggest that you talk to as many people as possible who have recently adopted and that you read some books totally devoted to adoption (some suggestions are in appendix B). Below are brief overviews of the different routes currently available for adopting. I have friends who have successfully adopted through each of these different routes. All of them have positives and negatives, so you need to choose which path suits you best.

Agency adoptions
An agency is an organization that is licensed by the state to place a child in an adoptive home.

• Public agencies
A *public agency,* such as the Department of Social Services, is supported by tax money. Public agencies usually deal with domestic adoptions and foster parenting/

adoption programs. The children are usually available for adoption because child protective services has terminated parental rights or because the parents have chosen to relinquish the children. These children are most often older children (grade school), children with special needs, or sibling groups who are in the care of child protective services.

The *fost/adopt* program is for children who have a limited chance of returning to live with their birth parents. The children are placed in a home before they are legally free to be adopted.

Molly and Tony successfully adopted two children through a public agency. They found the county agency flexible and supportive. After years of frustration and disappointment, Molly had become pregnant once, but miscarried the baby, so they looked to adoption to build their family:

> A woman at work had adopted through the county. She planted the seed in my mind. About a year later, a woman whom I had told of my infertility gave me the card of a social worker at the county to call. We had tried many other doors. In one week we had interviews with two women looking for parents for their unborn babies. The rejection of not being chosen, and the loss of these opportunities were hard to bear. We interviewed so many adoption counselors and agencies and yet God's peace eluded us in every aspect. None of the doors opened, so we called the county and went to the first meeting.
>
> I've never been a real baby person, so we told them that we were willing to adopt siblings under the age of eight. After all our years of infertility, we were ready to get on with having our family.
>
> We went through the home-study process and became licensed as foster parents. The day our application/home study process was finished (three-and-a-half months later) we got the call that they had found a match for us. They showed us pictures of David (aged 7) and Brian (aged 5), lots of records, court reports, and information about their

birth parents. They were already legally free to be adopted and were living in a foster home. We just knew it was right and God's plan for us. Two weeks later we met our sons.

Eight months later we were in court finalizing the adoption. They are both such sweet-tempered boys. They are in counseling to help them talk about their past. My older son remembers his birth parents. We just talk about their past in normal conversation because we have all the records and know their history.

I loved David and Brian before we met them, not because of some fantasy, but because the Lord confirmed it. They joy of the moment overflowed and fear melted away. They are our sons. This Christmas, we'll be putting bows on each other—Tony, Brian, David, and me—and give thanks for each one.

Benefits. If the adoption is a straight adoption, the children have already been relinquished. The cost (as low as $500) is the lowest of any adoption options.

Drawbacks. *Public agencies* don't place many babies, so the wait for an infant can be five years or longer. They are more concerned than most private agencies with matching ethnic backgrounds. Almost all the adoptions through a county agency are done through fost/adopt programs.

While it is better for the children not to be shuffled around to foster homes before being placed in an adoptive home, the uncertainty of this program can feel too risky for couples who have already dealt with loss. The Department of Social Services' main goal in the fost/adopt program is to give every chance for the children to be reunited with their birth parents, so visitations between the child and the birth parents are a part of this program until parental rights are terminated.

● Private agencies

Private agencies are licensed by the state to perform adoptions, but they are funded by private money. They are similar to the public agencies in that the home study is done prior to the placement of a child. They usually offer help in finding a child to adopt.

Many agencies are changing their adoption process to be more open and allow more flexibility in allowing the birth mother to directly choose the adoptive parents. Linda and Tim are currently waiting to adopt a child through a private agency. They chose the route of a private agency because it offered guidance through the adoption process, counseling, a set fee, and help in locating a child. Another factor was the more favorable laws toward agency adoptions versus independent adoptions in their state.

They have just completed a year of meetings, paperwork, and the home study. They expect to have a child placed in their home within a year.

Benefits. Relinquishment of parental rights often happens more quickly with private agencies than with independent adoptions, and the relinquishment is final once the birth mother releases her child to the agency. More infants are placed through private agencies than through county agencies.

Drawbacks. Each agency has its own set of criteria, which may or may not work in your favor. The cost is usually a fixed amount (of several thousand dollars) although some agencies offer a sliding scale.

Independent or private adoption

Independent adoption is basically a legal agreement made directly between the birth parents and the adoptive couple. Laws vary from state to state, but in most cases an attorney is hired to coordinate the transfer of the baby from the birth mother to the adopting couple and to execute the legal documentation.

In this type of adoption, the couple is usually actively involved in searching for the child through networking, sending out search/résumé letters, or advertising. The birth mother is also more involved in choosing the couple to adopt her baby. Instead of paying an agency fee, the adoptive couple usually reimburses the birth mother for specific medical costs, living expenses, and counseling.

Some organizations or individuals act as adoption "facilitators." They may help connect babies and adoptive parents, give advice and assist in writing "Dear Birth Mother" letters. Facilitators may save you money by assisting you at a lower hourly rate than an attorney, or they can be more costly.

Vicky tells how she and her husband, Steve, chose the independent adoption route:

> We were pretty devastated by the time we decided to adopt and weren't very strong emotionally, so it was hard. We chose independent adoption because the county had 200 people waiting for a healthy child. They had children with serious problems available, but we didn't feel strong enough to take one of those children.
>
> We went to the library to get every address we could related to adoption, then sent away for information and applications. One place we received information from was a resource center that assisted with independent adoption, so we used them. They showed us how to send out about 500 letters across the country. Then we waited for five months.
>
> In December, we got a phone call from a young woman who said shyly, "Hi . . . are you still interested in adopting a baby?" We met with her, and five months later, which was a long time to wait, she gave birth to a little girl.
>
> When our daughter was born, we got to the hospital at midnight and said, "We're here to see our baby!" The nurse knew nothing about it, so we had to go home without seeing the baby. I just cried. I thought, *this is it; we're not going to get her.* The next day during regular visiting hours, we walked into the hospital room and our birth mother Diane said, "Oh, there are the parents," and handed Nicole to me. I got to hold Diane's hands and look in her face and say, "Thank you for this gift." Then she kissed Nicole good-bye and said, "I'll love you forever my little

daughter." Then we [went home].

Two weeks later Diane called and said she ^ı the baby. I thought she'd changed her mind a to take Nikki. I sat rocking in the chair crying, don't let her take our baby, please." This is the hard part of independent adoption.

Diane came in, looked at her and said, "She's cute. Where's her room?" So we showed her the nursery. We talked awhile and she left. She just wanted to make sure that Nikki had a nice place to live. Six months later we signed the papers, and she was our kid.

We send Diane letters occasionally telling her how beautiful Nikki is, and she contacts us occasionally. God was so gracious to give us a beautiful baby daughter. And I'm so glad that I can tell Nicole the last thing Diane told her as she kissed her good-bye at the hospital. She won't have to wonder if her birth mother loved her.

Benefits. Most domestic adoptions are done privately, so more babies are available this way. Adoption through an independent agency can often take less time than agency adoptions. The couple only has to fit the individual birth mother's criteria, not an agency's. You may be able to attend the baby's birth.

Drawbacks. In many states, the birth mother in this situation has a longer period of time to change her mind. As a couple, you may be more involved with the birth mother's feelings about placing her child for adoption, which may add to your stress. The cost varies widely, depending on the expenses of the birth mother and the attorneys' fee. It can be more expensive than an agency adoption. Also, if the birth mother changes her mind or is dishonest, the adopting parents have no recourse to recover the money they've paid.

International/cross-cultural adoption

An *international adoption* is usually done through a licensed agency in this country which cooperates with an agency in the child's native country. Agencies often specialize in working with specific countries. A home study is generally required prior to placement. Each country has its own rules and restrictions for adoptions regarding parental age, travel to the country, and length of stay needed in the country. The child is legally adopted as a separate step after you return with the child.

In a variation of this called *adopt abroad,* you can use a lawyer or private party to help you find a child in another country, then travel to that country and complete the adoption there. A home study is still required by an agency in this country.

If you choose to adopt a child who is from a different ethnic background, but the baby is born in the United States, this is called a *cross-cultural domestic adoption.* This can either be done privately or through an agency.

Laura explained the process she and Jim went through to adopt internationally.

We worked with a clearinghouse, which directed us to an agency in Pennsylvania, which had contacts in Chili. When our home study with the agency was done, we had to get approval from immigration and give some financial information showing that we could support a child. We got our referral for our daughter about eight months after we first applied at the agency. She was four days old. Once we got the referral, there were lots of other documents that the country of Chili wanted us to fill out.

We got all that done and then waited for four more months.

I flew to Chili and stayed two days. (The required length of stay has changed now.) I didn't even have to make an appearance in a Chilean court. In Chili, they give the mother some time, then she has to appear in court to relinquish the child. Then they [made] us the baby's legal guardians before we could even see her.

My emotions felt frozen until after I got the final stamps of approval, then I started to cry. I called my husband, Jim, and told him that she was beautiful. She had these huge deep-brown eyes. I brought her home about a year after we started the process.

Benefits. Often other countries have more liberal age restrictions, or even allow single-parent adoptions. The waiting time *can* be minimal. If you go through a well-known agency with good connections in the child's native country, the risk of not ending up with a child is very low. You have the knowledge that you are helping a child in need.

Drawbacks. You will need to feel comfortable that the child will probably not look like you. Because of this, you will be asked about how your family originated. If you can see this as a chance to share about the benefits of building families through *international or cross-cultural adoption* and you can let your child know that you value his or her cultural heritage, this may be a good adoption route for you.

The cost of adopting internationally is higher than many domestic adoptions. Some countries are not well regulated, so bribes and delays can be commonplace in them. Children from other countries may have health problems, so they should be tested for hepatitis, tuberculosis, AIDS, and other illnesses.

Special-needs adoptions

Special-needs children are generally adopted through public or private agencies. The children may have physical, mental, or emotional disabilities, be age ten or older, or be of minority heritage. They may also belong to a sibling group of three or more.

Benefits. Special subsidies are sometimes available to help with medical or counseling costs. As with international adoption, there is an added happiness of being able to help a child who really needs it.

Drawbacks. A child with physical or emotional disabilities will take extra time, energy, and probably money. An older child's past will also need to be addressed more in depth. One adoptive father of a special-needs child suggested that a couple needs to be certain that the Lord wants them to adopt this type of child because there is an added daily cost involved in adopting a child who is more difficult to care for than the average child.

Open or Closed Adoption

Another aspect of the decision about which path to take in adoption involves how much openness you want with the birth parents and for how long. Most domestic adoptions are moving toward openness. In an extremely open adoption, the birth mother may live with the adoptive couple before the birth, then spend time with the child as he or she grows. In an extremely closed adoption, absolutely no information is shared between the birth parents and the adoptive parents. Babies from China, for example, have probably been abandoned before becoming available for adoption.

Most adoptions fall somewhere in the middle of these extremes. In a middle-of-the-road case, the birth and adoptive parents may meet once before the birth to exchange non-identifying information such as first names and medical information. Then the adoptive parents send letters and pictures occasionally through an intermediary for the first few years of the child's life. You should discuss with your spouse at which place on the closed-to-open continuum you would both feel comfortable.

The Home Study

Most couples come to adoption feeling battle weary after already having endured the stress of infertility. The idea of being analyzed by strangers to see if they would make good parents is an additional pressure and may resurrect feelings of inadequacy or anger.

Instead of seeing a home study as a test to pass, try to

see the questions as discussion topics for you and your spouse. Although it is stressful, try to view the process as a way to prepare you for parenting.

Cost

Adoption costs vary drastically, but average around $10,000. To many couples, the cost of adoption requires sacrifice, to some it is even prohibitive. While many infertility costs are covered by insurance and are spread over months or years, adopting couples usually have no assistance with adoption expenses which must be paid within a short amount of time.

Dr. Alan McNickle, professor of theology at Moody Bible Institute, has adopted two children. He suggests that one way churches can show their support for couples seeking adoption is to view it as a ministry and to help financially:

> If people feel before God that they need children, it seems appropriate to share their financial situation with their friends and church, thereby allowing other believers to "minister" with them. This is just like other social problems where people lose jobs and the last people to hear about it are their friends. They may be too embarrassed to share their needs because of pride. While the financial aspect could be a hardship, there are adoptions available that need not bring hardship.
>
> [Financial advisor] Larry Burkett said that people who are in need are often not aware of the money that's available if they would just let their needs be known. Often they are afraid to ask because they might be embarrassed if the adoption fell through. [Sometimes] mission organizations have contacts in other countries for children waiting to be adopted. [Those children] could be helped.

In addition, Dr. McNickle reminds couples not to be caught up in the materialism of our society: "We have to decide what our goals [are] and what we need as far as our lifestyle goes. . . . It's a matter of what we want to do with our life. A consistent biblical worldview demands that we make choices for eternity, not simply to satisfy personal, creature comforts that are culturally appropriate." Simplifying our lifestyle may help us save more money to use toward adoption.

Another option is to petition your company to reimburse employees for specific adoption expenses, such as legal fees and medical costs. In fairness to employees, many companies will reimburse adoption expenses to the amount that would equal the normal cost of giving birth.

The legal forms to complete an independent adoption can be filed without a lawyer in *very* simple adoptions. But if there's any chance that a problem might develop with the birth parents or if there is any question of exactly what needs to be filed or when, then it is safer to hire a lawyer. Even if you file the forms yourself, you will still need to have a home study completed by a public or private agency.

Nursing an Adopted Child

Part of the sorrow of being unable to carry a child can be the inability to nurse a child. Our bodies are amazing though, and a woman can often produce milk simply with the stimulation of a baby suckling. If you are interested in nursing your adopted child, this can be done. Most women can produce some milk and some women can even produce a full milk supply. Your local La Leche League can supply the special equipment to feed your baby supplemental baby formula as you are nursing him or her. The following books have further information on this: *You Can Breastfeed Your Baby Even in Special Situations* by Dorothy Brewster (Rodale Press) and *The Womanly Art of Breastfeeding* by La Leche League International (New American Library).

As one adoptive mom put it: "You get all the hassles of bottle feeding with all the hassles of nursing, but for me, it's been worth it." Even if a full milk supply is never produced, the baby can bond with mom, receive some immunities from the colostrum, and benefit from the enhanced jaw and speech development that nursing provides. (This benefit results from the position of the baby's mouth and jaw during nursing. The baby has to work hard, thus developing strong jaw muscles in the position that is thought to help speech.).

Finding Out More

If you are considering adoption, do all you can to find out more about it. Investigate agencies—many of them have informational meetings. Talk to a variety of people, ranging from those who have recently adopted, to those who have adult, adopted children, about their experiences with adoption. Ask agencies or attorneys for the number of children they have placed, the type of children (infants, school-age, special needs), and a breakdown of fees (some have sliding scales). Join an adoption support group.

If you decide to pursue a child through adoption, may God speed you toward finding that child or children.

Your Personal Journey

1. Do you see adoption as an option for you? Why or why not?
2. What type of child would you feel comfortable raising as your own?
3. Which pathway to adoption seems the best choice for you? (Consider the amount of contact you'd want with the birth parents, how much information—such as medical background—you'd want to have about the birth parents, and whether you feel able to have a child in your home for a few months before knowing for sure if you could adopt him or her?)
4. If you aren't ready to move toward adoption now, is there a time in the future when you would be ready to consider it?

17

Parenting after Infertility or Pregnancy Loss

A spring day in December is always more precious
than one in May is. —Irwin Philip Sobel

Be very careful never to forget what you have
seen God doing for you. May His miracles have a
deep and permanent effect upon our lives! Tell
your children . . . about the
glorious miracles He did   (Deuteronomy 4:9).

*I*f the path you've taken results in a child through
birth or adoption, your preceding struggle can
make you value this blessing even more. Most fertile couples cherish their children, but those children are
like an elegantly planted garden: planned, cultivated, and
beautiful. The child of an infertile couple, however, is like
a brightly colored wildflower blooming in the midst of a
barren, lifeless land.

Vicky felt a sense of wonder about the daughter she
adopted six years ago: "I'm still amazed that our childless
household now has a child's toys lying around and the joy
that a child brings. I thank God for that."

The Joys and Benefits

A pastor of ours once taught that pain increases our capacity for joy. Couples who become parents after infertility

have developed an immense capacity for feeling the joy of their child. They don't take their child for granted or view their child as a burden. They have the pleasure of being able to tell their child he or she was *very much* wanted. They would have valued their child's life if it had come easily, but the time of waiting has deepened the appreciation for the miracle.

Through our efforts to have children, we realize what a miracle it is that babies are *ever* conceived. It is an even greater miracle when they are born healthy. Children are an expression of grace. They are freely given, but not deserved or owed. They are gifts. Infertile people understand that well.

Rich, whose wife had multiple miscarriages and whose triplets were originally given only a slim chance to live, says he's still in awe about finally being a dad:

> There's nothing like having little ones running through your house. The children are almost eighteen months old now, and I still can't believe I'm a daddy. When I walk through the door and see three pairs of arms reaching out and saying, "Daddy," it was worth every struggle, every pain. When you hug them, you hug them that much tighter, when you kiss them, you kiss them that much more tenderly. It's better than I ever dreamed it would be.

A stronger parenting team

Infertile couples have also had more time to work on parenting issues beforehand, so they are likely to be more aligned on their child-raising issues. They've had time to develop trust, interdependence, and skills in working as a team, all of which help in parenting. Always aware that they might have a baby next year, they've been able to listen, watch closely, and discuss what they've seen about child rearing. They've been able to watch their friends' parenting choices and discuss child-rearing philosophies. Because their friends' children are older, they can watch and see what works and what doesn't.

New priorities for parenting

One of the particular joys that infertile parents share is how their changed priorities affect their parenting. Carole, who experienced two miscarriages and a stillbirth, found she was able to reevaluate what was important when her son was born:

> I didn't worry about cleaning. I just took the time I needed to rock my baby. Because of my previous losses, I don't think I ever really bonded with Ben until after he was born. Maybe it all felt so magical and new because I hadn't really bonded with him during my pregnancy. I just wanted to hold him and not let go. Even now, five years later, the wonder and joy of having him fills up my heart pretty much every day. I feel so thankful for the beautiful gift God has given me.

Infertile parents often are more willing to let the less important things in life slide while savoring moments with their child. Remembering their time without a child can sometimes help lessen normal parenting frustration.

Side benefits

If you have had two incomes for longer than you expected, you may be in a more financially stable position as you begin to raise your child(ren). (Providing you haven't had to mortgage your house for fertility treatment, adoption, or triplets.)

You will also have the emotional fortitude gained from surviving infertility to help you survive the terrible twos or teenage years.

The Challenges

Although parenting a child after infertility is an incredible joy, it also offers some challenges. When a child comes, does the specter of infertility fade into a bad dream? It does to a degree, but it still affects our lives. The degree often depends on how deeply we were affected.

Awareness of the fragility of your child's life

The booklet, *Your Next Baby* shares this quotations from a mom in Louisville who had a previous baby die: "Every night I whisper in his ear, 'Always know I love you and please, don't forget to breathe.' "[1]

Infertile parents may often feel this way about their child. They've learned that life isn't always fair, and they aren't immune to tragedy. They may worry that they will lose their child or they may feel unaccustomed to happiness and fear that their dream won't last.

Being aware that your child is special, combined with feelings of parental responsibility, can bring an intensity to parenthood that can lead to becoming overprotective. Being overprotective is being so concerned for the safety of your child that you isolate or inhibit her from experiences that are good for her growth and development. It is holding on too tightly because you still don't trust God.

After God finally gave Abraham a son, He tested him. God wanted to make sure that Abraham wasn't turning his focus to the gift instead of continuing to trust Him (Gen. 22:1-19). God knew how important Isaac was to Abraham, but He wanted Isaac to be a catalyst for a stronger relationship between Abraham and Himself.

And can you imagine how Hannah felt? After struggling for so long without a child, she weaned him, then left him with a priest to raise (1 Sam. 20:1-10). She had learned that God was in control and that she could trust Him. Because of the choices she made, her child was uniquely used by God. If you're tempted to try to hold on too tightly to your children because they were so hard to come by, it's comforting to read that after Hannah gave Samuel to God, " . . . the child Samuel grew up with Jehovah."[2] If we make the daily choices to point our children to God, we don't need to worry. Our children will grow up with Him.

(On the other hand, I was so concerned sometimes that people not think I was overprotective that I let my son do some things which were beyond his ability and had painful consequences. Don't relinquish your parenting responsibility either.)

A *sense of isolation*

Infertile parents can feel isolated because their closest friends often remain infertile. These friends really don't want to spend time with a new baby even if it is yours. Perhaps you hadn't kept up your friendships with people who had children because you were protecting yourself. Carole had a difficult time adjusting to this isolation motherhood brought:

> I love children and I wanted children, but after my son was born, it was a real adjustment. I no longer worked and was home all day. All of my friends had been from work, so I was lonely. No other moms lived anywhere in my neighborhood. No one was home but retired people. And they didn't want to baby-sit—ever.

Or you may have thought that once you had a child, you'd slip right in to the "mom's club," but many infertile women find it hard to make the transition. You may have had a multiple birth so people come up to you in malls and ask, "Did you take fertility drugs?" (Yes, I've been told they do that.) You may have given birth to a special-needs child or adopted a transracial child, so you don't fit the "normal" family image. If you have adopted a child, you still won't have a birth story to share. You just don't easily slip into the "normal" mom role.

Rosie felt this yearning to be just a regular mom:

> We were walking our daughter Cici one night in her stroller, when a couple walked by her and admired her. The woman said she just found out she was pregnant, and wanted to know my obstetrician. It made me sad to say that I never had an obstetrician. Why do I still have to feel different?

Infertility has changed us. We aren't just like other parents. Perhaps our vision of the "club" of motherhood has changed. Being the ones left out for so long should make us aware of not wanting to exclude others. And hopefully we've learned to stop looking for acceptance from others and rest on God's total acceptance of us.

Unrealistic expectations for parenting

Just as infertile parents can tend to idealize a pregnancy, they can also idealize parenthood. They subconsciously think that parenthood will bring happiness and totally erase the feelings infertility brought. But a clinical study that compared childless couples, previously infertile couples after a normal pregnancy, and never infertile couples, found that "mild depression does persist in women even after a biological solution to infertility."[3] Having a child does not automatically erase the feelings of being infertile.

Couples may also expect, again unrealistically, that if *they* ever had a baby, *they* would never yell at their child. Their child would also never rebel against them because she would sense the incredible love they have for her. But, becoming parents after infertility doesn't make you into perfect parents or promise you perfect children. It is important not to feel guilty if parenting overwhelms you at times. At times, all children rebel no matter how much they are loved. Look at Adam and Eve—they were offered the perfect life, and they still rebelled.

Questioning ability to parent

If children were conceived using a high-tech method or couples became parents through adoption, they may wonder at times if they were really meant to be parents. Did we push too hard to become parents? Do others know better how to care for this child? Whole books have been written about raising adopted children and how adoptive parents need to come to a point of feeling complete entitlement (or the right) to raise their child. Again, it is a process as parents get to know their child. They don't have to have all the parenting skills down by the time their child turns two months old.

Childless couples may feel unsure about their ability to be good parents if they have avoided children because it was too painful being around them. Or, by the time they have a child, all their friends and family members have already had children, so they're always on the receiving end of advice, which is sometimes phrased, "Sure, your child seems happy now, but just you wait until. . . . "

If you feel insecure being the novice, by all means, listen to the advice because it may be worthwhile. But also remember that God has given *you* your child to raise. For some reason, God's plan most often involves giving children to people with little or no parenting experience. Maybe it is so that they will go to Him for answers.

Fewer or more children than you planned
Ellen Glazer, in her book, *The Long Awaited Stork,* notes another difference in parenting after infertility: "A history of infertility almost always has an effect on how many children a couple has . . . Some couples end up with fewer children than they wanted and others may end up with more than they are prepared to raise.[4]

Rich shared about parenting multiples:

> The only thing that hurts is that you can't hold all three of them in your arms at the same time. And you long to. It's also hard to discipline them. In raising triplets, there are times you just have to sit back and bite your lip because they're just exploring and grabbing like all eighteen-month-old children.
>
> Financially we make it month to month. Sometimes I feel like we do it with mirrors. It has certainly rearranged our priorities. It is an incredible financial burden and I don't see us coming out of it anytime soon. But it's worth it.

Deanna said that she's had to learn to respond to the

insensitive comments that people make around her triplets:

> When people see me with the triplets, some of them say, "I'm sure glad it's you and not me." I've learned to reply: "Well, I'm glad it's me too." Or when they say, "Wow, you sure have your hands full," it's a joy to answer: "Yes, and it's so much better than when they were empty."

Learning to persevere through struggles is a valuable skill for parenting. Yet, you will stumble through most of the same pitfalls that other parents do. Infertility doesn't allow you to bypass the challenges of parenting (although personally, I think that would be only fair). Children aren't given because people earn them by their goodness. They are gifts.

Your Personal Journey

1. How do you anticipate parenthood will change your life? (Or, if you are a parent already, how has it changed your life?)
2. Do you anticipate any specific challenges in parenting? (Or, what challenges were surprises to you?)
3. While you wait for children, are there ways to help lessen the struggles you anticipate parenthood will bring? (For example, discussing parenting techniques with your spouse, spending time with others' children, or taking a parenting class.)

18

Secondary Infertility— Living In-between

Another Christmas morning, And my family is still not complete.
Not enough stockings on the mantle,
Not enough toys under the tree.
Too few little hands helping make cookies. . . .
Why can't I just be grateful for the child I have,
At this sacred time of year?
Because it's another Christmas morning
Without my baby. And I miss him.[1]

Like arrows in the hand of a warrior, so are the
children of one's youth. How blessed is the man
whose quiver is full of them   (Psalm 127:4-5, NASB).

*ichael and I only waited ten months before start-
ing to try for our second child. Since we had
hoped to have three children by the time our first
was finally born, we didn't want to lose much time. It also
seemed that my reproductive system had only worked correctly once in over five years of trying, so we didn't want to
miss the one time it might work again in the next five years.*

*I assumed that since we already had been able to have
our one miracle child, we wouldn't feel emotional pain
while trying for the next child. I soon discovered how
wrong I was. The lessons I learned the first time helped—I
entered this journey with less tunnel vision, more pa-
tience, and felt God's love for me much more than the first
time. But, as the years passed, I experienced again the
sense of injustice and the intense yearning for another
child. I wrote this poem in my journal:*

234

"Faltering Steps"

Lord, I hate to bother You again.
I know You have blessed me beyond my dreams,
but Your first blessing was so wonderful,
I can hardly wait for another.

I thought I was healed.
What has happened?
Some of the old feelings of worthlessness
are returning.

Please help me to remember all the lessons
You have taught me.
Help me to remember Your love
and to hold on to You.[a]

Are There Different Sizes of Quivers?

Looking at Psalm 127:4-5, I began to wonder if there are different sizes of quivers. When is a quiver full? Some couples feel their family is complete with just one child. Others plan for six children to "fill" their household. To them, one child is just the beginning of their family, so if they experience infertility after having one, they live with a sense that their other children are missing.

They may look at a photo of their small family and wonder if their family will ever be "complete." At the park, they watch their child play and wonder when the brother or sister will be there to sit on the other end of the teeter-totter. Those going through secondary infertility only know their quiver has more room, but no child to fill it. "When the majority of couples think of having a family, they think of having two or more children," says Marianne Carter, a licensed marriage and family counselor who works with infertile couples in San Jose, California. "A lot of parents feel strongly about wanting that balance."

An example of this comes from a man named Jeff in the book *Healing the Infertile Family*. He says:

I've always been an iffy sort of person when it comes to family life. The only constraint that I ever put on it was that if I ever had kids I would have more than one. I was an only child and as I grew up I always said to myself, "Boy, I never want to live in a family like this." I used to talk to walls because there wasn't another kid there.[3]

Just as there are many reasons for wanting a child in the first place, many reasons go into your idea of the perfect family size:

- you may have had a favorite brother or sister with whom you had a special relationship (for example, you shared confidences you would never have shared with your parents);
- you might have been an only child and were lonely; or
- you might have wonderful memories of a house full of people—all connected to you—gathered for special holidays, such as around the tree at Christmas.

What Is Secondary Infertility?

The definition of secondary infertility is a couple who wants, but is unable to conceive or carry, a child to term following the birth of one or more children. (This includes those struggling to have a second, third, fourth child, or more.) Couples who have adopted a child and want to adopt other children to "complete" their family also may relate to struggles with secondary infertility.

Some couples with secondary infertility experienced trouble conceiving the first time, so they have an inkling that they might have trouble the next time. Hopefully, these couples have been able to develop some coping tools from the first time around which will help them through infertility again. The downside for these couples is that they start the process more worn down from what they have already gone through.

But, other couples who became pregnant easily the first time are often shocked to find out they can't conceive again. Holly, for instance, was shocked to find out she was infertile because she unexpectedly became pregnant and had her first baby before she was married, at age 15. She was still growing up while her son was a baby, so she missed out on much of the joy of raising him. She later married Greg when she was 23. They tried unsuccessfully for ten years to have a baby. For couples who are new to infertility, the shock, confusion, and initial grieving adds further stress.

Secondary infertility is more common than most people realize. Of all the women who have had a baby, close to ten percent will later experience secondary infertility, according to fertility specialist Dr. David Adamson. "If approximately ten percent of women have secondary infertility, that means that 400,000 couples (there are now 4 million children born per year) who have a baby this year are going to later [experience] infertility."

The feelings of helplessness and hopelessness affect couples with secondary infertility just as they do those with primary infertility. "It touches the core issues for everyone: their goals, expectations, womanhood or manhood, body image, sexuality, their reason for being and for living. That's why it is so difficult and devastating for almost everyone," said Marianne Carter.

Sara, for instance, had no trouble conceiving her daughter during her first marriage. Then, when her daughter was eight, she married her husband Paul, and suddenly couldn't wait to have another baby. When a year passed without a pregnancy, she saw her gynecologist who discovered that her fallopian tubes were severely scarred, probably caused by an infection sometime after her daughter was born. He told her that her chances for becoming pregnant without some high-tech help were slim. She was amazed at how difficult secondary infertility was for her. "For the first time in my life, I didn't know how to control the emotions I was feeling. I couldn't understand why my emotions were so strong when I already had a child. I finally realized it was because I [had no] control in the situation."

Although couples with secondary infertility already have a child, they also have a concrete idea of what they aren't able to achieve. Dr. William Brown, past chairman of OB/GYN at The Good Samaritan Hospital of Santa Clara Valley, spoke about how the clarity of the joys of parenthood can add to the sadness: "My patients who have children at home and are experiencing infertility [have] a real sense of what it is they can't create, a clear picture of what they're missing. It's a personalized feeling of loss."

Medical Explanations
How could someone who has been able to have a child not be able to have another? Doesn't one child "prove" fertility? These questions make sense until you realize that a problem with fertility can happen at any time. Just about any of the reasons listed in chapter 4 could be a problem for a couple with secondary infertility, with the exception of a congenital problem which caused sterility. Perhaps after the last child, the husband or wife was exposed to toxic chemicals, an infection, injury, or operation. It could be that a medical problem, such as endometriosis, fibroids, or diabetes has progressed to the point that it is now affecting fertility. The passage of time since the last pregnancy could also compound the problem, since a pregnancy is harder to achieve with advancing maternal age.

Additionally, a complication with a previous pregnancy such as a placental abruption, cesarean section, or retained placenta could have required an operation or medical procedure. It's possible that a previous pregnancy or an infection after delivery could have damaged the uterus or scarred the uterus or fallopian tubes.

Hierarchy of pain
In a nationwide study of couples who wanted a baby, almost twice as many were experiencing infertility after the

birth of a child as those who were childless.[4] Yet, it is difficult for people to admit that although they have one child (or more), they are struggling to have another. One reason is that others often see secondary infertility as insignificant.

In the hierarchy of infertility pain, secondary infertility seems to be at the bottom of the list. At the top of the pyramid is the woman suffering from primary infertility. Beneath her is the woman who has miscarried (at least she got pregnant). And at the bottom is the woman who has secondary infertility (at least she has a child).

This hierarchy is understandable. Anyone who is a little closer to "normal" is envied. Women with irregular periods may even envy those who ovulate regularly. But what can happen with a hierarchy like this is that too much time is spent justifying whose pain is worse.

Infertility is painful, and therefore significant, no matter how many children you may already have. The yearning is still there, the control or choice is not. In Bob Deit's book, *Life after Loss,* he asks the questions:

> Which grief experience is the worst? Is it more difficult on the widow if her husband suddenly and unexpectedly drops dead of a heart attack? Or is it worse if he dies an inch at a time from cancer? Is it worse to lose a spouse to death or a marriage through divorce? Is the death of a child the worst of all losses?
>
> The truth is all of these are irrelevant questions. There is only one very worst kind of grief and that is *yours!*[5]

The Unique Problems of Secondary Infertility

Couples with secondary infertility also experience a unique set of problems as they try to have another child while doing their best to care for the child(ren) they have now.

Scheduling medical treatment

The schizophrenic pull between caring for my child and getting medical treatment to have another became graphically clear to me the week we started Pergonal treatments. Michael was taking off work to join me at the doctor's. I was going to have an ultrasound to check my ovaries, and he was going to learn how to give the injections of Pergonal. Two hours before we had to leave, I discovered Justin's forehead was hot and found he had a 101 degree fever. So, I canceled the baby-sitter, but we couldn't reschedule the appointment because it was timed to match my cycle. Justin seemed fine other than the fever, so we decided to give him medicine to reduce the fever and take him with us. (I don't like to take him to the infertility specialist's office because I worry that seeing him will hurt the other childless patients.)

I tried to keep him as low profile as possible while we waited, but felt uncomfortable for the other patients. Because the appointment took so long, Justin's medicine wore off. After my husband and I finished watching the instructional videotape for giving shots, Justin's fever suddenly shot up. He felt so hot that I panicked and dashed out to the receptionist to ask for a thermometer. But, Michael immediately called me back. I spun around to see Justin in his arms, throwing up all over both of them. We rushed him through the waiting area and out into the hall bathroom. (This wasn't very low profile, but then again, at that moment—covered in vomit, he didn't look too desirable to the other patients.) We did our best to clean them both up, then they left to wait in the car for a minute, while I went back into the office to collect my purse.

The nurse wanted to give us further instructions, but I told her we had to go. I was desperately wanting to take my son home, panicked about his high fever, yet trying to keep him low-profile. Simultaneously, I knew we only had insurance coverage for two months of Pergonal, and at $3,000 per cycle, we couldn't afford it later.

The nurse quickly gathered my Pergonal and syringes while I wiped up the mess, paid the bill, and apologized. I left knowing we might not have had enough instruction for Michael to give me the Pergonal shots and we might lose out on one of our best chances to get pregnant.

We had to call the doctor on the phone that night for further instructions about the shots, but after several aborted attempts (because I was shaking in nervous fits of laughter and wouldn't present a still target) my husband was able to give me the shot. (I have to admit, I didn't have much faith in his ability because he's never liked needles or shots, but he became quite a pro.) We were glad that we didn't have to skip the Pergonal, but felt guilty both for taking our son out while he was sick and for the spectacle he made at the office. (Justin's fever reached 105 degrees, but he recovered quickly.)

One woman, when talking about how difficult it was taking Pergonal said, "You know, as painful as these shots and blood tests have been, the hard part is getting some-one to watch my child for all these appointments." Women undergoing medical treatment for secondary infertility often have many doctor's appointments per month, for which timing is critical and dependent on their cycle day, so they may only have short notice. These women have to depend on others for something as personal as continuing their fertility treatment.

Finances

Medical treatment may also be more difficult because of the expense. A childless couple is often willing to make financial sacrifices, but when a child is already in the pic-ture, there is a greater need for financial stability. If the woman has the privilege of staying home with the first child(ren), the couple is down to one income and no dou-ble coverage on insurance. Couples considering adopting another child often share this same financial dilemma.

The existing child(ren)

"The parents want a sibling for the child," says Marianne Carter. "[Some feel] that if they can't have another child in some way, then they are really putting their child at a disadvantage." In a paradox to this, the parents may also feel guilty about not being there for the first child because so much time and emotional energy are being spent on pursuing another baby.

Because a child's world centers on himself, he also may begin to wonder if he is the cause of our frustration. "Did having me make you so you can't have any more babies?" Or he may feel threatened by the thought of another baby, "Why do you want another baby so badly? Aren't I enough?"

Balancing our desire for another baby with the needs of our current child(ren) is one of the hardest battles of secondary infertility. The more intense the medical testing and treatment (or adoption search) become, the harder it is to maintain this balance.

I've struggled in walking this fine line. Since part of my infertility problem is irregular ovulation, I've taken many cycles of Clomid and Pergonal. With Clomid, I become very tired and emotional, and have to cut way back on my schedule just to keep my head above water. The uneven emotions are very difficult for me to handle. While some women have few side effects, for me it's like having severe PMS all month long! (While taking Clomid, I have to pray constantly for enough strength to just act normal.) I cry at everything from McDonald's commercials on television to graphs showing the number of women unable to receive prenatal care. (I'm usually not like this, and these symptoms go away once I stop the Clomid.) During my primary infertility, I knew that my husband and my coworkers could handle times I might overreact. Now though, when I try with a Herculean effort to be patient with our son and fail, I worry about what damage I have done to his growing little psyche. I feel torn. *How can I justify taking Clomid to have another baby, when it stops me from being the best mom to the son I have? But, how can I wait when it took so long to get pregnant the first time?*

Concerns about Having an Only Child

If you cannot have a second child, you may share these common concerns of parents with "only" children:

- you may be concerned about the many experiences and growth opportunities your child will miss without siblings;
- you may be concerned about your child's loneliness or lack of family connection to others throughout life;
- you may fear your only child might die, leaving you childless again;
- you may be concerned about your only child having the sole burden of caring for you in your old age.

Your child's reaction

Your first child can be frustrated with not having a sibling, so you may feel additional pressure to have a child close in age to your first. Recently my heart broke when I heard Justin plead in his prayers at night: "Dear God, if it is all right with You, pleeeease let us have another baby in our house."

When Justin shows his sadness or desire for a sibling, I try to validate his feelings of sadness and check that I haven't been overexposing him to my infertility trials. Then I try to share with him what I've learned about God loving us, being in control, and being a friend who can be closer than a brother to us. I reaffirm to him how happy we are that he was given to us by God. I realize that maybe God will allow our son's loneliness as an only child to draw Justin to Himself, just as He has done with me through infertility. As with childlessness, the answer to contentment has to be with our view of God, certainty of His love for us, and knowledge that He is in control.

There are some things that you can do to help enrich an only child's life. The book *One Child by Choice* suggests:

- Work at helping your child create lasting friendships. Often friendships can last a lifetime and friends can be closer than siblings.

- Provide opportunities for your child to take care of and teach younger children. This will expand his or her intellectual abilities and social development.
- Maintain your sense of perspective about rules and about being overly protective by asking yourself: What would I do if this child were one of five children?
- Build your financial resources so your child will not have the burden of caring for you financially when you're older.[6]

Lack of understanding from the fertile world

There is still a stigma attached to having an "only" child, similar to that of a childless couple in our current society. Only children are often viewed as spoiled, lonely, and unhappy. And if a couple has not shared about the struggle to have another child, others may label the couple as selfish or too busy to give their child a sibling. Sara was dumbstruck at the response someone at work gave when she talked about her only child:

> A woman I worked with, but knew only casually, was waiting for me to finish at the copier. In an effort to make idle conversation, she asked, "You got any kids?" I answered "Yes, one." She shook her head and replied, "Only one kid? . . . Cheap, cheap, cheap!"

With primary infertility, couples may occasionally be offered some confused sympathy: "I can see how it would be hard to have no children . . . but have you thought of: taking a vacation? eating black bananas? or standing on your head?" (Unhelpful options are often offered, but if you look past the ignorance, most times the desire to help is there.)

With secondary infertility, couples get the same intrusive questions, just phrased differently. Instead of being asked, "When are you two finally going to have children?" they are asked, "When are you finally going to give so-and-so a little brother or sister? Isn't it time? You don't want her growing up to be an only child, do you?"

Once people realize that the couple is struggling to have another baby the comments immediately change to: "But you already have a beautiful child. Aren't you thankful for the one you have?" Most couples with secondary infertility find a total lack of understanding or compassion. The door to support is shut.

The problem with the lack of understanding from the fertile world is that now you need to spend large amounts of time with these people as your child is growing up. You can't choose to retreat from the fertile world as you might have done while experiencing primary infertility. You are thrown into toddler play-groups or preschool where you are surrounded by women who are pregnant with their second, third, fourth, or more. You may still feel isolated because they can't relate to the emotional and physical struggle you have in getting pregnant. They either forge ahead enlarging their families right on schedule, or worry more about *not* getting pregnant again.

There are exceptions to this lack of understanding though. I have a friend who wanted a large family (by today's standards) of five children. I could tell she strongly valued having children even though she had no trouble conceiving. She has been able to empathize because she cannot imagine what her life would be like without her children. She has been very sensitive and has supported me throughout my second time of infertility. I hope you will find understanding friends like this as well.

Lost Camaraderie and Guilt with Childless Women

It is hard to have the stigma of being infertile among the fertile. It's harder when the people on whom you have learned to rely for support no longer accept you as "one of them." Sometimes the fear of how others will respond keeps us silent. During a recent RESOLVE symposium, I sat on the grass during the lunch break with another woman.[7] When I finally got up the nerve to mention the miracle of my son after years of infertility, she exclaimed, "Oh, you have a child also? I haven't said anything about having my daughter all morning. I was afraid I was the only one and that I would alienate everyone." Another woman, feeling this same sense of isolation, said: "I feel like the shunned of the shunned."

When I talk with my friends who are experiencing primary infertility, I feel guilty for having a child—he seems a barrier between us. I even feel guilty with women who have adopted their child(ren) because I had a birth experience. I feel as if I don't have the right to ask for another "miracle." I've already had my share.

Many women even feel guilty going to a doctor. Infertility specialist, Dr. David Adamson sees this in his practice: "A lot of women say, 'I feel guilty about being here. . . . I know so many other people deserve [a child] more because I already have one.' I just say, 'Count your blessings . . . but let's try to get another blessing.' "

Infertile couples need to support each other. Those with secondary infertility need to be *very* sensitive to a childless couple's pain, guarding their talk about their child. The childless couples need to realize that pain can still exist even though a child has been born. Secondarily infertile couples can suffer just as childless couples do when their reproductive ability evaporates. It takes special sensitivity on both sides, but we *can* all support each other.

Advantages the Second Time Around

The greatest benefit of secondary infertility is obvious. We have a child. We are parents. Not being able to have another child emphasizes our amazement that we ever had a first. As the Israelites set up stones for a memorial to remember when God answered their prayers, we have a living memorial of God's gift to us.

My husband and I are *very* aware of what a miracle our son is. Hardly a night goes by without one of us turning to the other before we go to sleep and saying something like: "I just love our son so much"; or, "Isn't that kid wonderful?"; or "I'm so thankful we have Justin." We don't talk about how much he fills our lives to others because we don't want to hurt — or even worse — bore them, but that gratefulness is part of our everyday lives. Because of the time we spent waiting for our child, we are more aware of cherishing every moment we have with him.

Being part of the parent "club," if only on the fringe
There is not as large a gap between fertile couples and us anymore. If someone shares a birth story, I can join in and discuss my memories. (In the midst of these discussions though, I'm so concerned that there might be those present who would be hurt by the subject, that it often makes me uncomfortable.)

Patience
Going through primary infertility helped us to develop a long-term view of treatment. Instead of our anticipation level being sky-high each month, we know the score and anticipate a long haul. I have learned to be more patient with a body whose reproductive system is handicapped.

Knowledge
This time we're veterans. We know the staff at the infertility specialist's office, the language and procedures, where to find a network of support, our way around the medical library, and the questions to ask. Having already built up a base of knowledge has made the process a little less intimidating and confusing.

Knowing God better
God has not changed this time, but I have. Because I put the energy into struggling to find out if He loved me the first time through, I have wrestled with God and found Him true. He did not turn away from me when I was

angry, even though I was open and honest. I've found I am also more comfortable with the fact that in our current world, statistics reflect how God most often chooses to work. This has helped us in making choices. Going through infertility the first time made me wonder if I could trust God, but working that through helped me to develop a deep, abiding faith that is seeing me through this next time around.

Don't Miss the Good Stuff

I do not want to end this chapter by joining the others in saying, "Look on the bright side, at least you have your husband and child(ren)." The pain of secondary infertility is very real. Once it is acknowledged though, what can you do about it? Concentrate on remembering to thank God for past answers in the midst of your current struggles.

Sara discovered this one day during her daughter's parade at school:

> I went to the Halloween parade at my daughter's school this morning. The kids were all so cute dressed [in their costumes], but all I could feel was sadness. I realized that my daughter is in the sixth grade, so this will be her last year in elementary school doing cute stuff like this. Next year she'll take another step away from her childhood when she goes to junior high school. I found myself crying all the way from her school back to work.
>
> At work I finally realized that I was ruining today because I was worrying about tomorrow. I was overwhelmed with sadness because I wondered if I would ever have another child to go through all these delightful stages with. Once I saw that my thinking was ruining my time with my daughter, I asked God to help me live in today, delight in my daughter, and leave the future to Him.
>
> The sorrow doesn't go away. I used to think that joy was the absence of sorrow . . . but now I've realized that they can exist side-by-side.

Your Personal Journey

If you are dealing with secondary infertility

1. Try to analyze your reasons for your "ideal" family size. What are the good things about a family that size? Are there other ways to achieve some of those good things?
2. Are you succeeding in balancing the need to have another child with fulfilling the needs of your current child(ren)? If not, where do you need to make adjustments?
3. If you feel guilty about wanting another child, what is the reason?
4. Have there been times during the excitement of your last pregnancy or while you are with your child that you have been insensitive to childless women who may be hurt by hearing your birth stories or "my child is so cute, funny, smart . . . " stories?

If you are dealing with primary infertility

1. In what ways can you try to relate to secondarily infertile women as you would wish others would relate to your infertility?

Part VI

"Is There Life beyond Infertility?"

19

Using Infertility to Benefit Our Lives

You can't be brave if you've only had wonderful
things happen to you. — Mary Tyler Moore[1]

I seldom think about my limitations, and they
never make me sad. Perhaps there is just a touch
of yearning at times, but it is vague, like a
breeze among flowers. — Helen Keller[2]

*W*hether you eventually resolve your infertility
through a biological child, an adoptive child, or
choosing to remain a family of two, the insights
you have gained along the way are what make an agonizing trip bearable. Even if you're still living in limbo about
the outcome of your infertility, if you've honestly faced
your grief and given yourself adequate time for it, you may
now be ready to think about some of the silver linings of
the dark cloud of infertility.

If you ask those who have gone through infertility, they
will tell you it has changed them. As Deanna said, "We
were devastated after losing our babies. Rich says that he
doesn't think he'll ever be that naive again. I don't think
I'll ever be the same either. Something like this really
changes you forever." Part of this change is incorporating
our experience into our view of life so that we can grow

253

and gain new insights. Another part is allowing God to work in us. It would be a sad thing if after surviving nearly unendurable circumstances, we didn't change at all.

Recovering Our Balance

How do you know you're staring to recover and beginning to move on? With most people, this change comes gradually. You may discover that when you're listening to someone share the deep pain of infertility, you are no longer at that low point. While you still may have times of intense sorrow, the sorrow is no longer out of control or the main focus of your life all the time. You find you're laughing more.

Your tunnel vision widens. You look for and begin to see God's answers in other circumstances. You begin to concentrate on changing the things you can—your job, enjoying time with your spouse—and you begin to open up again to other people, including fertile couples, friends, and family. Circumstances may not change, but you are finally able to change your focus.

When these changes begin, you know you have started to recover from the blow of infertility. For me, I knew I was regaining my balance when the tenderness of God's love dawned on me again after my grief.

Cycle of grief

Recognize that discovering these new insights doesn't replace the grieving process. Grieving is necessary to move on, but you will know you are beginning to heal when you find you are experiencing joy in other areas at the same time as the sad feelings. Eventually, positive feelings will grow to become the norm, but this doesn't mean you'll never feel sad at the thought of not having a child or at having lost your child.

Vicky found that while the pain was slowly replaced with other positive feelings, the sorrow of not being able to create life still returned on occasion: "I've learned all these great things, but even after 12 years, I still find myself crying in church sometimes." The sorrow stops being all-pervasive, but it is normal to have it return at times.

Getting stuck

Even though grieving can be horrible, sometimes it can almost feel safer than the unknown of moving beyond it. For instance, maybe grief added a new dimension to your relationships. Perhaps you found it difficult to share emotions before, but grief broke down the emotional barriers, so your relationships have grown as you have learned to share on a deeper level. You may feel that if you move beyond your grief, your relationships will return to their previously unsatisfying state. Or, you may not feel able to get past your resentment toward God. If this happens, bitterness can form, opening the door to destructive or self-destructive behaviors. Bitterness comes when we use grief or anger as an excuse not to grow.

Getting unstuck may require a deliberate, conscious effort to focus on the problem and be honest about the good things you've discovered through your grief, asking God to guide and change you. If a relationship has changed for the better, share your concerns with the other person and take action to ensure those good changes won't be lost. If the problem is between you and God, spend time reading about who He is in the Bible, talking with someone who knows Him well, and talking it out with Him in prayer.

You may also need to find other areas of interest and joy in life. If you find that after a time, you are unable to move past your grief to find other areas of joy, find someone to talk to—a close, caring friend, a pastor, a physician, or a professional Christian counselor.

Learning from Grief

Can any positive changes come from discovering you may never have children or having a child die?

Realizing what is important

When we're dealing with issues of life and death, we gain perspective on the rest of life's problems. The things we used to worry about now seem so small. For instance, Rich found he has become less anxious about small problems: "I'm much more calm about things now. I don't get worked up and pull my hair out as quickly as before."

More compassion for those who are different or grieving

Many Christians have experienced feelings of "being different" because of their beliefs. Being infertile can make you even feel different from others in the Christian community. But being different isn't bad. It often encourages you to analyze and think deeply about life rather than just go along with the crowd. This can give you a new sense of who you are and what it means to try to please God rather than everyone else.

In the best of all worlds, hurting people would come to church, share their hurt, and find loving understanding. But the church is made of imperfect people. We don't have the same experiences, and it takes a major leap to try to understand life situations we haven't experienced. I still have a difficult time empathizing with some people when I can't relate to their situation. I'm trying to use my knowledge of being different and misunderstood to understand others' feelings.

Because we've experienced grief, we have a greater understanding of how to help others who are grieving. We're less afraid to be around those who are grieving or to ask them how they're doing. April found she was able to feel more compassion for people who experienced loss: "One of the things I always wanted as I was growing up was compassion. Through losing my babies and the major struggles we've had starting a business, I've gained a measure of compassion I wasn't able to feel before."

Dave discovered a similar change. "I used to be impatient with people who struggled with tough circumstances. My basic attitude was 'get over it.' I'm much more patient and feel more empathy for their trials now, even when I don't completely understand them."

Looking Forward

After gaining new understanding about how uncertain life is, we can begin to feel how precious *our* life is and gain a renewed energy for it. It is a miracle that *we* were ever born. Our narrow focus, which was so necessary as we worked through grief, now opens outward again. All possibilities seem new. Hope is reborn.

I remember coming out of my depression after my miscarriage and really seeing the world again. It was as if a fog cleared from my eyes. I was amazed at all the varied shades of green that spring, the vibrant flowers, the brilliant blue of the sky, and the people in my life. I saw them all again as if for the first time. The things I had become calloused to, like the touch of a hand, could move me to tears. I saw the miracle that each person around me ever came into being. I thanked God for clearing away my expectations, for creating beauty for our enjoyment, for health and life, and even for my friends' healthy babies.

Strength to handle adversity

We can begin to feel new strength when we realize: *I've faced one of my deepest fears and survived.* We feel a sense of resilience in recovering from a crippling blow. If we can survive the intense pain of infertility or losing a baby, we can handle just about anything else. We realize we have developed the ability to cope with catastrophe. This doesn't mean we won't grieve again, but we will feel more confident about recovering from the grief.

Relationship with God

We've also had the chance to develop a stronger, clearer relationship with God that has been tried and tested in our suffering. We understand better that His love doesn't depend on circumstances. Being honest with God about our anger, confusion, and hurt can bring us closer to Him.

A significant part of this deeper relationships with God is the understanding that God is in control and is also worthy of our trust. While some people deceive themselves into thinking that they're in control until much later in their lives, infertile couples run smack into the concrete truth much earlier than most that God alone is in control. This is a scary truth initially, but once we realize it is balanced with God's compassionate love, it becomes a wonderful truth that brings much comfort and security. This understanding can only come when life doesn't go our way.

When I stopped thinking that I caused everything good or bad that was happening to me, I understood that infertility wasn't directed against me because of something I'd done. This freed me to see with amazement the other good things I was being given which were also undeserved. I experienced the reality of grace.

Relationship with spouse

Many couples have found that infertility has helped them learn more about each other. Paul and Sara learned how to communicate and help each other more. "At first I didn't want to involve Paul in going through tests and things," said Sara, "because I felt it was my problem. I didn't want to bother him or mess up his life. Now I wish I would have included him more."

And Paul responded, "Once I asked Sara if she wanted me to be there when she went in for a surgery. She looked shocked that I would suggest such a thing. I think she was trying not to make a big deal out of it, but I think being more involved would have helped me too. I had no clue about what was going on."

Michael and I developed a stronger relationship through our common struggle to become parents. After all we've been through, I love and trust him so deeply. When problems come up in our lives, I don't have a doubt that we'll get through them because they're so minor compared to the fire we've already walked through.

Relationship with extended family

Infertility can also help develop stronger relationships with extended family. It can open up a channel to communicate emotions as it did with April:

> The miscarriages have given my mom and me a forum to express sadness. The first time I saw her cry was when I told her I was having my fourth miscarriage. I only received about three hugs from her in twelve years, but now she hugs me every time I see her.

Discovering New Goals

You may not decide to stop trying for a child, but you can open yourself up to additional goals and not pin all your hopes on having a biological child.

Take inventory of the decisions you made and the things you gave up or put on hold while trying to have child. Do you want to continue putting the same emotional, physical, and financial resources toward having a baby? Would you like to take a different direction in your career? What sacrifices have you been making to have a baby? Are they still worth it? Think about new or additional goals for your future.

I used to think that if I found any fulfillment outside of motherhood, God would see I was happy and would think I no longer wanted or needed a baby. Once I realized His love for me, I knew He wanted what was best for me and wouldn't make His decisions based on a manipulative game. But when I was open to the possibilities, instead of God sticking me in something I hated, He directed me to writing; this became something that I loved, was fulfilling to me, nurturing to others, and had long-term meaning.

Everyone has gifts to help touch hurting people, to show God's love, or to bring encouragement to those who are struggling. When we realize we are valuable to God, our spouses, our extended family, and to society, we can begin to look for these gifts in ourselves. Being open to other possibilities doesn't mean we close the door on having children, but it can make our time of waiting more fulfilling and balance our sense of esteem while we aren't succeeding in the area of bearing children.

Your Personal Journey

1. How has infertility changed you?
2. Where are you in your journey? Is joy coming back into your life? Do you feel like you're regaining your balance? Or are you still in the midst of your struggle?
3. What important goals have you put on hold while pursuing a pregnancy? Are there any you'd like to pursue while you're continuing to hope for a child?
4. Do you still want to pursue a pregnancy, or are you ready to look at different options, such as adoption or moving on as a family of two?

20

Two As a Family—Choosing to Lay Down the Burden

In making the child-free decision you shouldn't
think of what you don't have, but what you can have.
This is not selfishness . . . it is a sensible approach
to life. —Jean and Michael Carter[1]

Love is like a beautiful flower which I may not touch,
but whose fragrance makes the garden a place of
delight just the same. —Helen Keller[2]

*Y*ou may come to the point where you're so tired of
living in limbo that you feel a readiness to move
on. You may feel that the pursuit of a baby—the
distraction, expense, and the emotional and physical
pain of invasive medical procedures—is holding you back
from other meaningful goals. You may come to understand that having children is a phase of life, not life itself.
Or, you just may have encountered too many closed
doors. You may have tried unsuccessfully to adopt, but
because of your age, health problems, the cost, family dy-
namics, or other personal factors, you've decided that
adoption isn't for you.

This can be a time to discover other enjoyable and
meaningful things in life in spite of what has been dealt to
you. Whether you are confronted by the reality that you
will never have children born to you or you need to put an

end to a life of waiting, you need to feel the freedom to make the decision to accept life without your own children and put your energy toward fulfillment and meaning in other directions.

Just as making the decision to adopt, the decision to remain a family of two usually takes time. There always seems to be the lure of more medical treatments around the corner or a possible adoption lead. If you still feel you're meant to have children, then you should continue to pursue building your family. But if through prayer and circumstances, you feel you are being drawn to remain a family of two, investigate it, try the thought on, and see how it fits.

Defining Your Family

Although I appreciate the desire within the infertile community to positively portray the life of a couple without children, I find the term *child-free* confusing. The *free* part of the definition is meant to indicate that couples are free to choose a different route in life other than parenthood and should also be free from criticism for making that choice. But it can also be interpreted as being free of those burdensome, pesky children (like being germ-free). This is confusing to people not "in the know." Couples who go to great lengths to have a child only to have that dream slowly die, have feelings more closely aligned with couples who have lost a tangible child. I don't think a couple whose child had died would feel comfortable calling themselves *child-free*.

I prefer a more positive term that centers on what the couple does have, such as a *family of two*. This portrays the value a couple has for family while reaffirming their value without children. So if someone asks: "When are you going to start a family?" the answer can be: "We *are* a family." This term also builds a sense of camaraderie rather than separatism between couples with children and those without. Whatever term you use, understand your value to God and society as a couple without children. Infertile couples are some of the most loving, compassionate people I've known. They desperately need a way to express that love in a fulfilling way. If they later choose to stop trying for children, that doesn't change them suddenly into self-centered and uncaring people, but this is a stigma that many face.

God values you regardless of whether you conceive or raise a family. Just as some didn't understand your struggle to have children, some will not understand your decision to give up the pursuit of a child. The key is to keep in close communication with God. When you understand your worth as an individual to Him, it will be easier to gently educate those who don't understand.

Choosing to Stop the Pursuit

Even though the pain has lessened and you're happy to be quitting the struggle, giving up the dream of children can be difficult. After five years, Sara chose to stop pursuing a baby:

I feel as if I've graduated from my support group. Not because I had the hoped-for pregnancy, but I've moved on. I knew I was finally getting past the pain when we had a baby dedication at church. When I heard it was going to happen, my mind automatically started putting up defenses, then I realized I didn't need them because it doesn't hurt like that anymore.

Giving up the pursuit of a baby is still difficult. It's like giving up a boyfriend who just isn't right for you, but is very appealing. I know it will be good for me in the future, but it hurts. It's hard to give up the intensity of the pursuit. When I gave up medical treatment, that was a real relief, but it's been harder for me to give up the big idea.

Finding New Directions

Closing the door on having children can usher in an early mid-life crisis. You may begin to ask yourself, *what am I doing in my life that is meaningful and lasting?* Or it can feel similar to retiring (especially if it was taking as much time as a part-time job). And as the saying goes, always try to retire *to* something.

Focusing on the benefits

There *are* benefits to living without children. Jean and Michael Carter list some of them in their book *Sweet Grapes: How to Stop Being Infertile and Start Living Again.* They discuss the added resources of time, energy and creativity; the freedom to spend more time on career without feeling guilty; the ability to do things spontaneously; if work isn't fun or fulfilling, after work hours can be spent on something that is; the freedom to scrap your career and go back to school or make a highly satisfying, but unprofitable career move; the freedom to make less money; the energy for contributions to church or synagogue, community or arts; and the energy to invest in the relationship with each other.[3]

Focusing on your fertility in other areas

It can be hard to give up your infertile identity and stop trying to become parents because the pursuit can be so intense that when it is set aside, it leaves a great hole. After making the decision, you may need to find new goals to fill that hole and redirect your lives. Obviously, prayer is an important part of this as well as discovering your gifts. Talk to your mate, good friends, or a pastor. Ask what gifts they see in you. Set a goal and outline specific steps to develop one or more of those gifts.

Part of Sara's decision to stop pursuing a baby was combined with the desire for a new goal: "I've started setting long-range goals and other plans that don't involve children, but include parenting qualities: nurturing, creativity, etc. That sort of evolved. I decided I really want to become a teacher. So I'm going to go back to school to get a credential."

Make an inventory of everything you like to do. Put a star next to the activities for which you have gifts or skills. From these lists, develop some specific goals that can clearly be achieved. Start small to experiment. Instead of deciding to sign up for a new full-time degree program, start with a single class. This can allow you to try something before fully committing to it.

Spend some time trying to remember what used to make you happy before you started trying for a baby. What made life worthwhile? What made it fun? What first attracted you to your mate? What did you like to do together? You may decide you can fulfill some of these interests or other goals in your life by means other than having children.

Allowing children back into your life

The authors of *Sweet Grapes* explain that part of giving up your infertile identity is giving up the pain that being with other children caused you before. Because you've decided to change your focus to the potential gains of living without children, they are no longer a reminder of what you can't have or evidence of your inadequacy.[4] Making the choice to find fulfillment in other areas beside your own children makes events that have always been painful lose their power over you. Your choice actually enables you to stop avoiding children and allow them back into your life. Caring for all of God's children and having an investment in the next generation is the best way to let people know you value children.

Nurturing others

Choosing a nurturing profession or focusing on nurturing children are ways you can influence the next generation. Some ways to pursue this are becoming foster parents, teaching, running a day care center, or being an important aunt or uncle to a child. You can also nurture a child on a smaller scale by finding a child who has an interest in something you are an expert in, then passing on your knowledge and talents. Teach him how to speak another language, play a musical instrument, or sew. Most parents would be thrilled to have you help with their child's education and development.

Knowing my desire for a child, Michael signed us up to sponsor a child one year as a Christmas present to me. He wrote to Compassion International to ask for a young child to sponsor. He gave me the wrapped picture of a little boy named Pau from Burma. Writing letters to Pau, continuing to get pictures as he grew, and being able to buy him glasses when he needed them, partially filled our need to nurture a child and help the next generation.

You can also nurture others by becoming a medical professional, such as a doctor or nurse, or by ministering to people in your church. When Karen was able to look in another direction from her infertility, she found nurturing others was important to her:

> I learned that I wasn't going to die if I didn't have kids. It wouldn't be what I wanted, but God was in it. Having a ministry to other women has made me realize I could do some good and have a future. It has been important to me that I found something nurturing to do. That's something that parenthood meant for me.

A Future with Meaning and Purpose

Everyone has to redefine their lives without children at some point because life is a series of stages. Having children is the focus of just one of those stages. You may be having a midlife crisis or empty nest syndrome a little earlier than your friends. It may help to talk to older women who have needed to find a new focus when their children grew up and left home.

It takes time to develop new patterns of thinking and behavioral habits. Look for the joy that God will give you as you find the unique purpose He has for you. If it is from

God, you can be certain that you will find meaning and excitement in it. It will be something that will fit you.

God cares about your future and has good plans for you, plans for delight, fulfillment, and productivity. Hold onto the promise in Psalm 103:5, which says that God "satisfies your desires with good things" (NIV).

Your Personal Journey

1. What gifts do you feel God has given you? (If you don't know, ask those close to you.)
2. What was meaningful to you as a couple before you started trying to have a child? What was fun?
3. Did you have any adults in your life, beside your parents, who greatly influenced you? Would you like to play that role in a child's (or adult's) life? What concrete steps would you need to take to pursue that?
4. Can you think of any ways to fulfill some of your goals in other ways if it won't be through having children?

Epilogue

I don't know if we'll ever be able to have another biological child, if God has a child in mind for us to adopt, or if something else will fulfill this desire in us for another child. Michael and I have been told that our chances to get pregnant again are two thirds of one percent per cycle. While we *know* God can perform a miracle, we also know that statistics are a reflection of how God generally chooses to work. What I do trust is that God will walk me though whatever the future holds and that He is acting out of His love for me. A promise in which I found great comfort isn't a promise for a baby, but it's a promise that God will not let us live barren, empty lives if we follow Him:

> Jesus said, "I came that they might have life, and might have it abundantly" (John 10:10, NASB).

I pray that God will bless each of you with a child, but even more, I pray that you will feel the hand of God supporting you, loving you, and drawing you to Him as you work through your pain. I leave you with this prayer that Paul prayed for his fellow Christians. I pray it for you:

> When I think of the wisdom and scope of His plan I fall down on my knees and pray to the Father of all the great family of God—some of them already in heaven and some down here on earth—that out of His glorious, unlimited resources He will give you the mighty inner strengthening of His Holy Spirit. And I pray that Christ will be more and more at home in your hearts, living within you as you trust in Him. May your roots go down deep into the soil of God's marvelous love; and may you be able to feel and understand, as all God's children should, how long, how wide, how deep, and how high His love really is; and to experience this love for yourselves, though it is so great that you will never see the end of it or fully know or understand it. And so at last you will be filled up with God Himself (Eph. 3:14-19).

Appendix A—Resources

INFERTILITY

The American Fertility Society
1209 Montgomery Highway
Birmingham, AL 35216-2809
A professional medical organization offering patient brochures, bibliography of books, ethical guidelines, information on fertility doctors, and the annual report of statistics from programs offering Assisted Reproductive Technologies (ART).

de Miranda Institute
23 Rockroad Way
Irvine, CA 92715
(714) 559-7260
Offers a book for infertile couples who are experiencing difficulty with insurance reimbursement, *A Consumer's Guide to Insurance, Including California's AB#900.*

DES Action USA
1615 Broadway, #510
Oakland, CA 94612
(415) 465-4011
Provides quarterly newsletter, support for those with DES including information on infertility related to DES and fertility drugs.

The Endometriosis Association
8585 N. 76th Place
Milwaukee, WI 53223
(800) 922-ENDO
Offers support for women with endometriosis, including a newsletter, video and audio tapes, support groups, and a help line.

Ferre Institute, Inc.
258 Genesee St., Suite 302
Utica, NY 13502
(315) 724-4348
Offers brochures, a newsletter, and a lending library of books related to infertility.

National Infertility Network Exchange (NINE)
P.O. Box 204
East Meadow, NY 11554
(516) 794-5772
Offers national support for infertility and adoption, including referrals and a newsletter.

RESOLVE
1310 Broadway
Somerville, MA 02144-1731
Business line (617) 623-1156
Help line (617) 623-0744
Large national organization with local chapters offering compassionate and informed support related to infertility, miscarriage or adoption. Offers a support line, quarterly newsletters, symposiums and workshops, pre-adoption meetings, and a lending library.

Serano Symposia, U.S.A.
100 Longwater Circle
Norwell, MA 02061
(800) 283-8088
(800)435-4220 (automated information line)
A pharmaceutical company involved in infertility drug therapy which offers information brochures to fertility patients.

Stepping Stones
2900 N. Rock Rd.
Wichita, KS 67226–1198
A free infertility newsletter from a Christian perspective. Also provides information on Christian peer-support groups nationwide.

MISCARRIAGE AND STILLBIRTH

Centering Corporation
1531 N. Saddle Creek Road
Omaha, NE 68104–5064
(402) 553-1200
Offers a catalog of books on miscarriage, stillbirth, and grief.

Compassionate Friends
P.O. Box 3696
Oak Brook, IL 60522–3696
(708) 990–0010
A nationwide self-help group offering support for those mourning the death of a child, including by miscarriage or stillbirth. Also offers local chapter monthly meetings, books, and a quarterly newsletter.

H.A.N.D. of Santa Clara County
P.O. Box 341
Los Gatos, CA 95031
(408) 732–3228
H.A.N.D. (Helping After Neonatal Death) offers support to parents during the normal mourning following a child-bearing loss. Offers phone peer counseling, a newsletter, a resource library, grief support groups within California, and assistance in starting support groups elsewhere. It also offers in-service workshops for medical professionals.

Pregnancy and Infant Loss Center
1421 E. Wayzata Blvd., #30
Wayzata, MN 55391
(612) 473–9372
Offers the *Loving Arms* newsletter, referrals to support groups, and information for related areas such as funeral options, high-risk pregnancy, and surviving siblings.

SHARE: Pregnancy and Infant Loss Support, Inc.
St. Joseph Health Center
300 First Capitol Drive
St. Charles, MO 63301–2893
(314) 947–6164
Offers emotional, physical, spiritual, and social support for those who are troubled by the tragic death of a baby through miscarriage, stillbirth, or newborn death. The support includes a bi-monthly newsletter, and 250 chapters internationally. Also provides education about bereaved parents.

UNITE, Inc. Grief Support
c/o Jeanes Hospital
7600 Central Ave.
Philadelphia, PA 19111–2499
(215) 728–3777
National grief support for those with a pregnancy loss, offering a quarterly newsletter and referrals to local support groups.

ADOPTION

Child Welfare League of America, Inc.
440 First St., NW, Suite 310
Washington, D.C. 20001–2085
(202) 638–2952
A national clearinghouse which publishes materials on adoption, including an adoption directory.

National Adoption Center
1218 Chestnut Street
Philadelphia, PA 19107
(800) TO-ADOPT
(215) 925–0200
Refers families to agencies in their communities, offers a guide for approaching business and corporations to support adoptions, and supplies information about special-needs adoption.

National Committee for Adoption, Inc.
1933–17th St., NW
Washington, D.C. 20009–6207
(202) 328–1200
Offers information for those seeking to adopt.

Holt International Children's Services
P.O. Box 2880
Eugene, OR 97402
(503) 687–2202
A Christian International Adoption Agency, also offers a bi-monthly magazine.

Pact—An Adoption Alliance
3315 Sacramento St., Suite 239
San Francisco, CA 94118
(415) 221–6957
Facilitates low fee adoptions for infants of color, including transracial adoptions.

PROBLEM PREGNANCIES OR MULTIPLE PREGNANCIES

High Risk Moms, Inc.
P.O. Box 4013
Naperville, IL 60567–4013
(708) 515–5453
A support group for problem pregnancies. Offers a help line and a newsletter, *High Risky Business.*

Triplet Connection
P.O. Box 99571
Stockton, CA 95209
(209) 474–0885
Offers phone support, information, a newsletter, and data bank for couples expecting triplets, quadruplets, or more.

Appendix B—Further Reading

Infertility: General/Medical

Harkness, Carla. *The Infertility Book: A Comprehensive Medical & Emotional Guide.* Berkeley, CA: Celestial Arts, 1992.

Menning, Barbara Eck. *Infertility: A Guide for the Childless Couple.* 2nd ed. New York: Prentice-Hall, 1988.

Nachtigall, Robert, M.D. and Mehren, Elizabeth. *Overcoming Infertility.* New York: Doubleday, 1991.

Sher, Geoffrey, M.D., and Marriage, Virginia A., R.N., M.N., with Stoess, Jean, M.A. *From Infertility to In Vitro Fertilization.* New York: McGraw-Hill, 1988.

Silber, Sherman, M.D. *How to Get Pregnant with the New Technology.* New York: Warner Books, 1991.

Stephenson, Lynda. *Give Us a Child.* New York: Harper & Row, 1987.

Stout, Martha. *Without Child.** Grand Rapids, Michigan: Zondervan, 1985.

Van Regenmorter, John and Sylvia, and McIlhaney, Joe S. Jr., M.D. *Dear God, Why Can't We Have a Baby?** Grand Rapids, Michigan: Baker Book House, 1986.

Infertility: Emotional/Social

Anderson, Ann Kiemel. *Taste of Tears, Touch of God.** Nashville: Thomas Nelson Publications, 1984.

Baran, Annette and Pannor, Reuben. *Lethal Secrets: The Shocking Consequences and Unsolved Problems of Artificial Insemination.* New York: Warner Books, 1989.

Baughan, Jill. *A Hope Deferred.** Portland, Oregon: Multnomah Press, 1989.

Becker, Gay, Ph.D. *Healing the Infertile Family: Strengthening Your Relationship in the Search for Parenthood.* New York: Bantam Books, 1990.

Halverson, Kay with Hess, Karen. *The Wedded Unmother.** Minneapolis: Augsburg, 1980.

Salzer, Linda. *Surviving Infertility: A Compassionate Guide through the Emotional Crisis of Infertility.* New York: Harper Collins, 1991.

Stigger, Judith A. *Coping with Infertility.* Minneapolis, Minnesota: Augsburg Publishing House, 1983.

Miscarriage and Stillbirth

Borg, Susan and Lasker, Judith. *When Pregnancy Fails: Families Coping with Miscarriage, Stillbirth, and Infant Death.* Boston: Beacon Press, 1981.

Friedman, Rochelle, M.D. and Gradstein, Bonnie, M.P.H. *Surviving Pregnancy Loss.* Boston: Beacon Press, 1981.

Gryte, Marilyn. *No New Baby.* Omaha, NE: Centering Corporation, 1988. (For children whose expected sibling dies.)

Morrow, Judy and DeHamer, Nancy. *Good Mourning.** Dallas: Word Publishing, 1989.

Scher, Jonathan, M.D. and Dix, Carol. *Preventing Miscarriage: The Good News.* New York: Harper Collins, 1991.

Schwiebert, Pat, R.N. and Kirk, Paul, M.D. *Still to Be Born: A Guide for Bereaved Parents Who Are Making Decisions about Their Future.* Portland, Oregon: Perinatal Loss, 1989.

Semchyshyn, Stefan, M.D. and Carol Colman. *How To Prevent Miscarriage and Other Crises of Pregnancy.* New York: Macmillan Publishing Co., 1989.

Vredevelt, Pam W. *Empty Arms: Emotional Support for Those Who Have Suffered Miscarriage or Stillbirth.** Portland, Oregon: Multnomah Press, 1984.

Grief and God

Deits, Bob. *Life after Loss.** Tucson, Arizona: Fisher Books, 1988.

Manning, Doug. *Don't Take My Grief Away.** San Francisco: Harper & Row, 1979.

Yancy, Philip. *Disappointment with God.** Grand Rapids, Michigan: Zondervan, 1988.

Infertility: Secondary

Hawke, Sharryl and Knox, David. *One Child by Choice.* Englewoods Cliffs, NJ: Prentice Hall, 1977. (Offers positive encouragement about "only" children.)

Adoption

Anderson, Ann Kiemel. *Open Adoption: My Story of Love and Laughter.** Wheaton, IL: Tyndale, 1990.

Gilman, Lois. *The Adoption Resource Book.* New York: Harper Collins, 1992.

Hormann, Elizabeth. *After the Adoption.** Old Tappan, New Jersey: Fleming H. Revell, 1987.

Johnston, Patricia A. *Adopting after Infertility.* Indianapolis, IN: Perspectives Press, 1992.

Johnston, Patricia Irwin. *Perspectives on a Grafted Tree.* Fort Wayne, IN: Perspectives Press, 1984.

The Womanly Art of Breastfeeding. New York: New American Library, 1987. (Offers information on breastfeeding and adopted children.)

Pregnancy and Parenting after Infertility

Glazer, Ellen. *The Long-Awaited Stork: A Guide to Parenting after Infertility.* Lexington, Massachusetts: Lexington Books, 1990.

Hales, Dianne, and Johnson, Timothy, R.B., M.D. *Intensive Caring: New Hope for High Risk Pregnancy.* New York: Crown Publishers, 1990.

Rich, Laurie, A. *When Pregnancy Isn't Perfect: A Layperson's Guide to Complications in Pregnancy.* New York: Penguin, 1991.

Two As a Family

Carter, Jean W., M.D. and Carter, Michael, Ph.D. *Sweet Grapes: How to Stop Being Infertile and Start Living Again.* Indianapolis: Perspectives Press, 1989.

Love, Vicky. *Childless Is Not Less.** Minneapolis: Bethany House, 1984.

Helps for Friends, Family, and Pastors

Johnston, Patricia. *Understanding: A Guide to Impaired Fertility for Family and Friends.* Indianapolis, IN: Perspectives Press, 1983.

Osmont, Kelly, MSW with McFarlane, Marilyn. *What Can I Say? How to Help Someone Who Is Grieving: A Guide.* Portland, Oregon: Nobility Press, 1987.

Spring, Beth. *The Infertile Couple.** Elgin, IL.: David C. Cook, 1987. (For pastors.)

*Denotes books that offer a Christian perspective

Notes

Chapter 1
1. Geoffrey Sher, M.D., "Pacific Fertility Medical Center, Inc. IVF Position Statement" (1992).
2. Marilyn B. Hirsch, Ph.D., and William D. Mosher, Ph.D., "Characteristics of Infertile Women in the United States and Their Use of Infertility Services," *Fertility and Sterility*, 47 (4) (April 1987):618–625.

Chapter 2
1. Harriet Prescot Spofford, "Only," in *The Home Book of American Quotations* (New York: Dodd, Mead and Co., 1967), 53.
2. "God's Greatest Gift": © Gibson Greetings, Inc. Reprinted with permission of Gibson Greetings, Inc., Cincinnati, Ohio 45237. All Rights Reserved.

Chapter 3
1. Alice S. Whittemore, et al., "Characteristics Relating to Ovarian Cancer Risk: Collaborative Analysis of Twelve US Case-Controlled Studies," *American Journal of Epidemiology* vol. 136 (1992): 1184–1203.
2. Luis G. Escobedo, M.D., MPH, et al., "Infertility-Associated Endometrial Cancer Risk May Be Limited to Specific Subgroups of Infertile Women," *Obstetrics & Gynecology* vol. 77 (1991): 124–28.
3. For more information on this, ask for the "Fertility Awareness" fact sheet from RESOLVE. (See Appendix A: Resources for address.)
4. Ibid.
5. David Adamson, "Unexplained Infertility—The Non-Diagnosis," *Fertility Review* vol. 2, No. 2 (Sept. 1986).

Chapter 4
1. "Understanding Fertility Problems," (Daly City, CA Krames Communications 1985): 11
2. "Ovarian Cancer and Fertility Drugs," *RESOLVE National Newsletter* (April 1993): 6.
3. Zeev Shoham, M.D., et al., "Early Miscarriage and Fetal Malformations after Induction of Ovulation by Clomiphene Citrate and/or Human Menotropins, in In Vitro Fertilization, and Gamete Intrafallopian Transfer," *Fertility and Sterility* vol. 55 (1991): 1.
4. Geoffrey Sher, M.D., Virginia Marriage, R.N., M.N., with Jean Stoess, M.A., *From Infertility to In Vitro Fertilization* (New York: McGraw-Hill, 1988), 70.
5. Eli Reshef, M.D., et al., "Endometrial Inadequacy after Treatment with Human Menopausal Gonadotropin/Human Chorionic Gonadotrophin," *Fertility and Sterility* vol. 54 (1990): 1012.
6. "Pergonal/Profasi Therapy" Serano Laboratories,(1987): 5.
7. Isaac Ben-Nun, M.D., et al., "Effect of Preovulatory Progesterone Administration on the Endometrial Maturation and Implantation Rate

after In Vitro Fertilization and Embryo Transfer," *Fertility and Sterility* vol. 53, (1990): 276.

8. Augusto P. Chong, M. D., et al., "Comparison of Three Modes of Treatment for Infertility Patients with Minimal Pelvic Endometriosis," *Fertility and Sterility* vol. 53, (1990): 407.

9. Kohzoh, Makita, M.D., et al., "Guide-Wire-directed Detachable Balloon: Clinical Application in Treatment of Varicoceles," *Radiology* vol. 183, (1992): 575–77

Chapter 5

1. "Prayer Book" in *The Oxford Dictionary of Quotations*, 3rd Ed. (New York: Oxford University Press, 1979), 399.

2. "The Listener," in *The Oxford Dictionary of Quotations*, 3rd ed. (New York: Oxford University Press, 1979), 148.

3. Sher, Marriage, Stoess, *From Infertility to In Vitro Fertilization*, 52, 62.

4. Ibid., 187, 190.

5. S.A. Troup, et al., "Cryopreservation of Human Embryos at the Pronucleate, Early Cleavage, or Expanded Blastocyst Stages," *European Journal of Obstetrics & Gynecology and Reproductive Biology* vol. 38 (1990): 133–39.

6. John Jefferson Davis, *Evangelical Ethics* (Phillipsburg, New Jersey: Presbyterian and Reformed Publishing Co., 1985), 73. Used by permission.

7. Annette Baran & Reuben Pannor, excerpt from *Lethal Secrets* (New York: Warner Books, 1989), 37. Used by permission.

Chapter 6

1. Manuel Velazquez, *Philosophy: A Text with Readings*, 5th ed. (Belmont, California: Wadsworth Publishing, Co., 1994), 427.

2. "George Moore: The Bending of the Bough IV," in *Dictionary of Quotations*, ed. Bergen Evans (New York: Delacorte Press, 1968), 103.

3. John Stott, *Involvement: Social and Sexual Relationships in the Modern World* (Old Tappan, New Jersey: Fleming H. Revell, 1985), 194.

4. P.M. Zavos,"Characteristics of Human Ejaculates Collected via Masturbation and a New Silastic Seminal Collection Device (SDC)," *Fertility and Sterility* vol. 43 (1985): 491.

5. P.M. Zavos and J.C. Goodpasture, "Clinical Improvements of Specific Seminal Deficiencies via Intercourse with a Seminal Collection Device versus Masturbation," *Fertility and Sterility* vol. 51 (1989): 190–93.

Chapter 8

1. Leslie Phillips, "Strength of My Life," (Waco, Texas: Word Music, a Division of WORD, Inc, 1987). Used by permission.

Chapter 9

1. Ruth Harmes Calkin, "Ten to One," in *Tell Me Again Lord, I Forget* (Wheaton: Tyndale House Publishers, © 1974), 84. Used by permission of Tyndale House Publishers, Inc. All rights reserved.
2. Dr. James Dobson, excerpt from "Focus on the Family" radio program (Colorado Springs, Colorado: Focus on the Family, 11/21/91). Used by permission of Focus on the Family.
3. Philip Yancey, *Disappointment with God* (Grand Rapids: Zondervan Publishing House, 1988), 34, 37. Used by permisssion.
4. Excerpts of letter used by permission.
5. Gary Vanderet,"Dealing with Discontent," (Palo Alto, California: Discovery Publishing, 1990), #794. Used by permission.
6. Author unknown. Previously printed in *Stepping Stones* newsletter (Feb.–March, 1991).

Chapter 10

1. Robert Nachtigall, M.D., and Elizabeth Mehren, *Overcoming Infertility* (New York: Doubleday, 1991), 172.
2. Dianne Hales & Timothy Johnson, M.D., *Intensive Caring* (New York: Crown Publishers, Inc., 1990). Used by permission.

Chapter 11

1. Deborah Tannen, *You Just Don't Understand: Women and Men in Conversation* (New York: William Morrow and Company, Inc., 1990), 24–25.
2. "Study: Stress of Infertility Greater on Women than Men," *San Jose Mercury News,* (Feb. 27, 1991): 2C.
3. Peter Fagan, Ph.D., et al., Sexual Functioning and Psychologic Evaluation of In Vitro Fertilization Couples," *Fertility and Sterility* vol. 46, No. 4 (Oct. 1986): 668.
4. John Snarey, "Men Without Children," *Psychology Today,* (March 1988): 61–62.
5. Gary Vanderet, *Cultivating Intimacy in Marriage.* (Palo Alto, California: Discovery Papers, 1990). Used by permission.

Chapter 12

1. Jack Hayford, *Early Flight* (Hollywood, California: Haven of Rest Ministries, 1986), 11.
2. Philip Yancey, excerpt from "Focus on the Family" radio program (Colorado Springs, Colorado: Focus on the Family, 11/20/91). Used by permission.
3. Lamb and Leurgans, "Does Adoption Affect Subsequent Fertility?" *American Journal of Obstetrics and Gynecology* vol. 134 (1979): 138–44.
4. Used by permission.
5. Rana Limbo and Sara Wheeler, *When a Baby Dies: A Handbook for Healing and Helping* (La Crosse, Wisconsin: Resolve through Sharing, 1986), 74.
6. Ibid.

7. Ray S. Anderson,"God Bless the Children—and the Childless," *Christianity Today,* Aug 7, 1987, 28. Used by permission of *Christianity Today.*

Chapter 13

1. Debra Evans, "The Infertility Maze," *Christian Parenting Today,* (Jan. Feb. 1991), 60, 71.

Chapter 14

1. Ellen Sarasohn Glazer, *The Long Awaited Stork: A Guide to Parenting after Infertility* (Lexington, Mass.: Lexington Books, 1990), 13. Used by permission.
2. Judith Bernstein, R.N., M.S.N., et al, "Psychological Status of Previously Infertile Couples after a Successful Pregnancy," *Journal of Obstetric, Gynecologic and Neonatal Nursing* (November/December, 1988): 404–08.
3. Dianne Hales & Timothy Johnson, M.D., *Intensive Caring* (New York: Crown Publishers, Inc., 1990).

Chapter 15

1. Catherine Marshall, ed., *The Best of Peter Marshall* (Grand Rapids, MI: Zondervan Corporation, 1983), 335.
2. Margaret B. Spiess, "Teddy Bears," in *Cries from the Heart* (Grand Rapids: Baker Book House, 1991), 34.
3."The Medical Causes of Miscarriage," (Somerville, MA: RESOLVE, Year). See Appendix A: Resources for more information.
4. Rami Langer, M.D., et al., "Reproductive Outcome after Conservative Surgery for Unruptured Tubal Pregnancy—a 15-year Experience," *Fertility and Sterility* vol. 53 No. 2 (Feb 1990): 227.
5. Stefan Semchyshyn, M.D., and Carol Coleman, *How to Prevent Miscarriage* (New York: Collier Books, 1990), 40–41.
6. Jonathan Scher, M.D. and Carol Dix, *Preventing Miscarriage: The Good News* (New York: Harper & Row, 1991), 15, 71.
7. John Markoff, "Miscarriage Tied to Chip Factories," *New York Times* (Oct. 1, 1992): 1.
8. Stefan Semchyshyn, M.D., and Carol Coleman, 141–43.
9. Scher and Dix, *Preventing Miscarriage,* 27, 32, 35, 191–92.
10. Robert Nachtigal, M.D. and Elizabeth Mehren, *Overcoming Infertility* (New York: Doubleday, 1991), 299.
11. Scher and Dix, *Preventing Miscarriage,* 12.
12. Kochelle Friedman, M.D. and Bonnie Gradstein, M.P.H., *Surviving Pregnancy Loss* (Boston, MA: Little, Brown & Co., 1982), 6.
13. Bob Deits, *Life afer Loss* rev. ed.,(Tucson, Arizona: Fisher Books, 1992), 6. Used by permission.
14. Sister Jane Marie Lamb, "Stillbirth, Miscarriage, and Infant Death: Understanding Grief," (St. Charles, MO: SHARE, Year).
15. Wayne Watson, "Home Free," (Waco, Texas: Word Music, 1990). All rights reserved. Used by permission.

16. Miscarriage burial cradles are available from Bay Memorial, c/o Tom Zerbel, 321 South 15th St., Escanaba, MI 49829, (906) 786–2609.
17. Sister Jane Marie Lamb, OSF "Parents' Needs and Rights When a Baby Dies" *Health Progress* (Dec. 1992), p. 55.
18. Rana Limbo and Sara Wheeler, *When a Baby Dies: A Handbook for Healing and Helping* (La Crosse, WI: Lutheran Hospital RTS Bereavement Services (formerly Resolve Through Sharing), 1986), 65–66.

Chapter 16
1. *Your Next Baby,* Centering Corp. © 1984, box 3367, Omaha, NE, 68103-0367.
2. Jay P. Green, Sr., gen. editor and translator, "1 Samuel 2:21," *The Interlinear Bible* (Grand Rapids: Baker Book House, 1983).
3. Judith Beernstein, et al., "Psychological Status of Previously Infertile Couples after a Successful Pregnancy," *Journal of Obstetric, Gynecologic, and Neonatal Nursing,* 17(6), (Nov–Dec, 1988): 404–08.
4. Glazer, *The Long Awaited Stork,* xvi.

Chapter 17
1. Helen Keller in *The Last Word: A Treasury of Women's Quotes* by Carolyn Warner (Englewood Cliffs, NJ: Prentice Hall, 1992), 39.
2. Tim Malcom, "Real Women," *Stepping Stones,* 1993: 4

Chapter 18
1. Marty Heiberg, "Another Christmas Morning," *Loving Arms,* (Winter, 1992), 4.
2. First published in *Stepping Stones* newsletter. (June–July 1991): 1.
3. Gay Becker, *Healing the Infertile Family* (New York: Bantam Books, 1990), 13. Used by permission.
4. Marilyn B. Hirsch, Ph.D. and William D. Mosher, Ph.D., "Characteristics of Infertile Women in the United States and Their Use of Infertility Services," *Fertility and Sterility* 47(4) (April, 1987): 618–25.
5. Bob Deits, *Life after Loss,* rev. ed., 65–66.
6. Sharryl Hawke and David Knox, *One Child by Choice* (Englewood Cliffs, New Jersey: Prentice Hall, 1977), 23–48, 82.
7. See appendix B: resources for further information on RESOLVE.

Chapter 19
1. Mary Tyler Moore, *The Last Word,* 77.
2. Ibid., 261.

Chapter 20
1. Jean Carter, M.D. and Michael Carter, Ph.D., *Sweet Grapes: How to Stop Being Infertile and Start Living Again* (Indianapolis: Perspective Press, 1989), 33. Used by permission.
2. Helen Keller in *The Last Word: A Treasury of Women's Quotes,* 204.
3. Ibid., p. 31–32.
4. Ibid, p. 35–36.

Glossary of Terms

abortion—The medical term for a pregnancy loss, whether by a spontaneous miscarriage or a deliberately induced termination of the pregnancy before the fetus is able to survive outside the uterus.

> **complete**—a pregnancy loss in which the fetus, placenta, etc. are completely expelled from the uterus.
>
> **habitual**—spontaneous miscarriages occurring in three or more successive pregnancies.
>
> **incomplete**—a pregnancy loss in which part of the fetus or placenta, etc. remain in the uterus.
>
> **induced**—the intentional termination of a pregnancy.
>
> **inevitable**—a potential pregnancy loss that can no longer be prevented.
>
> **missed**—an embryo or fetus who has died, but remains in the uterus.
>
> **spontaneous**—a miscarriage before the twentieth week of gestation.
>
> **threatened**—vaginal spotting and bleeding during pregnancy that may or may not result in a miscarriage.

AID, AIH—See artificial insemination.

anovulation—The absence of ovulation. This can occur even when menstrual periods are regular.

artificial insemination—A process in which sperm is placed into a woman's vagina or uterus by a medical procedure at the time of ovulation. Either the husband's sperm, *Artificial Insemination by Husband* (**AIH**), or a donor's sperm, *Artificial Insemination by Donor* (**AID**), or *Donor Insemination* (**DI**) may be used. When the washed sperm is placed into the woman's uterus, the process is called intrauterine insemination (**IUI**).

Assisted Reproductive Technology (ART) — A variety of high-tech procedures used to assist reproduction, such as *In Vitro Fertilization* **(IVF)**, *Gamete Intrafallopian Transfer* **(GIFT)**, and *Zygote Intrafallopian Transfer* **(ZIFT)**.

basal body temperature (BBT) chart — A chart for graphing a woman's temperature throughout her menstrual cycle to verify and estimate the time of ovulation. (See sample chart in chapter 3.)

Bromocriptine (Parlodel) — A drug used to suppress elevated prolactin hormone levels.

cervical mucus — Secretions of the cervix, which aid in transporting and filtering sperm.

cervix — The narrow neck of the uterus that protrudes from the uterus into the vagina.

chemical (or biochemical) pregnancy — An early pregnancy only confirmed by a blood or urine test.

cilia — The minute, hairlike projections lining the insides of the fallopian tubes that propel the egg from the ovary toward the uterus.

clinical pregnancy — A pregnancy which has been confirmed by seeing evidence of the fetus in the uterus during an ultrasound exam.

clomiphene citrate (Clomid or Serophene) — A synthetic hormone drug often prescribed to induce ovulation.

conception — See fertilization.

corpus luteum — The collapsed follicle on the ovary after it has released an egg which produces progesterone and estrogen after ovulation.

cryopreservation — The process of freezing and storing sperm, eggs, and embryos in liquid nitrogen in a frozen state.

Danazol (Danocrine) – A synthetic drug used to treat endometriosis.

diethylstilbestrol (DES) – A synthetic estrogen compound which was given to some pregnant women to prevent miscarriage. When the children of these women grew up, a number of them were found to have abnormalities of the reproductive organs.

dilation & curettage (D&C) – Stretching open the cervix to scrape the interior walls of the uterus.

donor insemination (DI) – See artificial insemination.

ectopic pregnancy – A pregnancy that implants outside the uterus, usually in the fallopian tubes.

egg donor – A woman who donates her egg(s) (ova) to an infertile couple.

ejaculate – Seminal fluid (usually containing sperm) discharged through the urethra during male climax.

embryo – The developing baby from fertilization through the eighth week of pregnancy.

embryo donation – The transfer of an embryo (created through IVF) into a woman who has no biological connection to the embryo.

embryo transfer – The placing of an embryo which was fertilized in the laboratory into a woman's uterus.

endometrial biopsy – A procedure in which a physician scrapes or suctions a small portion of the lining of the uterus, then evaluates the ability of the lining to hold and nurture a fertilized egg.

endometriosis – A condition in which the endometrial tissue spreads outside of the uterus and implants in various locations in the pelvic cavity, where it can cause scarring, pain, damage to the reproductive organs, and is thought to contribute to infertility.

endometrium—The mucus membrance lining of the uterus that changes through the menstrual cycle to nurture an embryo if fertilization occurs.

fallopian tubes—The tubes attached to the upper ends of the uterus which serve as a passageway for the egg to travel from the ovary to the uterus.

fertilization—The union of egg and sperm, also called conception.

fetus—The developing baby, from nine weeks after fertilization until birth.

fimbriae—The fringelike endings of the fallopian tubes close to the ovaries that capture the egg as it is released from the ovary.

follicle-stimulating hormone (FSH)—A hormone released by the pituitary gland that stimulates the growth of follicles in the ovary or stimulates sperm production in the testes. Used alone in drug form (Metrodin) or in combination with LH (Pergonol) to induce ovulation.

gametes—Eggs or sperm.

gamete intrafallopian transfer (GIFT)—A procedure in which eggs are retrieved, then placed with washed sperm in a syringe and immediately transferred into one or both of the fallopian tubes in the hope that fertilization will occur in the tubes.

gonadotropins—The hormones FSH and LH that stimulate the ovaries to produce eggs or the testicles to produce sperm.

GnRH analogs (Lupron or Synarel)—A synthetic drug used to block the body's production of FSH and LH. They can be used to enhance a woman's response to fertility drugs or to treat fibroids or endometriosis.

hCG—See human chorionic gonadotropin.

hMG—See human menopausal gonadotropin.

HSG—See hysterosalpingogram.

human chorionic gonadotropin (hCG)—A hormone produced by the implanting embryo or placenta during pregnancy. It is also a drug used in combination with hMG or clomiphene to trigger ovulation.

human menopausal gonadotropin (hMG) (Pergonal)—A natural hormone drug used to induce ovulation, derived from the urine of post-menopausal women.

hysterosalpingogram (HSG)—A test in which dye is injected into the uterus and the fallopian tubes, then x-rays are taken to check the shape of the uterus and that the tubes are patent (open).

hysteroscopy—A direct visual examination of the cervix and the interior of the uterus using an endoscope (a narrow telescope).

immunologic infertility—The decreased ability of sperm to fertilize an egg because of antibodies (produced by a husband or wife) which attach themselves to the sperm.

infertility—The inability to conceive within one year of unprotected intercourse, or the inability to carry a child to live birth.

intrauterine insemination (IUI)—See artificial insemination.

in vitro fertilization (IVF)—A procedure in which eggs that are removed from the wife's ovaries and sperm that are collected from the husband are placed together in a petri dish and incubated to await fertilization. If the eggs are fertilized, the developing embryos are placed back into the mother's uterus two to three days after fertilization.

IUI—See artificial insemination.

laparoscopy—A minor surgery using a laparoscope (a narrow telescope) to view the outside of a woman's reproductive organs through a small incision in her abdomen; may also be used to place sperm and eggs into a woman's fallopian tubes during a GIFT procedure.

laparotomy—A major surgery in which the abdomen is opened with an incision. The operation is performed under direct vision.

LH—See luteinizing hormone.

luteal phase defect—A shortened second half of the menstrual cycle (the time between ovulation and the beginning of menstruation) or an inadequate progesterone production during this time.

luteinizing hormone (LH)—A hormone produced by the pituitary gland which stimulates the ovary to release the mature egg, stimulates secretion of estrogen, and the formation of the corpus luteum. It also stimulates testosterone production in males.

micromanipulation—A special procedure (which is used to assist with severe sperm dysfunction) that creates a tiny opening in the outer covering of the egg to assist sperm penetration.

miscarriage—The spontaneous death of a baby, most often in the first trimester. (Also see abortion).

morphology—The shape of sperm cells.

motility—The sperm's ability to move forward.

mycoplasma—A microorganism found in the female cervix or male urethra that may contribute to infertility or miscarriage problems.

oligospermia—A persistently low sperm count.

oligo-ovulation—Infrequent ovulation.

oocyte—An egg or ovum.

oocyte retrieval—A procedure to collect egg(s) from a woman's ovaries, usually done by inserting a long needle through the vagina.

ovaries—The female reproductive organs in which eggs are formed, then released; these also produce estrogen and progesterone.

ovulation—The discharge of one or more eggs from an ovary.

ovulation induction—The use of hormones to stimulate the ovaries to develop and release eggs.

ovum—A mature egg cell.

pelvic inflammatory disease (PID)—An infection that can cause scarring in the reproductive organs, particularly in the fallopian tubes. PID's can contribute to infertility.

pregnancy reduction (selective termination)—An intentional abortion of one or more fetuses in cases of multiple pregnancy, by injecting a chemical substance into the fetus.

secondary infertility—The inability to conceive or give birth to a child after having carried at least one pregnancy to term.

semen—The fluid discharged at ejaculation that contains sperm and seminal fluids.

semen analysis—An analysis of a sample of semen under a microscope to estimate sperm count, motility, morphology, and other characteristics.

sonogram—See ultrasound.

sperm—The male germ cell which enters an egg in sexual reproduction to produce a new individual.

sperm antibodies—A protective substance produced by a man or woman's immune system that is directed against sperm.

sperm bank—A facility that stores frozen donor sperm.

sperm count—An estimate of the total number of sperm in an ejaculate.

sperm donor—A man who donates sperm to an infertile couple.

sperm washing—A technique that separates sperm from seminal fluid and concentrates the sperm best able to fertilize an egg.

Spinnbarkheit test—A test to estimate when ovulation is occurring by analyzing the "stretchability" of cervical mucus.

sterility—Permanent inability to produce the genetic material required to conceive a child.

stillbirth—The death of a baby in utero or during delivery during the third trimester of pregnancy.

superovulation—The stimulation of the ovary with fertility drugs to develop more than one egg.

surrogate mother—A woman who offers to carry a child for an infertile couple. She may have no genetic contribution to the child (gestational surrogate) or she may contribute the egg and the father contribute the sperm (surrogate).

tubal patency—An open (fallopian) tube.

ultrasound—A procedure that bounces sound waves off the body to produce an image on a screen, often used to evaluate ovarian activity or pregnancy.

unexplained infertility (also idiopathic infertility)—A term used for infertile couples when no organic problem can be detected in either partner.

uterus—The hollow muscular organ in a woman's pelvis in which fertilized eggs normally become imbedded and which nourishes the fetus until birth.

varicocele—A varicose vein of the testicle which raises the temperature of the scrotum and has been associated with lowered sperm count and motility.

zygote—A single-cell embryo before it first begins to divide.

zygote intrafallopian transfer (ZIFT)—A procedure that transfers a zygote to the fallopian tube(s) before it divides.

Subject Index

A

B

C

D

H

Hagar   78
Hamster-egg penetration assay   44
Hannah   133
HCG, *see human chorionic gonadotropin*
History evaluation   41
Holidays   133
   also see Mother's Day and Christmas
Home Study, adoption   215, 222–23
Human chorionic gonadotropin (hCG)   72, 273
Hüner test   42
Hysterosalpingogram   31, 40, 42, 273

I

In vitro fertilizaton (IVF)   55–61, 84–85, 193, 270
Infertility, definition of   21
Intimacy in marriage   150–52
Intrauterine insemination (IUI)   47
   also see artificial insemination
Isolation, feeling of   230

J

Jacob   118
Jeremiah   75
Job   105, 111, 120

L

Laparoscopy   40, 42, 47
Laparotomy   47, 274
Leah   77
Leuprolide, *see Lupron*
Levirate law   77
LH hormone   35, 45
Lupron   40–46, 272

M

Male perspective   144–47
Marriage   140–53, 258–59
Mary   75
Masturbation   43, 55, 85
Memorial service, *see remembrances*
Metrodin   45–46
Miscarriage, *see pregnancy loss*
Mother's Day   134–36, 155–56
Mucus testing (Spinnbarkheit test)   34, 276
Multiple pregnancy/births   46, 72, 81–85, 232–33
Mycoplasma   40, 274

N

Nafarelin, *see Synarel*
Nursing adopted child   224

O

Ovulation predictor tests   35

P

Parenting   226–33
Parlodel   46
Pastors   165–68
Pergonal   40, 45–6, 71, 73, 88, 240, 242
Perinatologist   196
Pornography   86–87
Postcoital test (PCT)   42
Pregnancy   183–89, 270
Pregnancy loss   53, 186, 190–206, 227
Pregnancy reduction   81–85, 275
Progesterone   40, 46, 197
Prolactin   40, 46
Punishment   110

T

Temperature chart, *see Basal Body Temperature Chart*
Tests for infertility   41–45
Treatments for infertility   45–58
Tubal pregnancy, *see ectopic pregnancy*
Tubal surgery   47

U

Ultrasound   42, 276
Unexplained infertility   35
Urologist   36,44

V

Validation of loss   199–200
Varicocele   48, 277
Vulnerability   101

W

Waiting   116

Z

Zacharias   111
Zygote intrafallopian transfer (ZIFT)   55, 193